Saudi Arabia

Saudi Arabia

Energy, Developmental Planning, and Industrialization

Edited by
Ragaei El Mallakh
Dorothea H. El Mallakh
International Research Center
for Energy and Economic
Development

LexingtonBooks
D.C. Heath and Company
Lexington, Massachusetts
Toronto

Library of Congress Cataloging in Publication Data

Main entry under title:

Saudi Arabia, energy, developmental planning, and industrialization.

Includes index.
1. Saudi Arabia—Economic policy—Congresses. I. El Mallakh,
Ragaei, 1925–   II. El Mallakh, Dorothea H.
HC415.33.S23   338.953'8   81–47746
ISBN 0–669–04801–1   AACR2

Published simultaneously in Canada

Printed in the United States of America

International Standard Book Number: 0–669–04801–1

Library of Congress Catalog Card Number: 81–47746

To our nieces and nephews, the next generation to grapple with a developing and changing world: Teressa Sara Huff, Dorothea Blythe Huff, David Hugh Bundy, Jonathan Ragaei Lange, Kathryn Cecelia Bundy, and Gillian Anna Lange.

Contents

List of Figures
and Tables

Preface

In 1974 the International Research Center for Energy and Economic Development (ICEED) initiated its annual international energy conferences. In part due to the wide acceptance of these meetings as well as to the desire to pursue energy and development aspects of specific countries or regions in more depth, the center decided that an area conference planned in conjunction with the energy sessions would be a logical step.

In October of 1980 the first international area conference was held to discuss "Saudi Arabia: Energy, Developmental Planning, and Industrialization." The two days of sessions, following the seventh international energy meeting, drew an exceptional range of talents on the economics and development of the Kingdom. The chapters in this book, except for that prepared by the editors, were written for presentation to the conference.

The contributions represent a mixture of academicians, officials, and representatives of industry and finance. The views expressed similarly reflect this variety of disciplines, sectors, Saudis, and non-Saudis, and the opinions advanced do not necessarily represent the agencies and institutions with which the authors are identified or of the ICEED. In addition to the formal papers, the conference also allowed for a substantial amount of informal exchange of information and views among the participants.

The chapters have been arranged to allow the reader to begin with a general overview of the Saudi economy and then proceed to the more specialized areas addressed by the conference. Dr. Ali Johany, Dean of the College of Industrial Management at the University of Petroleum and Minerals in Dhahran, has set the stage with his chapter, "The Saudi Economy: Yesterday's Performance and Tomorrow's Prospects." Dr. Farouk Akhdar, Secretary General of the Royal Commission for Jubail and Yanbu, traces the thrust that underlies the Kingdom's developmental activities in the industrial sector. How this philosophy has been translated into targets and practice forms the basis of the contribution of Dr. Fouad Al-Farsy, Deputy Minister for Industry, in the third chapter, "Saudi Arabian Industrial Development: Aspirations and Realities."

The critical place of the petroleum sector in the Saudi economy receives much deserved attention in three presentations: "The Interactions between Oil Policy and Industrial Policy in Saudi Arabia," by Dr. Paul Stevens of the University of Surrey; "Oil and Gas: Industrial Implementation," by Saud Ounallah of Petromin (the Saudi national oil company); and "The Saudi Petrochemical Industry in the 1980s," by Dr. H.G. Hambleton of Laval University.

The development process under way in the Kingdom is contingent upon the continuation of technology transfer. This element has been skillfully examined by Dr. Talal Hafiz, editor-in-chief of *Saudi Report,* in his chapter, "Technology Transfer to the Developing Nations: The Case of Saudi Arabia." A more specialized means of facilitating this transfer is through the Saudi Arabian National Center for Science and Technology (SANCST), described in another chapter by a member of that institution's staff, Fahad Huraib.

The cultural and social fabric of a nation has a direct and substantial impact on the path that development takes. Dr. John Duke Anthony of the School of Advanced International Studies of the Johns Hopkins University and Dr. Abdulrahman Al-Said of the University of Petroleum and Minerals in their respective chapters have attempted to point out the special historical and cultural factors that figure in the process of transition of Saudi Arabia from its former tribal society to a nation-state.

With the dramatic increase in the price of crude oil in the 1970s and the concomitant massive inflow of petroleum-generated revenues, Saudi Arabia has emerged as a major factor in the global economy and international finance. Dr. Yusuf Nimatallah, Executive Director for Saudi Arabia at the International Monetary Fund, offers insights into the Kingdom's role in international finance and development assistance. The same influx in revenue that has pushed Saudi Arabia into the forefront of individual aid donors has presented its domestic economy with special pressures, including both indigenous and imported inflation. Dr. Ahmed Al-Malik, Director General of the Foreign Department of the Saudi Arabian Monetary Agency, directed his comments to this problem during the conference, drawing from the chapter he coauthored with Michael Keran, "Monetary Sources of Inflation in Saudi Arabia."

The economic and commercial relationship between the United States and Saudi Arabia is long-standing and has been strengthened throughout the 1970s: the Kingdom has become the major source of oil imports for the United States; the United States is a major source for Saudi Arabia of technology and capital goods, particularly in the petroleum sector. Abdullah Taher Dabbagh, head of the Commercial Section of the Saudi Embassy in Washington, D.C., examines this relationship.

Adequate labor—both in numbers and skills—has been proven a critical input into the development process. Thus the chapter by C.A. Sinclair of the University of Surrey on "Manpower in Saudi Arabia, 1980–1985" (coauthored by J.S. Birks) stirred considerable comment during the conference. In fact, the then just-published *Third Development Plan* for the Kingdom identified the expansion of indigenous manpower and a reduction of dependence on imported labor as one of the basic targets for the first half of the 1980s.

The concluding chapter, "The Third Development Plan of Saudi Arabia, 1400–1405 A.H./1980–1985" has been written to describe the development and spending priorities established by the Kingdom to mid-decade in not only manpower but also in industrialization, the agricultural and petroleum sectors, and toward the ultimate objective of diversification of the economy as well as its development. This blueprint stands as a comprehensive development document, one that addresses the multifaceted needs and distinctive features of the Saudi economy in many of the very issues raised in the chapters of this book.

1

The Saudi Economy: Yesterday's Performance and Tomorrow's Prospects

Ali D. Johany

The Rapid Pace of Saudi Economic Development

Prior to the unification of Saudi Arabia in 1932, an integrated national economy did not even exist. Economic activity outside Hejaz (where the holy cities are located) was confined to livestock raising by Bedouins, primitive agriculture, and production of simple tools by craftsmen who lived in small towns concentrated around sources of water.

In Hejaz (the northwestern part of the country), an opportunity did exist for economic development that could have affected all of Saudi Arabia because of the yearly influx of pilgrims visiting the holy places in Mecca and Medina. But the lack of security made movement of people and goods an exceptionally risky activity.

The justified fear of raids on camel caravans by ruthless Bedouins, the infrequency of rain, and the inhospitable weather of the desert limited the size and scope of economic activity and made production feasible only on a small scale for small markets, practically subsistence in nature.

By the end of 1932, the security problem was completely solved. And from that date until today, Saudi Arabia has become the safest place on earth for both property and people.

Oil was discovered in commercial quantities in March of 1938, but World War II interrupted the development of the petroleum industry. In the period that immediately followed the end of the war, production increased rapidly. Total output rose more than threefold from 60 million barrels during 1946 to 200 million barrels during 1950. Since the end of World War II, oil has been the source of revenues for both the private and public sectors.

The overall performance of the Saudi economy can be accurately measured by the growth of the government budget—the vehicle through which oil revenues reach every segment of the economy—which increased from $103 million in fiscal year 1947–1948 to almost $73,000 million (Saudi riyal 245 billion) for fiscal year 1980–1981.

1

But the greatest rates of growth were achieved from 1974 to 1980 (see table 1-1). In this period the main problem was the level of inflation, caused by the high growth of liquidity given the economy's modest infrastructure, which made it impossible for imports (supply of goods and services) to increase as fast as nominal income.

By the end of 1970, however, the battle against inflation was won, and its current rate (fall 1980) in Saudi Arabia is below the world average. The reasons for a low inflation rate include a drastic decrease in the level of liquidity (table 1-2) and improvement of the country's seaports, which decreased the waiting periods of incoming loaded ships from six months in 1975-1976 to less than six hours in 1978-1979. It is planned that by the end of 1980, a total of 114 piers will be in operation at the five main ports as compared to the 57 that existed in 1977.

Table 1-3 summarizes the economic development of the country during the 1970s. The projects that received the government's greatest attention were road construction and ports, airport and telecommunication schemes, housing, the establishment of new industries, and the building of schools.

The improvement and expansion of roads is very impressive by any standard, but it is even more so when one looks back a few years. In 1968 the total cumulative length of Saudi Arabia's asphalted roads was less than 2,000 kilometers; by the end of 1979 the total rose to more than 20,000 kilometers (see table 1-4).

The accomplishment in the field of education is just as impressive. The number of students enrolled in all levels of educational institutions in 1979 reached 1.35 million as compared with only 42,000 in 1952.

In the period of 1975-1977 there was an acute housing shortage that was made even worse by rent controls. For example, the monthly rent of a two-bedroom unfurnished apartment in 1974 in the major cities averaged between $150 and $200. The same apartment in 1977 would have rented for somewhere between $500 and $800 per month. During 1980 that apartment

Table 1-1
Real Gross Domestic Product (GDP)

	(Annual Growth Rates)			
	1975–1976	1976–1977	1977–1978	1978–1979
GDP	8.6	14.8	5.9	7.6
Oil sector	1.1	13.2	− 0.5	1.8
Nonoil sector	19.8	16.9	13.8	13.7
Private	17.8	18.9	13.9	14.1
Public	23.9	12.9	13.5	12.9

Source: Kingdom of Saudi Arabia, Saudi Arabian Monetary Agency (SAMA), *Annual Report, 1979.*

Table 1–2
Annual Growth Rates of Money Supply and Real Supplies of Goods and Services

Fiscal Year	Money Supply (M_3)	Real Supplies of Goods and Services
1975–1976	73.9	34.5
1976–1977	52.7	30.3
1977–1978	43.6	23.9
1978–1979	14.5	15.7

Source: Kingdom of Saudi Arabia, Arabian Monetary Agency (SAMA), *Annual Report, 1979.*

could not be rented for more than $300. The housing shortage was eliminated chiefly by the establishment in 1976 of the Real Estate Development Fund, which grants interest-free loans to citizens for building their own dwelling and loans for constructing residential buildings for others to occupy. By the end of 1979 the fund's total loan disbursements, since its creation in 1976, reached Saudi riyals (SR) 24.4 billion.

Telephone quality and service has been improved rapidly during the 1970s. By the end of 1981 work is expected to be finished on the 470,000 automatic telephone lines operating on electronic exchange in seventy-two towns throughout the Kingdom. In addition, a total of 291,300 lines were already in operation at the end of 1979.

Telex lines are expected to reach 9,000 by the end of 1980 as compared to 6,350 lines in mid-1979. This service is now available in nineteen cities.

There is no other less-developed country that did what Saudi Arabia has effected to further the industrialization of the country by the private sector. And given the trader mentality of the majority of Saudi businessmen, government encouragement is necessary. The government incentives to the private sector include:

exemption from custom duties of imported machinery and equipment, spare parts, raw or semi-processed materials, and packing materials, protective tariffs or quotas against competing imports, financial assistance on a highly concessionary basis, long term leasing of industrial sites at nominal rent, preferential treatment for locally manufactured goods in government procurement and assistance in the identification of viable projects through market research and feasibility studies.[1]

Yet it seems that most of the industrial projects undertaken by Saudi industrialists are confined to the assembly of already manufactured parts.

Table 1-3
Project Budget Expenditure, 1974/75–1978/80
(in million riyals)

Fiscal Year	1974–1975	1975–1976	1976–1977	1977–1978	1978–1979	1979–1980
Total project expenditure	26,397.0	74,379.0	74,433.4	74,866.0	83,047.7	105,680.0
Council of ministers and related budget headings	1,658.9	4,761.8	4,756.9	4,924.5	4,399.4	13,964.0
Municipal and rural affairs	3,683.8	13,221.6	14,758.0	11,681.3	7,966.8	9,789.8
Public works and housing	114.4	185.7	9,061.4	7,856.8	5,649.4	3,022.5
Information	205.3	636.7	959.8	1,064.0	723.5	634.3
Civil aviation	1,150.8	4,469.9	4,469.9	4,370.0	3,912.8	6,804.6
Interior	973.2	2,301.3	3,078.9	3,293.4	3,330.5	4,131.9
Labor and social affairs	165.7	1,408.5	2,040.8	2,237.0	1,452.3	2,126.5
Health	435.1	2,061.6	1,737.0	1,758.3	1,855.0	1,822.0
Education	1,265.6	6,355.1	6,367.6	7,955.3	5,123.1	5,771.5
Communications	4,212.0	10,994.2	15,380.7	7,822.5	7,377.0	9,811.3
Finance and national economy	1,955.3	7,030.1	3,984.8	3,754.3	3,309.5	7,868.3
Industry, electricity, and commerce	114.4	586.7	1,081.0	488.0	337.3	3,450.5[a]
Agriculture and water resources	1,053.5	1,718.0	1,721.4	1,511.4	1,854.4	3,112.0
Public investment fund	3,000.0	1,600.0	—	—	4,000.0	4,250.0
Other	6,409.0	17,047.8	25,396.3	39,002.7	50,433.0	49,379.4
Less: expected shortfall	—	—	-20,361.1	-22,853.5	-18,676.3	-20,258.6

Source: Kingdom of Saudi Arabia, Saudi Arabian Monetary Agency (SAMA), *Annual Report, 1979*.

[a]Including gathering and liquefaction of gas.

Table 1-4
Road Network in the Kingdom, 1974/75-1978/79
(cumulative length in kilometers)

| Year | Asphalted Roads | | | | Rural Roads |
	Main	Secondary	Feeder	Total	
1974-1975	6,141	5,556	473	12,170	8,510
1975-1976	7,182	5,798	1,125	14,105	11,193
1976-1977	8,362	5,897	1,779	16,038	13,307
1977-1978	9,618	5,959	2,660	18,238	16,948
1978-1979	10,834	6,030	3,270	20,134	20,119

Source: Kingdom of Saudi Arabia, Saudi Arabian Monetary Agency (SAMA), *Annual Report, 1979.*

The main problem that hinders private industrial development is the lack of skilled and semiskilled Saudi workers. It is not unusual for an industrial plant in Saudi Arabia to have not a single Arabic-speaking individual, for the managers are usually Europeans and the workers are almost certain to be from the Indian subcontinent or from the Far East.

Nevertheless, the mere existence of privately owned factories of any kind in a country that ten years ago had almost none is very encouraging. From 1975 to 1978, a total of 1,035 industrial establishments were licensed, with a total capital of SR 16,780 million.

The most massive industrial projects are, however, undertaken by the government under the auspices of the General Petroleum and Mineral Organization (Petromin) and the Saudi Basic Industries Corporation (SABIC).

The biggest project that Petromin is engaged in is the construction of the 1,270-kilometer-long East-West crude-oil pipeline linking the Ghawar Field (the world's largest) to the Red Sea port of Yanbu. Eventually the capacity of this pipeline will reach 3.5 million barrels per day (b/d). The eleven pumping stations that were built to push the crude through the pipeline to Yanbu will be fueled by natural gas liquids (NGL), which is also supposed to reach Yanbu through a 1,168-kilometer NGL pipeline. The NGL pipeline is being built by Techint Arabia Limited at a cost of $104 million, under the supervision of the Arabian American Oil Company (Aramco).

The mammoth gas-gathering and processing system that is expected to collect and process about 3.3 billion cubic feet per day (cfd) is being implemented for the government by Aramco. This enormous project was undertaken to utilize the "wet" gas that is produced in association with oil and that was hitherto flared; roughly 500 million cubic feet of associated gas is produced with every 1 million barrels of crude oil.

The original cost of this project was estimated to be $4.5 billion. Petromin now says it will not cost more than $12 billion.[2] About 40 percent of the collected gas will be used to produce fuel gas for industry, to power electric generating plants, to desalinate seawater, and to provide ethane as feedstock for the petrochemical industry at Jubail and Yanbu. The other 60 percent of the gas will be exported in the form of propane, butane, and natural gasoline.

SABIC, in partnership with such giants as Exxon, Shell, Mobil, Dow, Texas Eastern, and a large consortium of Japanese companies, is building huge petrochemical, fertilizer, and metallurgical complexes at Jubail and Yanbu, which, when completed, should give Saudi Arabia a large industrial base and make it one of the world's largest exporters of petrochemicals in addition to being the largest crude-oil exporter.

Pollution of the air, land, and sea that will undoubtedly accompany these industrial developments is but one of the problems that economic progress brings. Saudi Arabia, like many other countries that underwent rapid economic change, has to worry about these problems and has to do so very soon.

The Permanent Question: What Is the Optimum Rate of Oil Output?

To Saudi Arabia each barrel of oil in the ground is part of the country's total capital stock much like a computer or a cement plant. The only difference is that oil is not reproducible, so the stock of known reserves, given a state of technology and an oil price, cannot be increased without further efforts (investment).

The only way stocks of oil in the ground can generate income is by appreciating in value. The country's assets should be managed in such a way that all assets—oil or buildings—earn the same rate of return, with adjustments for risk. Thus, if oil is to be left in the ground, its net price (price minus operating and user costs) must increase at a rate equal to the interest rate. That is, if the rate of return on additional investment within Saudi Arabia or abroad (with adjustment for risk) is greater than the rate of increase in the value of oil in the ground, then more oil ought to be produced. Conversely, none should be produced if the value of oil rises at a higher rate than the rate of return on investment. If the question is strictly a financial one, then the decision to be reached is in principle a simple one. With the help of a computer and a relatively uncomplicated economic model, the answer is easily available.

However, in reality Saudi Arabia is a part of this world, a fact that it cannot ignore. There were many instances when the Saudi government had decided to increase oil output not because of its need for funds but because it felt that not doing so would increase the price of oil to a level that could pave the road toward a steep and universal economic decline. For example, following the political upheaval in Iran during the fall of 1978, the price of oil rose sharply in the spot market, and Saudi Arabia raised its oil output to 9,310 million barrels per day during October and to over 10,000 million barrels per day for the months of November and December. Throughout 1979 Saudi Arabia raised its oil output from the government-announced target of 8.5 million barrels per day to 9.5 million barrels per day. Obviously, output was increased to avoid price increases. And in October of 1980 Saudi Arabia again announced an oil-output increase to around 10 million barrels per day obviously in an attempt to reduce the impact of the Iraqi-Iranian conflict on the price of oil.

Consequently, we can say it is almost certain that in this unstable world, Saudi Arabia will, in the immediate future at least, find itself producing more oil than it wants to from a purely financial point of view. How long this situation will last, no one can be certain. Sooner or later, however, the cost of producing oil will make squeezing the last few barrels greater than the price of other sources. And, as result, oil revenues can be expected to flow only for a limited and uncertain time period. If part of the revenue is not saved and invested, future consumption will fall. The problem that Saudi Arabia faces is, in principle, not different from the one an individual in his prime working age faces. The objective is to maximize the country's total wealth (permanent income) rather than "current income."

Saudi Arabia can maximize its total wealth with investment projects that generate future income. But since domestic productive capacity cannot be expanded at the same rate at which the oil revenues grow in certain years, some of the investment funds must be invested abroad. The proper question that economic policymakers should ask themselves is what proportion of total investment should be allocated to each type of investment.

The answer to this question is provided in figure 1-1. Investment funds should be allocated in such a way as to equate the marginal rates of return on domestic (r_d) and foreign investment (r_f). Given the total amount of funds for investment GF, maximum return is achieved by allocating GS to domestic investment and SF to foreign investment.

And since the relative backwardness of the economy limited the amount of expenditures on development projects that could be undertaken without substantially increasing the inflation rate during years of rising oil revenues, one may wonder whether it is not more sensible for the government to immediately shift funds from domestic to foreign investment once the real rate of return on domestic investment falls below the rate of return that could be generated on foreign investment. However, once one takes into consideration some problems that are associated with foreign investment, then almost any positive rate of return on domestic investment becomes attractive.

Here are some possible problems: (1) American and Western European

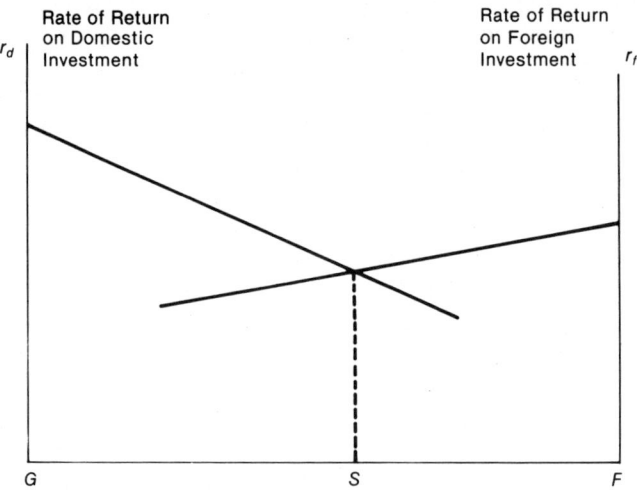

Figure 1-1. Allocation of Investment Funds

governments may levy taxes on foreign investments—including Saudi investment. (2) There is a threat of expropriation to coerce the Saudi government to take a particular political stand (the probability of such action may not seem very high at this time, but it is nevertheless positive). (3) The more likely course of action for political pressure is to simply block the movement of Saudi funds.

One thing is certain: Saudi Arabia's investment in Europe and America reduces its political freedom and increases the political leverage of the foreign countries in which its assets are invested. In other words, property rights of the Saudis in their investments abroad could be threatened at any time. Under normal circumstances, however, the greatest threat to Saudi foreign investment is the world rate of inflation because Saudi investment abroad is mainly in the form of near-money assets.

If Saudi Arabia is forced by international circumstances to produce more oil than its present stage of economic development dictates, and as a result, it accumulates more funds that must be invested domestically, what sort of domestic investment should be undertaken?

The emphasis of the first and second five-year plans was on infrastructure—specifically roads, buildings, and sea- and airports. The third five-year plan will, on the other hand, shift expenditure away from construction toward industry, agriculture, and human resources. Although the economic value of agriculture and industry is obviously to broaden the Saudi economy's base and thus diversify income, investment in such activities may not be as useful as in human capital. Today the Saudi economy is experiencing a severe shortage of skilled and semiskilled Saudi workers in addition to the shortage and sometimes even complete absence of certain professionals. As a result Saudi farms and factories have to be manned mostly by foreigners, which implies that a large portion of the wages of those foreigners is leaked to other countries' economies. In addition, the skills that these foreign workers acquire while working in Saudi Arabia is an asset that is not owned by Saudi Arabia.

The economic history of Japan and Switzerland, and most recently of South Korea, seems to show that investment in human beings when coupled with political stability, in the final analysis leads to an impressive rate of economic growth. And since Saudi Arabia's economic objective is creating a permanent source of income, once oil is gone, then investment in human capital is the best expenditure toward reaching that goal.

Saudi Economic Issues in the 1980s

By any standards, the growth rates and structural changes the Saudi economy experienced in the 1970s are very impressive. These developments were discussed in the first section. In this section, a glimpse of the economic issues that Saudi economic policymakers must contend with in the 1980s and beyond is given.

Income Distribution

No detailed figures are available concerning the distribution of income in Saudi Arabia, but certain generalizations can be made. First, the urban population was (and still is) the segment of the population that benefited the most from economic growth, for they are the ones who, relatively speaking, have the required skills to participate most effectively in the country's development. From this group comes the leadership of business and industry as well as the high-ranking government officials. In addition, the urban population benefits the most from the services that the government offers free of charge like education, health services, and the use of roads. And they are the ones who consume the greatest amount of water and electricity that are available in greater abundance to city dwellers at a very small fraction of their actual cost.

Second, among the urban population, income is concentrated in the hands of those who work in the private sector where salaries and wages are manyfold what the government pays its employees.

It is true that the source of wealth in Saudi Arabia is oil, and oil is 100 percent owned by the government, but the way this wealth is spread to the population favors those who own business establishments and to a lesser extent those who work for them. The reason for this distribution is traceable to the fact that those who work for the government receive fixed wages and salaries, the purchasing power of which is continuously falling, due to inflation. Those in the private sector, on the other hand, sell their services in the open market and are often able to benefit from shortages caused by the continuous growth of liquidity that has often grown at a faster rate than the growth in the supply of goods and services.

The absence of income taxes and other kinds of taxes has only compounded the problem. The only tax Saudis are asked to pay, which they do not always pay, is the *Zakat,* which is 2.5 percent of an individual's net worth, and that obviously is very small and has very little effect as an instrument of income redistribution, even if paid by everyone.

The press in Saudi Arabia and abroad had often talked about the many Saudi "billionaires." One can never be sure of the accuracy of newspaper stories, but one thing is certain: the number of Saudis who are millionaires is growing, and those who joined this exclusive club did so mainly because they happened to be engaged in some sort of private business activity when the economy boomed in the 1974–1977 period.

During the midseventies the easiest way, though not the only way, for one to become a millionaire was simply to engage in the buying and selling of land. It was not unusual for the value of a plot of land an individual bought one day to more than double a week later. Yet, there were many, though certainly not all, government employees who were busy doing their jobs and who did not participate in the real-estate bonanza.

One can conclude, therefore, that the group of Saudi citizens who benefited the least from economic growth are the Bedouins. That is not to say that the Saudi Bedouins are not better off today because they are; it is only to say that their relative share of the pie is small and continuously decreasing.

But how many Bedouins are there in Saudi Arabia? Estimates have varied from as high as 90 percent to as low as 10 percent.[3] The reasons for these differing estimates are many, but the chief one seems to be the confusion between Saudi citizens who are descendents of tribal ancestors and between those citizens who are totally nomadic and completely isolated from the sedentary population. If one means by Bedouins the Saudi citizens who derive their livelihood by raising goats, sheep, and camels and follow the clouds (move to parts of the country where it has rained), then their number is perhaps less than 15 percent of the population. There is no doubt, however, that Saudi Bedouins are yesterday's majority who are becoming today's minority. And their economic status has to be given greater attention in the coming years than it receives now.

The State of the Oil Fields

In all of the Saudi oil fields, gas and crude oil are "trapped" under pressure in strata of porous rock where water surrounds the oil deposits. The permeability of the rock and the amount of the water pressure determined the amount of oil that can be recovered. Geologists tell us that the holes in the rock of Saudi oil reservoirs are large enough to allow oil to move freely toward the drilled wells.

The problem now (and it will worsen in the future) is maintenance of the required pressure at a level that permits recovery of the greatest possible amount of crude, given the present state of technology.

Among the factors that govern the pressure are (obviously) the age of the field, the number of producing wells in a given area of a field and the amount of oil pumped from the entire field and from each well. That is, not only does the total amount of oil extracted affect pressure but also the rate at which extraction occurs and the number of wells used to accomplish the job.

Between mid-1970 and mid-1973, total Saudi oil output increased from 3,500 million barrels per day to 7,500 million barrels per day, an increase of more than 100 percent, and most of this additional oil came from the Ghawar oil field. This field is the world's largest and stretches for nearly 250 kilometers, but still, increasing its output in a mere thirty-six months by 4 million barrels per day eventually led to decreasing the pressure on its crude.

Since the early 1970s water has been pumped in to replace the pressure lost as a result of accelerated oil output. Gas could also be used to maintain pressure, but gas itself is a substitute for oil, and its value is rising with the increasing price of oil.

Of course, there is nothing wrong with pumping water to maintain pressure at desirable levels, as the pressure in every oil reservoir eventually falls, but the problem is that Saudi Arabia sweet water is more scarce than oil. Thus Aramco has had to rely on seawater. And seawater creates problems that may be as serious as rapidly decreasing pressure in the oil fields.

Furthermore, injecting water, whether purified or not, creates new problems. As more oil is pumped out, the injected water seeps into the producing wells and the wells start running "wet." Wet wells mean that water is mixing with oil, and in this case wells have to be blocked with concrete at the base or completely shut in.

Injecting seawater to alleviate pressure creates other problems in addition to the possibility of wetting the wells such as: (a) the corrosion of pipe-lines and other equipment, and (b) salt and other seawater minerals may block the pores in the rock, causing a reduction in the amount of recoverable oil from the injected reservoirs.

What are the solutions to these serious problems? First, water has to be injected to prevent pressure from falling to levels that reduce the amount of recoverable oil. Consequently, in 1978 Aramco pumped about 11.5 million barrels per day of saline aquifer water and treated seawater into the "old" fields.

Second, the problems that water injection creates must also be dealt with. One of the solutions, albeit an expensive one, is water desalination. In 1979 Aramco's seawater-treatment plant at Qurayyah in Eastern Ghawar started operations. This plant, the world's largest when the whole system is completed, will produce 3.6 million barrels per day of treated seawater. The cost of the project may well exceed $1 billion. The problem of wet wells that water injection generates must also be dealt with. A plant to desalt crude is being built at Safaniyah, the main source of Saudi heavy crude. When it is finished in 1984, it will have a capacity of 2.1 million barrels per day of desalted crude. Desalting plants will also be built at Berri, the premier pro-ducer of extra-light crude, and in northern Ghawar. It is estimated that 4 million barrels per day of crude oil will be desalted by the mid-1980s. The cost may reach $5 billion.[4]

What we want to emphasize here is that the days when the operational costs of producing oil in Saudi Arabia were mainly the costs of drilling and operating wells are gone forever. Substantial investment in seawater-treatment plants as well as in crude-oil-desalination plants has to be under-taken. And acceleration of oil output not only reduces total reserves but it also reduces the amount of oil that otherwise would have been recoverable.

Since the Saudi economy is completely dependent on petroleum, it is rather an understatement to say that the delicate conditions of the old Saudi oil fields ought to be the concern of every Saudi citizen.

Water

Water shortages in the Arab Peninsula are nothing new. What is really new in Saudi Arabia today is the high cost of producing water and the in-credibly low prices people are charged for using it. It is estimated that Saudi urban centers consume about 1,200 million tons of water per year. The pro-jected amount of water that Saudi cities and towns will consume in the year 2000 is 4 billion tons if the price of water stays at its present level.[5]

At the present, Saudi Arabia gets half of its drinking water from desalination plants, and the other half from underground reservoirs—fossil water. But fossil water is like oil, a nonrenewable resource, and if Saudis continue consuming at the same rates of consumption as in the 1970s, none of it will be left for future generations.

Treating seawater is a very expensive alternative. The Saudi government so far has spent SR 25 billion in water-desalination plants and related projects; another SR 7 billion will be spent soon. Furthermore, this SR 32 billion will be only what is spent under the aegis of the Saline Water Conservation (SWCC) and does not include Aramco's desalters for oil operations or the Ministry of Defense plants, nor even the Ministry of Agriculture plants.[6]

The vice governor of SWCC was quoted as estimating the "real cost" of desalinated water at about $2.00 a cubic meter. That is very expensive indeed. Yet it seems almost certain that the real cost to Saudi Arabia of producing each additional cubic meter of water is much more than $2.00. Why? Because in Kuwait, where cost conditions should not be much different than they are in Saudi Arabia, the government charges Kuwaiti consumers up to $4,00 for a cubic meter of desalinated water.[7] And it is almost certain that if the real cost of a cubic meter of desalinated water in Kuwait is about $2.00 (as is being claimed to be the real cost in Saudi Arabia), then the Kuwaiti government would not ask consumers to pay $4.00 for it. But since Saudi consumers are only charged SR 0.5 (equivalent to $0.15), they are in effect encouraged to waste water *even* if each cubic meter costs only $2.00. If consumers pay $0.15 for a commodity when its cost of production is $2.00, they will behave as if the cost is actually $0.15—the amount of income they have to give up in order to acquire each additional cubic meter of water.

The Saudi government's motive in keeping the cost of water to consumers so low is rather obviously an attempt to keep the cost of living as low as possible. The problem is that this method of subsidizing consumers results in misallocation of resources. Everybody would be better off if the real price of water were paid and then given back to consumers as a lump sum, which they could spend in any way they see fit. In this way consumers would receive a subsidy that would increase their real income without encouraging them to waste water. Then the relative prices of all the goods and services they consume as well as the level of their income would determine their water consumption. And given that the real price of water is going to be somewhere between thirteen to twenty-six times its present level, consumer income will have to reach many times its present level before water is consumed at the rates it is being consumed now.

If by the year 2000, Saudis are going to consume 4 billion cubic meters of water, as currently projected, then the opportunity cost of consuming that much water would be at least $8 billion (4 × $2.00) in 1977 dollars. That would be almost one-third of the entire government budget. It is rather apparent that something has to be done about conserving water. The most obvious and immediate remedy should be to increase the price of water to consumers.

But good news may eventually come from the Saudi Arabia's Center for Science and Technology (SANCST) and from the University of Petroleum and Minerals' (UPM) Research Institute. Both are engaged in applied desalination research, and scientists at SANCST as well as at the UPM Research Institute think there is a good chance their research will lead to technological breakthroughs that will result in reducing the cost of "Harvesting" sweet water from the sea.

Conclusion

Saudi Arabia has been trying to do in ten years what took many other countries hundred of years to do. It would be foolish therefore to expect this nation to achieve what it did, and it is certainly remarkable, without any difficulty. Some economic mistakes have been made, but the Saudis are learning from their mistakes, and their leadership is keenly aware of the problems that rapid economic growth can create.

Notes

1. Kingdom of Saudi Arabia, Saudi Arabian Monetary Agency (SAMA), *Annual Report, 1979,* p. 73.

2. *Saudi Business,* October 5, 1979, p. 16.

3. Abdulrahman H. Al-Said, "The Transition from a Tribal Society to a Nation-State," chapter 10 of this volume.

4. The source of information in this section is *Saudi Business,* November 30, December 7, and December 14, 1979.

5. *Saudi Business,* April 18, 1980, p. 10.

6. *Saudi Business,* January 11, 1980, pp. 16–19.

7. Ibid., p. 17.

2 The Philosophy of Saudi Arabia's Industrialization Policy

Farouk M. Akhdar

I believe it is particularly important that Americans have a clearer understanding of the rationale underlying the Kingdom's industrialization program and the benefits that the West derives from our development strategy.
For that reason, I have chosen to concentrate my remarks on the philosophy
of Saudi Arabia's industrialization policy.

The objectives and strategy of the Kingdom's industrialization program
are generally understood in the West. But there is less understanding of the
philosophy underpinning the government's rapid industrialization policy,
the relationship between oil policy and industrial policy, or how the West
benefits from our industrial development strategy.

In the 1970s the Kingdom of Saudi Arabia made a fundamental policy
decision to respond positively to the world demand for its depleting petroleum resources to moderate disruptive oil price increases and to invest the
receipts from its oil sales in its gigantic economic development plan.

It is important to understand, however, that Saudi Arabia did not have
to adopt this decision. An alternative development strategy was also considered and had its supporters. That strategy emphasized the conservation of
our oil resources, slower economic growth, and a less rapid development
pace and more moderate social change.

One could hardly blame us for deciding that it is not in our interest to
rapidly deplete our valuable oil resources or run up current account surpluses that promptly depreciate in value. Far better to slow down our
growth and limit oil exports to the amount needed to cover our immediate
and more modest development needs.

The consequence for the West of such a development strategy would
have been unfortunate. It would have meant even more rapid increases in
the price of oil than those that resulted since the mid-1970s. It would have
meant chronic supply shortages, more inflation, slower growth, and more
unemployment in the West. It would have meant that Saudi Arabia
imported less from the West and therefore less recycling of what some in the
West have elected to call "petrodollars."

Such a strategy, while benefiting Saudi Arabia, would have been harmful not only to the West but to the entire world economic and financial system. I wonder how many Americans are aware of the adverse impact on

their economic prosperity such a decision by the Kingdom would have entailed.

But the decision to severely limit oil exports was not adopted because the government of Saudi Arabia considers itself a responsible member of the international community. As such, it recognizes its obligation to maintain the health and stability of the world financial and economic system, even if that would be at the expense of our own domestic economy. We consider that our destiny is tied to the future of the world economy in general and the U.S. economy in particular. We understand that we are a vital part of the interdependent global economic system.

To implement the fundamental decision concerning oil policy, the Kingdom was compelled to sharply increase the volume of its oil production and exports, both of which rose about 250 percent during the 1970–1979 period.[1] The immediate results, particularly pronounced after the increase in OPEC oil prices in 1973–1974, were to

Vastly increase government revenues beyond normal development requirements

Sharply increase the country's international financial assets

Accelerate the depletion of the Kingdom's chief natural resource and generator of national income

It is at this point that the initial oil-policy decision adopted by the government can be seen to be intimately linked to the industrial policy adopted by the Kingdom.

Faced with the fast depletion of the Kingdom's oil resources, it was incumbent on the government to employ the rapidly increasing oil revenues to transform the national economy and reduce our excessive dependence on oil production and exports as a source of economic growth and prosperity.

With respect to the Kingdom's accumulation of financial assets overseas in the world capital markets, the government recognized that the value of these assets was being depreciated constantly due to world inflation and the decline in the value of the foreign currencies in which the assets were held. According to a study of the Arab Monetary Fund in Abu Dhabi, Arab cash balances in Western countries have been depreciating nearly 5 percent per annum in real terms in recent years. Consequently, the Saudi government realized the desirability of converting its accumulating cash surpluses into actual investments within the Kingdom in order to minimize the decapitalization of its international financial assets.

For these reasons, the Kingdom's second and third five-year development plans have given increasing priority to the expansion of the productive sectors of the economy such as manufacturing industry, nonfuel minerals, and agriculture. It was necessary, of course, to undertake a parallel expansion of those supporting infrastructure and services essential for the efficient functioning of the productive sectors such as education and training, water and electricity, transport and communications, and banking and finance.

Under the circumstances, it is neither surprising nor illogical for the Saudi government—particularly in view of the economically undeveloped state of the economy in the early 1970s—to have pursued a policy of rapid economic development during the second-plan period (1975–1980).

It was against this background in the 1970s that the Kingdom defined its industrial objectives and strategy. The fundamental goal of Saudi industrialization is to foster the diversification of the economic base in order to reduce the Kingdom's overwhelming dependence on the oil sector, to achieve greater economic self-sufficiency and protection from external supply disruptions, and to gain the cost advantages from domestic manufacturing activity.

To achieve these objectives, Saudi Arabia is promoting private investment in manufacturing industry by offering a wide range of financial, fiscal, tariff, and other incentives to qualified investors. The government has also assumed responsibility for initiating large-scale industrial projects beyond the capability of the private sector by entering into joint-venture partnerships with foreign firms who provide managerial, technical, and marketing know-how.

In general, it can be said that industrialization in the 1980s will proceed along two complementary lines in the Kingdom. In the existing areas of industrial concentration such as Jeddah, Riyadh, and Dammam, manufacturing industry will continue to expand along conventional paths, with the government's providing incentives and subsidies under the industrial promotion laws.

But the Saudi government has adopted another parallel approach to the industrial transformation of the Kingdom based on the construction of two large, completely new hydrocarbon-oriented industrial cities, one at Jubail on the Arabian Gulf coast, 80 kilometers north of Dammam, and the other at Yanbu on the Red Sea coast, 350 kilometers north of Jeddah.

The Royal Commission for Jubail and Yanbu, established in 1975, has been assigned the responsibility for the planning, design, construction, and operation of the infrastructure facilities for the heavy industries and for the new communities established at the two sites.

The urban-industrial complexes at Jubail and Yanbu constitute the centerpieces of the Kingdom's heavy industrialization program. They reflect the government's commitment to develop large-scale, hydrocarbon-based and energy-intensive industries such as petrochemicals, fertilizers, and iron and steel that can effectively utilize the country's abundant, reliable supply of crude oil and associated natural gas as industrial fuel and raw materials.

The Jubail and Yanbu basic industry programs envisage the construction of as many as two dozen major new refineries, petrochemical, fertilizer, iron and steel and other resource-based industries, as well as secondary manufacturing and fabricating facilities that use the output of the basic industries as raw materials, by the end of the century.

We are well aware that there are critics of the Kingdom's industrialization strategy. It is often argued that industries based on oil and its by-products cannot contribute to the diversification of the sources of the Kingdom's income or provide an alternative to the oil sector when this resource is depleted since such industries depend themselves on oil and natural gas.

Logically, the hydrocarbon-based industries under construction at Jubail and Yanbu cannot be considered an alternative to the oil sector as a generator of national income. Therefore, it may be asked, why is the Kingdom embarked on a program of heavy industry at Jubail and Yanbu, an industry that is heavily dependent on natural resources that one day will be exhausted?

There are, in my view, three reasons why the kingdom is pursuing hydrocarbon-based industrialization at Jubail and Yanbu. Remember, however, that these reasons should be viewed within the context of the philosophy of industrialization and oil policies, I have talked about:

First, we know that it will be a long time, perhaps three generations, before the Kingdom's oil resources are effectively depleted. In the meantime development of petrochemical fertilizer and other hydrocarbon-based industries will generate additional value added from the use of our oil and natural-gas resources while they last. Since immense amounts of natural gas are wasted at present, the development of a gas gathering, processing, and distribution system will enable this discarded resource to be used as a raw material and fuel for new industries at Jubail and Yanbu.

Second, the large-scale hydrocarbon-based industrial projects at the two industrial cities will contribute to the creation of a new class of trained Saudi managers, entrepreneurs, and technicians—to the establishment of new work attitudes and discipline—all of which can be readily transferred to other expanding economic sectors as the oil sector declines in relative importance. The formation of a well-trained indigenous labor force capable of operating and maintaining the two urban-industrial complexes and that provides a nucleus of administrative and technical personnel to be drawn upon by the entire Kingdom will constitute a major contribution to Saudi Arabia's future economic diversification and self-sustaining growth.

Third, the new hydrocarbon industries will create new "growth poles" in the eastern and western provinces that will contribute to the regional dispersion of economic activity by attracting a wide range of ancillary industries and fabricating facilities to Jubail and Yanbu. These industries will produce by-products of the petrochemical plants, steel mills, and refineries and provide goods and services needed by the industrial complexes and communities at both cities.

Before concluding this chapter, it may be useful to underline the historical importance of Saudi Arabia's decision to adopt a policy of responsiveness to the energy demands of the international economy, which required an expansive oil-export policy and consequently more rapid depletion of the Kingdom's oil reserves. From this initial decision flowed a series of benefits to the West, which can be summarized as follows:

More moderate international oil price increases and less deflationary impact on the world economy than would otherwise have been the case

A more secure supply of oil for the world economy and fewer supply crises than would otherwise have occurred

More time for the international economy to adjust in the long run to the new era of oil scarcity and to embark on efforts to conserve oil and develop alternative energy sources

A rapid increase in the sale of Western plant, equipment, and other goods and services that has enabled Western countries to finance part, if not all, of their oil imports from the Kingdom

By earning more foreign exchange from the sale of oil than is required to finance the Kingdom's growth requirements, Saudi Arabia contributed to the recycling of its financial resources by investing conservatively and responsibly in financial assets in America and other Western countries, thereby reducing the strain on the world financial system

There can be no doubt that the Western world has benefited greatly from the Kingdom's policy of oil and industrialization. We can see this clearly in Saudi Arabia. But what we can see less clearly is how Saudi Arabia has benefited from this policy of international cooperation and responsibility. There are many in the Kingdom that are asking today what can the West do to help Saudi Arabia? How can the West, particularly the United States, illustrate to the people of Saudi Arabia, to the people in the Middle East, and to the whole world that this policy of moderation and international responsibility can indeed be beneficial to all parties concerned, particularly to the Saudi people who made that important sacrifice?

Note

1. Crude-oil production rose from about 1.4 billion barrels per year in 1970 to 3.4 billion barrels in 1979, while crude-oil exports increased correspondingly from an average of 3.8 million barrels per day in 1970 to about 9.5 million barrels per day in 1979.

3 Saudi Arabian Industrial Development: Aspirations and Realities

Fouad A. Al-Farsy

Saudi industrial development is a subject of urgent importance to Saudi Arabia. This subject is also important to all other industrialized nations if they are to properly understand the Saudi role in the world today and in the future.

Oil has been a principal fuel for the industrial economies and for the less-developed countries trying to modernize. But for nonindustrialized Arab countries, such as mine, oil is also a fuel for achieving national aspirations. Given the stark reality of their common dependence on this dwindling asset, I want to discuss the hopes of Saudi Arabia with you and to explain some of the emerging economic realities in the Gulf area that form the basis for Saudi Arabia's industrial development plans.

It is essential to understand that Saudi national aspirations are based on their religious and cultural heritage as well as on present realities. The uniqueness of the Saudi Kingdom is that it is founded on the Qu'ran, using that sacred scripture as its Construction. Among the most important of Islam's demand on its followers, as individuals and as a nation, are to act fraternally, to govern justly, to create equality, and to instill in people good behavior, and within nations, moral conduct.

Heritage is another base for Saudi aspirations. The people of Saudi Arabia remember and revere their traditional homes, the simple houses and tents where those of other generations were born and grew up. At the same time, however, they remember the austerity and difficulties of that time. There were not enough doctors, hospitals, schools, or food—memories they do not cherish—and the pace of development is driven by the need to provide these necessities of life for every man, woman, and child in Saudi Arabia as rapidly as possible.

I emphasize these tenets because some say their attachment to religious and social traditions slows the progress of development. This is not so. In two decades Saudi Arabia has moved from one century to another without violence. It is moving ahead responsibly but at a rapid pace. For example:

In the past five years alone, they have tripled the number of schools in Saudi Arabia, put electricity in a million more homes, and made important progress in health services.

Even more impressive is the development of their infrastructure. Since 1975 their ports have expanded to handle an additional 23 million tons of cargo each year. They have built 15,000 kilometers of paved roads, installed 700,000 telephones, and constructed 300,000 housing units (most through the Real Estate Development Fund).

Five years ago there were only three hundred factories in the Kingdom, with a total capital of $100 million. Today, excluding the huge, government-sponsored basic industries development, there are six hundred new light or conversion industries whose total capital is about $7 billion.

They are nearing completion one of the largest single industrial projects in history—a gas-gathering system to capture and use petroleum-associated natural gas that was previously wasted.

But while moving ahead, Saudi Arabia is determined to develop in an economically sensible manner. To do this, they must examine their resources realistically. Today they are a resource-rich country dominated by a single economic sector. But Saudi Arabia really has only two major resources—oil and people. In forty years, they will still have the people, but they will not have the oil of today.

Their hopes, their plans, and indeed their duty, is to stop wasting their assets, or letting others waste them, and to provide for future generations. Their major aspiration, then, is to redirect their economy while there is still time so that their children and their children's children will inherit a truly productive society.

Some say that Saudi Arabia should invest its oil money and live on the proceeds. An appealing idea perhaps, but that is not the path they have chosen. Instead, they have chosen to diversify their economy, recognizing their comparative economic advantages and their obligation to act honorably in an interdependent world economy.

Saudi Arabia is now beginning its third five-year plan. This new plan reflects not only their ambitions for the future but the progress they have made under the first two plans. The first five-year plan, for 1970–1975, was largely experimental and reached in many directions. Under that plan they made great strides in improving water supplies, roads, and health and educational facilities. Of course, not every program was fully implemented.

The second five-year plan concentrated on building a physical infrastructure—those things necessary to improve living and working conditions in the Kingdom and those things critical to their industrial objectives. They gave high priority to diversifying their economic base. Part of their effort was in nonpetroleum industries: cement, agriculture, and water desalination. During this second five-year plan, they made major advances in what is perhaps the most important element of any developing country's ambitions: education. Some statistics show how far they have come.

Twenty-five years ago there were only three small high schools in the Kingdom. Today there are 1.3 million students.

When Riyadh University opened in 1958, it had fewer than fifty students. Today they have six universities with 60,000 students in the Kingdom. An additional 15,000 students are studying in the United States, and thousands more are studying in Europe, Africa, and Asia.

Among the emphases of the third five-year plan are manpower development as well as infrastructure. This new plan continues the objective of expanding those industries that are not dependent on their oil resources by developing the manpower skills needed in the nonpetroleum industries.

One manpower problem all industrial nations are familiar with—urban migration—has been growing in the Kingdom. One aim of the current plan is to slow this migration by making their secondary villages and towns more habitable.

The foundation of their efforts to industrialize and create a balanced economy lies in the basic industries that the government is developing, primarily in petrochemicals, metals, and fertilizers.

Their natural gas represents an enormous potential—both as fuel and as feedstocks. Using this gas, they are now building and plan to operate profitably world-scale ethylene-based petrochemical plants in Saudi Arabia. These plants will help create an industrial base that can lead to diversified exports and to downstream manufacturing industries.

They believe that energy-intensive industries must be, and shall be, located in the oil-producing countries. Saudi Arabia can successfully establish hydrocarbon industries because they have a significant cost advantage in energy and raw materials. They are acquiring the technology for these new industrial complexes through joint ventures with established energy and chemical companies.

There is more to development than basic industries, of course. Their development aspirations include training their young people to become a scientific base on which their applied technology can rest. A parallel drive is to develop downstream manufacturing industries as well as service industries essential to a modern economy. They expect also, in their future, to make major technical strides—in desalination, solar energy, and arid-land farming—to benefit not just Saudi Arabia but the world as well.

They will consider their development successful only if it allows them to meet their broader responsibilities in the community of nations, especially in the Arab world and among the lesser-developed countries. They take these responsibilities very seriously. As Moslems, they have an obligation to share their wealth and to serve one another in this increasingly interdependent world.

They consider private-sector investment, both Saudi and foreign, essential in developing their manufacturing and service industries. Therefore, they have developed a number of government-sponsored incentives. They also recognize that government assistance in forming new companies and in selecting and evaluating industrial projects must be a cooperative effort. As a part of that effort, companies qualify for a number of benefits after they receive a government license. Some of these benefits are

The Saudi Industrial Development Fund makes loans, for a nominal operational fee, of up to 50 percent of the capital.

They grant tax holidays of five years for nonindustrial projects and ten years for industrial-based projects.

They provide import-tax exemptions for industrial equipment and raw materials that are not manufactured or available in the Kingdom.

The government provides other tax exemptions for profits earned by foreign partners and assists in exporting manufactured products.

There are no restrictions on the movement or transfer of capital or profits.

Finally, they provide land in industrial cities for new industries at a nominal fee.

Saudi industrial aims then are to establish a broad base for their future national income and to raise the standard of living and level of productive employment in the Kingdom. Crucial to the success of these goals is diversification of their economy to

Decrease their overwhelming dependence on petroleum income

Reduce their dependency on foreign goods and workers

Increase the opportunities and capabilities of the Saudi people

The greater their success in establishing a working, diversified, industrial economy, the greater will be their ability to preserve their crude-oil resources for future generations. This resource has brought them the financial power to industrialize. Extending its benefits wisely is a duty that all Saudis share.

Finally, any realistic view of Saudi Arabia's development must recognize that economic interdependence has become an irreversible fact in the world. The Kingdom has benefited greatly from Western technology and expertise and has in turn tried to share its prosperity with the world. Their oil-production policies, their oil-pricing policies, and their aid programs testify to their efforts to ensure that their wealth does not mean poverty for others.

All industrializing nations face many challenges waiting in the future. But economic policies founded on narrowly defined national or regional interests do not recognize the reality of interdependence. Every nation today is vulnerable to the economic actions of others, and parochial calls for consumer cartels or increased military capability overlook the most important need—international cooperation.

In short, anything but friendship and true cooperation among nations is, to me, unthinkable. All nations are inextricably dependent on each other in today's world. Much of the Arab world is particularly involved with the industrialized world. The West depends on them for oil—and they depend on the West for technology, for know-how, and for arms and military training. In this respect, I would request the United States and other oil-consuming countries to be more candid about the real causes of increasing oil prices. OPEC (Organization of the Petroleum Exporting Countries) is not the problem. This is clearly evident when dollar inflation is considered. Only in the past eighteen months has Saudi Arabia's price for its oil, in real dollars, climbed above the level of 1974. Their losses, as a result of using the inflated dollar as the currency in oil payments, demonstrate their support for the U.S. economy and the dollar and their patience in their pricing policies.

Some blame OPEC for U.S. inflation, which is grossly misleading at best. At the worst, it flogs the "foreign devil" as the cause for problems in America rather than focusing on the very real causes within the U.S. economy. Portraying fake "sheikhs" with oil wells, harems, and camels, and ridiculous fantasies like ABSCAM will not help the United States but only hurt Saudi Arabia.

In the final analysis, economic development must occur within each nation according to its own unique historical and social evolution. But the opportunity to pursue development depends on the maintenance of a cooperative economic world order.

These then are some Saudi aspirations. They do not dream of empires or even of great influence. They recognize that solutions to world problems require cooperative leadership in world affairs. Their hope is to help foster regional development and help bring real peace to the Middle East. They hope as well for a new and equitable relationship between the nations of the North and the South. They do aspire to wealth, but they aspire to the wealth that comes from a modern and balanced society, the wealth that can provide their children a secure, productive, and worthwhile future.

They share common dependencies, and they have, if they are wise enough to see them, common interests. In Saudi Arabia they believe in and are working toward a future where interdependence is a welcome idea and a preferred notion to narrow, parochial thinking.

Together the United States and Saudi Arabia can change the economic lexicon without giving up specific national interests. To deal with vulnerability, there is a choice—between cooperation and provocation. Yet in this day and age, when no nation can be independent of other nations and economies, there is no honorable choice but to cooperate. For progress and human enrichment in this dangerous age can be achieved only if we work together to make the world economy operate more smoothly, honorably, and justly.

4

The Interaction between Oil Policy and Industrial Policy in Saudi Arabia

Paul John Stevens

The purpose of this chapter is to examine the way in which Saudi Arabia's industrial policy interacts with its oil policy and what the implications of this interaction are in terms of the oil policy. My concern is to assess the relationship between the two in the period 1974–1979.

By 1974 Saudi Arabia had gained a *de jure* control of Aramco (Arabian American Oil Company) as a result of the "participation" movement that had begun in 1967.[1] This assumption of control marked a watershed in the sense that Saudi Arabia was now theoretically in a position to directly implement policy with respect to oil operations, whereas previously the control of the government had been exercised in a more informal and indirect way. Also after 1974, for reasons to be discussed later, the change in the international oil market brought Saudi Arabia into prominence as the main influence on oil pricing. Because Saudi Arabia lost this position in 1979, the period 1974–1979 forms a natural time span for study and for making tentative projections about the future.

A major problem in a discussion of this sort is the identification of what policy actually is in terms of its objectives. Given the structure of government in Saudi Arabia and the general secrecy surrounding its working, policy identification is a far more complex undertaking than would appear at first sight. There are three sources from which policy can be divined: statement, circumstantial evidence, and "mere" hypothesis.

The first source that can be used to identify objectives is a statement. This can be of the official sort such as a ministerial statement. The problem in interpreting such official statements is the degree of Machiavellian analysis to which the statement can be subjected. Did the statement mean exactly what it said, or did it imply something more subtle? Statements can also be of the unofficial sort. The problem with these is to establish their veracity. Another key difference between the two types of statements is that official ones can be referenced while unofficial ones cannot.

The second source for identifying policy is what may be called *circumstantial evidence*. This involves deducing policy objectives from actions. For example, a decision to increase oil production may be interpreted to indicate that the oil-policy objective is to lower prices. The problem with this sort of evidence is that it is open to different interpretations particularly if the action is intended to achieve more than one objective. Also, it assumes that the action taken was a decision by the government rather than by force of circumstances. If the latter was the case, then the causal link between action and intention is broken.

The final source of evidence for divining policy is what I have called "mere" hypothesis. The method here is to decide in the light of other policy objectives (say, with respect to development) what policy objectives (say, with respect to oil) would logically follow if overall policy were consistent. The main problem with this approach is that is assumes that the author has the same view of the world as the policymaker and shares the same logic—dangerous ground indeed!

Nevertheless, despite the problems of each source, there is no alternative available. Thus, when the policy objectives are outlined later, all three criteria have been applied as far as possible to the assumed objectives, and in most cases they pass all three tests. Where they fail one, some explanation is provided.

The Policymaking Structure in Saudi Arabia

Before examining specific policies, it is worth describing briefly the way policy is actually formulated in the Kingdom. This discussion serves two purposes. First, it further illustrates the problems of identifying policy, and second, it illustrates the potential for contradictions and complementarities in policymaking that I hope to expand on later.

At the top of the structure is the King, who theoretically makes all decisions. In practice there is a backup of advisors and institutions that play a role in the decision-making process. The key decisions lie in fact with the Royal Family, and so at the top of the structure is the Higher Committee (not to be confused with the Higher Petroleum Committee), which is made up of princes and is, in effect, the inner cabinet. It is not a particularly formal body in the sense of having any rules or specific terms of reference. Under King Faisal it tended to concentrate on internal affairs, but with the accession of King Khaled, it turned more to foreign affairs, probably reflecting the changing position of the Kingdom in the world after 1974. It is convened by command of the King, and in practice its decisions are binding on the King.

Below the Higher Committee in terms of the formal structure is the Council of Ministers. This is effectively a cabinet of the government ministers; in practice this body is of very limited significance.

Because of the importance of oil in the Kingdom's affairs and the general complexity of the subject, an inner group of decision makers was set up as the Higher Petroleum Council (HPC) in April of 1973. The function of the HPC was to examine broad issues of policy that concerned oil and industry (given the links between the two).

Below this structure are the executive bodies that convert the broad policy into specific action and then ensure implementation. There are two ministries, the Ministry of Industry and Electricity and the Ministry of Oil and Mineral Resources. The other major executive body is Petromin, which was established in 1962 and is responsible by the terms of its original charter for oil and industrial development in Saudi Arabia.

The result of this organization plan has been that Petromin, which was for all purposes the national oil company, was responsible for the industrial projects as well as the oil projects because of the assumed links between them. However, as development proceeded and the number of projects increased, Petromin began to run into administrative constraints. Thus in December of 1975,[2] the responsibility for petroleum, gas, and mineral projects was transferred to the Ministry of Industry and Electricity, which left Petromin free to concentrate on oil marketing, refining, and distribution, keeping only three of the related subsidiaries (Argas, The Arabian Drilling Co., and Marinco).

In August of 1976, the Saudi Basic Industry Corporation (SABIC) was formed to act as executor to the Ministry of Industry and Electricity in much the same way that Petromin had related to the Ministry of Oil.[3] Two other administrative bodies that have appeared recently are the Gas Council (to oversee gas development) and the Royal Commission for Yanbu and Jubail (responsible for those industrial complexes).

While the function of all these bodies is to implement the policy passed down from above, since they are concerned with the day-to-day operations, they are also in an unparalleled position to provide the higher bodies with information and advice. It is not entirely clear where Aramco fits into this structure. Presumably, it acted as executive body to the Ministry of Oil in "Aramco areas." The government certainly set maximum production limits and prices on Aramco, but the extent of government influence in other decisions, for example, expanding productive capacity, remains obscure.

Three points should be made about this policymaking structure. The first is that there is a great deal of overlap in the structure not only in terms of fields of responsibility but also in terms of personnel. Thus the same person could (and does) keep appearing in different policymaking bodies. The result of this practice is that policy will be a compromise between the different views held by a few senior policymakers. Second, the policymaking structure is cumbersome and slow. It is not capable of taking rapid decisions. Last, the structure is still in transition, and the final form depends a great deal on how the "new" Aramco will be integrated into the system. For example, in January of 1980, Dr. Abdul Hady Taher of Petromin indicated that the birth of a Saudi National Oil Company was "imminent."[4]

Saudi Arabian Oil Policy

The Importance of Saudi Arabia's Oil Policy

At one level, the importance of the policy requires little elaboration. In 1979 Saudi Arabia's oil production accounted for more than 18 percent of the noncommunist world's oil production and more than 30 percent of OPEC's (Organization of the Petroleum Exporting Countries) oil production.[5] In 1978 Saudi published proved reserves accounted for more than 17 percent of world oil reserves, a figure that almost certainly understates the position.[6] Finally, the Kingdom's oil dominance illustrated in these figures is reflected in the foreign assets that have accrued to Saudi Arabia. At the end of 1978, Saudi Arabia's foreign assets were some $60 billion compared to $28 billion for Kuwait.[7]

However, of more interest than this rather conventional approach to the importance of Saudi Arabia in world oil affairs is to examine the role of Saudi Arabia in world oil pricing. The basis of the following argument is that OPEC in this period did not behave like a cartel and in reality had little or nothing to do with setting of oil prices. The pricing mechanism that operated was as follows.

Saudi Arabia fixed the price of the marker crude—the basis for which will be discussed later. More accurately, Saudi Arabia went to the OPEC ministerial meetings with a price band in mind. OPEC then discussed the price, and Saudi Arabia fixed the marker price within that band. The media then announced that OPEC had set the price of oil. What of the pricing of the other crudes? Theoretically, there was an OPEC formula of differential pricing that set the price of the crudes according to their quality (gravity, sulfur content, and so on) and their geographic location. In practice, this formula was rarely used.

In effect, the other oil producers got what they could in the market. If the countries tried to overprice their crudes, then the companies refused to lift or, if the operators were on long-term contract, they reduced their lifting as they were allowed to do by the agreement. This of course meant that the companies would then be short of crude. In that case, they turned to Saudi Arabia and lifted from their excess capacity. (At times during this period, Saudi oil production dipped below 6 million barrels per day.) If too many companies turned to Saudi Arabia in this way, then it meant that the other countries had not overpriced their crude in the first place. In application, the companies did not in fact need to turn to Saudi Arabia. The threat alone was sufficient to ensure that the other producers priced in line with market conditions. Thus the prices of the other crudes were set by the chemistry of the blend constrained by supply and demand conditions.[8]

The whole system was based on Saudi Arabia's setting the price of the marker and the companies' acting as policemen to keep the other producers in line. This conclusion is similar to the one reached by M.A. Adelman.[9] However, I would like to emphasize a significant difference in approach from that used by Adelman. Underlying Adelman's analysis is the assumption that the oil producers are being irrational or unreasonable in shifting the supply downward (or not pushing it up). Thus, for example, "let me in passing pay proper disrespect to the slogan that Saudi Arabia would rather keep oil in the ground than money in the bank. A barrel sold today sacrifices the present value of a barrel sold in the future. Saudi Arabian reserves can easily be expanded to fifty years' supply. If the price of oil were then not $11.50 but $111.50, its present value would be less than $1."[10] This type of approach ignores several factors. The barrel sold now may well yield a revenue that cannot be invested domestically. This must then be invested abroad, which means that the capital sum involves risk with respect to foreign-exchange fluctuations and/or sequestration or freezing. For example, a study by Dr. O. Aburdene has shown that, in terms of 1974 dollar prices, the $129.5 billion gross foreign assets of OPEC that are denominated in dollars would be worth only $75.1 billion in early 1979 simply because of dollar devaluation.[11]

Second, this sort of simplistic discounted cash-flow technique ignores the fact that inflation may well create a negative interest rate that could leave the country in fifty years time with a worthless piece of paper. Finally, it also assumes that the marginal utility of the dollar now will remain the same in the future. Thus, my approach is based on the assumption that the oil producers are being perfectly rational in either reducing present production or not expanding it, especially where the real domestic absorptive capacity is low. Equating marginal cost and revenue to maximize profit— which is the basis of Adelman's analysis—is not relevant for a depletable resource. Marginal revenue may be above marginal cost, but, unlike manufacturing, the barrel not produced today (and thus the profit) is not lost forever but can be produced another day.

The pricing system just described lasted until 1979 when two factors caused Saudi Arabia to lose control of the situation. First, the loss of Iranian production as a result of the strike, and then the reduction in output decreed by the revolutionary government meant that some 3–4 million barrels per day were lost from the world market. In order to make up this deficit, Saudi Arabia was obliged to produce close to the limit of its producing capacity. Second, during the period 1978–1979, there was considerable doubt thrown on the ability of Saudi Arabia to maintain high production levels for any length of time. These fears first began to be circulated as the result of statements heard by various U.S. Senate committees, the most recent being that of the Church Committee in 1979.[12] Even earlier than this, rumors of technical problems in the fields were printed in the *The New York Times* late in 1977, prompting the Chairman of Aramco to write a letter in January of 1978 denying such problems.

These rumors were fueled by two other events. First was the apparent failure of the Saudis in the first quarter of 1977 to increase output sufficiently to force the OPEC "hawks" back into the fold after the split in December of 1976 at the Doha meeting. This was supposed to be the result of a combination of field problems and bad weather that hampered loading at Ras Tanura. It should be pointed out that Prince Fahd later stated that Saudi Arabia had never intended to solve the pricing split by overproduction.[13] Second, in 1978 it was announced that liftings of Arabian light-gravity crude were to be restricted to 65 percent of total lifting. The Saudis later vigorously denied that this move was the result of any technical problems that were not to be expected given the age of the fields.[14]

This loss of surplus capacity by the Saudis—for whatever reason— meant that they also lost control of the market that subsequently went berserk. There is considerable speculation at present as to what the upper production limit of Saudi Arabia now is; recent reports suggest that maximum capacity could be increased to 11 million barrels per day soon and reach 12 million by the end of 1981.[15] Whether this will be sufficient for the Saudis to regain control of the market (assuming they would be willing to produce at such a level) depends, to a great degree, on how long and to what extent the conflict between Iran and Iraq results in a loss of their oil production and exports.

Whichever approach to Saudi oil policy is taken—that is, the numbers game or the setting of price—there can be little debate that Saudi Arabian oil policy is of crucial importance in the world and is worth further study.

The Objectives of Saudi Arabian Oil Policy

I would suggest that all Saudi policy stems from two broad objectives. The first is the acquisition or maintenance of security and stability (defined either altruistically or cynically); the second is to raise the voice of Saudi Arabia in world affairs. These very general objectives, which underlie all aspects of Saudi policy (oil, foreign, and so on), need to be converted into specifically "oily" subobjectives.

The general objective of security and stability can be translated into three subgoals. The first is to secure the long-term health of the oil market, which follows from the fact that Saudi Arabia's reserves make it the oil producer with (potentially) the longest life. This requires the long-term health of the customers, which in turn requires that supplies of oil are available at "adequate" levels and at "reasonable" prices. (What is "adequate" and "reasonable" is clearly a matter of debate.) This aspect of Saudi oil policy, that is, moderation, has been the subject of considerable discussion. On numerous occasions Saudi Arabia has been accused of being a puppet of U.S. foreign policy. There also have been reports of a secret agreement between the two governments relating to the favorable placing of Saudi funds in the United States in return for "moderation" within OPEC.[16] Such assertions tend to miss the point that moderation by Saudi Arabia is motivated by self-interest. [In any case, it seems improbable that Saudi Arabia would tie up its policy options until 1984 (according to the "secret" agreement) in return for a few extra percentage points on the interest rate.]

Securing the long-term future for oil carries another implication with respect to oil pricing. There are two views. One is based on the "noble oil" argument and states that oil should be priced in such a way as to speed up the substitution of other energy sources for oil since oil is "too precious to burn." This is the view officially followed by the Saudi government. The other argument is that oil should be priced in such a way as to slow down this substitution and ensure that oil remains a key element in the world economic scene. Altruism supports the first approach, but it is difficult to accept that the Saudis would like to see the main reason for their growing importance in the world being undermined. It is true that as a petrochemical feedstock, oil would still be important, but nothing like on its present scale as an energy source.

The second of the subobjectives is to diversify the economy away from its virtual total dependence on crude-oil exports. This implies moving downstream in the oil industry, which in turn suggests the need for greater control over the industry both domestically and internationally. The reason underlying this subobjective is related to the ideas developed on export dependence in the literature of development economics.

The final subgoal (which is related to the second) is to use oil as the leading development sector to secure real economic development. Apart from reducing export dependence, and for that matter import dependence, real structural change in the economy would also, in theory at least, help to diffuse the benefits of oil down through the population, thereby forestalling instability arising from economic conditions.

These three subobjectives designed to secure and promote stability have a strong domestic orientation although they do also carry international implications. The subgoals of the other central aim—raising the Saudi voice in world affairs—while having domestic implications have more of an international orientation.

The first of these "international" subobjectives is to be a responsible and reasonable member of the international community. Thus Saudi Arabia has consistently claimed to be both a moderating and stabilizing force in the international oil market. The assumption underlying this approach is that the reasonable voice is more likely to carry weight in the corridors of power than the extremist voice.

Second, Saudi Arabia has attempted to resist the encroachment of radical left-wing movements both in the Arab world and abroad. This is because such movements are anathema to the Saudi philosophy and are also viewed as a threat to domestic stability and to the stability of Saudi Arabia's oil consumers.

Third, their objective in the international field is to secure a satisfactory settlement to the Arab-Israeli issue. This goal is in part motivated by nationalistic religious reasons genuinely held. However, it is also motivated by the fact that the continuation of the struggle tends to promote the radical groups that are so objectionable to the Saudis. Moreover, the large numbers of Palestinians living in the Gulf states are a political force to be considered in any calculations.

The final objective in this category is the promotion of Islam, motivated partially by missionary zeal but also by a more complex element. A large part of the legitimacy of the ruling family in Saudi Arabia arises from its role of guardian of the Holy Places of Islam. Thus anything that strengthens Islam and the importance of those places in turn strengthens the position of the House of Saud.

It is perhaps worth reiterating the reasons for the absence of any supporting references for these alleged objectives of Saudi oil policy. As outlined in the introduction, there is no clearcut source of policy goals available. Rather to each policy objective is applied the criteria of (a) statements, (b) circumstantial evidence, and (c) "mere" hypothesis. The objectives just stated satisfy all three with one exception, which is that the Saudis are seeking to price oil in such a way as to slow down the rate of oil substitution. Official statements deny this as an objective. However, given the motives of Saudi Arabia in maintaining the crucial role of oil in the world, it would be unlikely that the official statements would say anything different.

Oil-Policy Tools and Constraints on Their Usage

There are two broad policy tools that the government of Saudi Arabia can use in order to achieve their objectives—oil-production levels and price levels. Both arise from the legislative power of the government with respect to oil operations.

The production tool implies setting the level of oil output. This in part is determined by the price set, but there is also the influence of the production ceiling set by the government. In March of 1975 the upper limit for Aramco was increased to 8.5 million barrels per day[17] and remained at this level until 1979 when it was increased to 9.5 million barrels per day to offset the loss of Iranian crude. As well as setting the absolute level of production, the government can fix the structure of that output as well. Thus in March of 1978 the government introduced a maximum of 65 percent on the lifting of light crude.[18] An adjunct to the production-level tool is the form of availability—whether the crude should be sold to the majors, to small independents, on a direct government-to-government basis, or whatever. This has been of particular importance in seeking to achieve foreign-policy objectives.

In general, the production tool has tended to follow the pricing tool rather than vice versa. The period 1975–1976 saw considerable discussion in the trade press and the general circulation of rumors concerning the debate that appeared to be taking place within the Saudi policymaking groups over the level of production. The timing of the debate coincided with the launching of the second five-year plan. Central to the debate was uncertainty over the extent to which the Kingdom could and should expose itself to pressures from rapid development. The argument was won by those favoring relatively high production levels, but the debate reemerges from time to time. Once price had been set, the production level was then allowed to find its own level according to the situation in the market. The result was that production tended to fluctuate quite wildly over the period in an effort to stabilize the market. After 1979, production—or more precisely, availability—became more of an issue as the world appeared to face a real physical shortage of oil.

The Saudis have always been very insistent on the idea that the determination of the production level in Saudi Arabia has been—and will always be—a matter for the Saudi government alone.[19] This assertion of sovereignty (which has hindered attempts to introduce prorationing into OPEC) is quite understandable. The production level is an adjunct to prices. To agree on any level limits freedom of action in terms of policy objectives. Although there has been discussion recently that Saudi Arabia may enter some sort of production agreement, past experience suggests that this is highly unlikely.

The price tool implies setting price. In the period under discussion, this meant setting the posted price with the other prices (for example, government official selling price) moving in line with some minor variations depending on the market situation. The use of this pricing tool has undergone several changes in the period under discussion.

Before December of 1973 the Saudis were more than happy to follow the trend that allowed prices to rise to what they viewed as a fair and realistic level. In this sense the rise in price was not so much a specific policy tool as a reaction to world circumstances. In December of 1973, faced with the choice of agreeing to a higher price or splitting OPEC, Sheikh Yamani (unable to get guidance from Riyadh) chose the former course.[20] After this price increase, the Saudi position was rather ambivalent. On the one hand, they felt that the price was too high for the general health of the world economy. On the other hand, they were unwilling to reduce the price without some form of *quid pro quo* from the oil consumers. Nonetheless, the possibility of a lower price was hinted at. For example, in mid-1974 Sheikh Yamani suggested that Saudi Arabia would auction 1.5 to 2 million barrels per day for whatever price the market would bear (which would have effectively meant a price cut). However, there appeared to be nothing offered in return, and the offer was dropped alledgedly in exchange for an agreement with Algeria to freeze oil prices.[21]

In March of 1975, with the death of King Faisal, there was a significant change of attitude toward the price such that the existing price was now viewed as acceptable. In May of 1975, Prince Fahd actually suggested that the intention in the future was to maintain the oil price in real terms.[22] This implied a higher price in nominal terms; in September of 1975 the Saudis increased the marker price by 10 percent. The question of price then appeared to be used much more as a bargaining weapon as can be seen clearly from the "will-they/won't-they?" game played by the media prior to every subsequent OPEC ministerial meeting.

Although it is within the power of the Saudi Arabian government to use these two tools of production and price at will, they are different sides to the same coin. While the government can set price or production levels, it cannot set both since they are faced with a demand curve that (apart from the very short run) is not perfectly inelastic. The choice of a price therefore implies fixing a production level and vice versa. In addition, there are a great many other constraints that limit the extent to which these policy tools can be utilized. These limitations can be divided into those of a technical nature, those of an economic nature, and those of what might be loosely termed a "political" nature. Although these divisions simplify the analysis, it should be remembered that in practice the division is far from clearcut.

There are two main technical constraints concerned with influencing the production figure. The first is the question of capacity to produce. This not only concerns the capacity of the fields themselves but also the capacity of the treating, moving, and loading facilities. Clearly, production cannot rise above the capacity limit. This constraint is complicated by the fact that the size of recoverable reserves is in part determined by production levels. Normally, the faster the fields are pumped, the less oil is recoverable. This can be taken to extremes when serious field damage can result from an output level that is too high. Thus the rumors surrounding the Ghawar field to the effect that Aramco overproduced in anticipation of participation and as a result damaged the fields (thereby necessitating the 65-percent light-crude lifting limit) would be in this technical-constraint category.

The second technical constraint on policy action concerns the associated gas produced with the oil. This can place both maximum and minimum constraints on production. If oil production goes above the level of the gas-gathering and treating facilities, then the associated gas must be flared, that is wasted. Indeed, when Saudi Arabia increased its output to 9.5 million barrels per day in response to the Iranian crisis, the premium charged on the extra 1 million barrels per day was supposed to allow for this waste of gas. To some extent this constraint will be removed when the Aramco gas-gathering scheme is completed since this system is expected to be able to cope with the associated gas from some 12 million barrels per day of oil production.[23] The gas can also place a minimum constraint on oil production. If oil production is at a very low level, then the gas-utilizing equipment is not being efficiently used. Given the capital intensity of gas projects, this plays havoc with their economics. Also, if LNG contracts are involved, then oil production must be maintained at a level sufficient to provide the gas for liquefaction. Otherwise, the country would be in breach of agreement.

There are five types of economic constraints on the use of policy tools. First is the question of revenue needs since both production or price decisions have revenue implications. There are minimum revenue requirements if certain services are to be met and plans fulfilled. Additionally, there are maximum revenue requirements; exceeding the domestic absorptive capacity implies finding a place abroad to invest the surplus funds. In the case of Saudi Arabia, what these maximum/minimum levels actually are has been the subject of so much discussion and depends so much on the assumptions made that to pursue the topic here would be fruitless.

The second constraint is what the market can take in economic terms. Thus a very high oil price or problems over oil availability could seriously damage the economic health of the customers as a result of recession or balance-of-payments problems, and so on. For the Saudis this appears to have been a very major consideration in their calculations. Linked to the market constraint is the third limitation that concerns the strength and health of the U.S. dollar. A large part of the Kingdom's foreign assets are held in dollars. Thus any action that would damage the dollar would also damage the value of these assets. It has been noticeable that whenever the issue of pricing in dollars has been challenged by other OPEC members, Saudi Arabia has very quickly let it be known publicly that they would oppose such a move. (In any case, there is no viable alternative at the moment to the dollar as the petrocurrency.)

A fourth constraint involves the level of company profits. If these are allowed to become too large, then they act as a source of considerable embarassment to the Saudi government. This has been particularly crucial in the more recent period when the price of Saudi crude has been held below world levels. In the fourth quarter of 1979, Exxon's earnings were up 60 percent on the fourth quarter of 1978, Mobil's were up 72 percent, Texaco's were up 62 percent, and Standard Oil Company of California's were up 66 percent.[24]

The final economic constraint relates to the uncertainty associated with any policy action on oil prices and production. This uncertainty stems from two sources. First, there is the problem of the time lag. It is often far from clear how long a decision to alter price or production will take before it has an impact on the market. The figures suggest that there is about a four- to five-month lag between a change in Saudi Arabia's output and a "sympathetic" movement in the Rotterdam spot market price. However, there is considerable variation on the length of lags, which means that using production as a means to smooth out the market could in fact aggravate undesirable trends. The second cause of uncertainty is the oligopolistic structure of the industry. There is a high level of interdependency with one "actor" never being sure of how the other "actors" will respond to a given action. Early in 1980 the Saudis twice increased the price of their marker crude by $2 in an attempt to restore pricing order to the market. However, the other OPEC members simply increased their prices accordingly, which annoyed the Saudis considerably.[25]

There are three constraints that may loosely be described as "political." The first concerns sanctity of contract. There are numerous ways in which a contract can be broken—for example, *force majeure* and the doctrine of changed circumstances. However, if such alterations become too frequent as the result of policy decisions on production or pricing, then obviously the "good-citizen image" would suffer.

The second constraint is what the market will bear politically, which differs from what the market will bear economically in the degree of change. If tomorrow Saudi Arabia were to announce a production-conservation ceiling of 4 million barrels per day, within a short space of time the Western economies would collapse. The Western economies would not accept this happily, and so, despite any consequences, action would have to be taken that would restore the status quo. (It should be stressed that this is a positive as opposed to a normative viewpoint.) Clearly, the Saudis realize this and simply for the sake of their own survival, would not introduce changes that were too drastic.

The third "political" constraint is the obverse of the second, namely, how decisions affect Saudi Arabia's relations with other OPEC states. This involves considering not only questions of institutional cohesion but, on a more regional level, the status of Saudi Arabia in the Arab world generally. This aspect would be a study in its own right.

Thus during the period under consideration (1974–1979), when Saudi Arabia entered the OPEC meeting with its price band, all these factors will have played a part in determining both the level of the band and its range. Which constraints play the more important role depends on the circumstances of the time, not least of which would be the relative influence of the individual policymakers in the decision-making structure.

The next stage is to examine how Saudi Arabia's industrial policy fits into this analytical framework.

Saudi Arabian Industrial Policy

The Objectives of Saudi Arabian Industrial Policy

The same basic objectives that underlie Saudi oil policy—stability and raising the Saudi voice—also act as the basic requirements of the industrial policy. Two of the specific oil objectives provide the *raison d'être* of industrial policy: the diversification of the economy away from dependence on crude exports and the use of oil as a leading development sector. Taken together, these two goals mean industrializing the economy. Thus, a policy of industrialization in Saudi Arabia is more of a logical consequence arising from other factors rather than a policy in its own right. This is important since it suggests that details of the industrial policy will be captive to other considerations.

Stated in generalities, the policy is to use apparent comparative advantage to maximize value added in the oil sector. Other officially stated motives include increased self-sufficiency and protection from external disruptions.[26] Stated in specifics, this means industrialization via four routes: (a) moving downstream into refining and petrochemicals; (b) processing gas (either as an energy source or as a chemical feedstock); (c) developing energy-intensive industries such as metal smelting; and finally (d) developing ancillary industries to the oil sector that arise from forward and backward linkages.

These specifics are well known and often stated. What is of more interest are the policy tools available to achieve these objectives, their constraints in use, and the subsequent relationship with oil policy.

Industrial-Policy Tools and Their Constraints

There are four industrial-policy tools available. Their potential as tools arises from the fact that the hydrocarbon resources and their revenues are the property of the state. Consequently, in a situation in which the private sector is either unable or unwilling to pursue an industrial path, industrialization can be pursued by means of massive state involvement in the hope of eventually turning over the fruits of the development (if any) to the private sector.

The first tool is the capacity of the Saudi government to decide to invest in one project rather than another; the government can do this by virtue of its control of the purse strings. Petromin was the first body to dispense finance in projects such as the Saudi Arabian Fertilizers Company.[27] Now there are numerous bodies empowered to spend funds in such a way, either directly (as SABIC) or indirectly (as the Saudi Industrial Development Fund). For example, in 1978, of the gross domestic capital formation (which in that year accounted for over 30 percent of gross domestic expenditure), over 60 percent (more than 40 billion riyals) was accounted for by the government.[28]

This industrial policy tool utilizing investment decisions interacts with oil policy in one of two ways. First, the level of such investment would obviously increase the minimum revenue requirements, thereby influencing oil-price and production policies. Second, the government's purchasing policy can influence the economics of the projects and therefore the willingness of foreign companies to become involved (which in turn could imply incentives as oil entitlements). Since the object of the exercise is development, it is quite possible that the government would require that the largest quantity of inputs be obtained locally in order to maximize backward linkages. This certainly has been the case in Saudi Arabia. On the surface, the policy has also been successful. For example, the Royal Commission for Yanbu and Jubail recently announced that of the infrastructure contracts granted so far, foreign firms had obtained $150 million of contracts while Saudi firms had obtained $1.3 billion.[29] However, these figures are completely misleading since a large number of the Saudi firms are joint ventures with foreign companies and are in effect no better than trading agencies. Thus although Saudi firms may have signed the contract, the actual goods are still imported. (Of course, this also implies that the backward development linkages are much lower than the figures would suggest.) Also, preference is given to Saudi companies even if their price is higher (within limits), which tends to increase the capital costs of the projects. The implication of this for oil entitlements and oil policy will be examined later.

The second policy tool available to the government to achieve industrial policy objectives is the decision and the location of oil-processing plants. One of the main reasons for the explosion in plans to locate refineries and petrochemical plants in the Arab world in 1974–1975 was the takeover of the operating oil companies by the governments—a process brought about either by nationalization or by the collapse of the participation agreement. The decades of the fifties and sixties had seen a massive switch in refinery location away from the oil fields to the market. Part of the reason for this transfer was the economics of location, but part was also explained by the fact that the companies (for strategic and tax reasons) chose to locate there.[30] They had the right to do so because they were the disposers of the crude. Once the governments gained control of the companies, then they, at least theoretically, became the disposers of the oil and could choose the processing location. Given development objectives, it appeared logical to locate within the countries themselves; hence the appearance of so many plans for refineries and petrochemicals.

This location decision influences the oil-policy tools and objectives in two ways. First, it affects crude availability. Clearly, the more crude processed, the less available for export; this would have enormous implications for the whole structure of the international industry and the oil trade. Second, part of this location decision involves the building of gas-processing equipment. (This factor is important for rather different reasons than for locating oil-processing plants. Previously the associated gas could be happily flared by the companies since it represented to them a product of no value. Once the government took over, they were in a position to limit waste of what was to the country a valuable resource.) The existence of such plants places considerable inflexibility on the oil-production-level decision, as already explained.

The third industrial-policy tool is the decision by the government of how to price the inputs into these projects—specifically the infrastructure and the feedstock. *Infrastructure inputs* are items such as electricity and water that could be regarded as public utilities. The pricing of these inputs would have a significant impact on the economics of these projects. Their being priced low through subsidization has implications for revenue requirements and the length of time the economy remains dependent on crude-oil exports. The pricing of the feedstock for these plants (oil or gas) also carries implications for oil policy since the pricing of these inputs has to be compared against some notion of opportunity cost. Whether the feedstock prices are on or below the alternative-use price will depend to an extent on the general oil-pricing policy of the government. This is important because, given the need to break into export markets—where competitors will be extremely sensitive—too low a level of pricing could lead to charges of dumping and subsequent retaliation.[31]

A related aspect to these incentives of input pricing concerns the granting of tax holidays. For reasons to be explained shortly, an essential aspect of Saudi industrial policy is to encourage involvement of foreign companies. One way to achieve this is to offer generous financial incentives as, for example, tax holidays. Extensive use of this method of encouraging investment carried implications for government revenue sources and their continued need for a minimum level of oil revenues.

The final industrial-policy tool that the government can use is to exert pressure to open up markets for the products to be produced. Given the small fragmented market that exists in Saudi Arabia, this pressure is crucial. In terms of the domestic market, one possibility is by trade protection based on the infant-industry arguments. However, carried out on a large scale, this kind of protection could have serious implications for the issue of recycling of oil revenues, which in turn could affect the health of the oil consumers—a matter of some importance in Saudi oil-policy calculations.

Import limitation in the case of Saudi Arabia would be insufficient; if the projects are to be viable, then export markets must be secured. The main area of contention here is that of petrochemicals. There are already numerous signs that Saudi penetration in the petrochemicals market will be strongly resisted by the chemical companies in Europe and the United States who are facing a period of increasingly difficult operating environments and a greater squeeze on profitability.[32]

All this implies that Saudi Arabia will have to use its oil power to secure markets for its petrochemicals. This would add a considerable constraint to oil-policy options now available to Saudi Arabia.

There are two main constraints that operate on these policy tools. The first is the market constraint, already discussed, and the second is availability of resources complementary to the capital that is effectively for the moment in "unlimited supply." Much has been written about these constraints (especially labor).[33] There is little that can be added here except to reaffirm that these constraints are so serious that the viability of some of the projects must be in doubt.

This doubt about the projects arises because the constraints seem so large as to offset any comparative advantage that Saudi Arabia appears to have. These comparative advantages may have been overstated. Take the case of aluminum smelting as an example. Thirty percent of the price of aluminum is accounted for by the energy cost of smelting. It is argued that given the cheap supplies of gas available to Saudi Arabia, an aluminum smelter would be able to compete despite the higher capital costs and the need to import the bauxite. However, the 30-percent energy input is the result of technology from an era of cheap energy. Since the realization that this cheap-energy era is over for good—and this only really occured after 1977–1978—technology is slowly beginning to accommodate the new situation. For instance, the possibilities for recycling aluminum on a large scale (which saves 95 percent of the energy input to primary smelting) are being explored; one estimate suggests that by 1985 34 percent of U.S. aluminum consumption will be met from recycling compared to 23 percent in 1978.[34] Similarly, ALCOA recently claimed to have developed a new smelting technique that saves up to 30 percent of the energy input required for primary smelting; that company is planning a capacity expansion of 450,000 tons per year on the strength of the new process.[35]

All this makes the project doubtful, at least in terms of a private profit/loss accounting approach. (A cost-benefit approach could conceivably produce a different result.) The significance of this is that the projects need foreign involvement if the constraints (labor, technology, and markets) are to be overcome. Indeed, all the major Saudi projects have gone ahead on this joint-venture basis. One way to encourage this foreign involvement—many would argue the only way—is by offering oil entitlements, which is precisely what the Saudis have done. The actual magnitude of these entitlements and just how important they have been in persuading the foreign companies to finally go ahead with the projects (many of which have been "on the books" for five years and more) is a matter of considerable speculation.[36]

What is clear is that this carries important implications for oil policy since it effectively ties up quantities of crude for a long time to come. Just how much depends on the level of the entitlements. One estimate puts the figure as high as 300–350,000 barrels per day on a 15-percent share in a $2 billion project, but this is almost certainly an overstatement.[37]

Conclusion

Oil and industrial policy in Saudi Arabia are strongly interrelated. The interrelation arises because the two sets of tools available to achieve the policy objectives provide a series of constraints that impinge upon the use of the tools. While the constraints interact in either direction, it is the contention of this chapter that during the period under consideration (and in fact at present), it is oil policy that has called the tune, and industrial policy has had to dance accordingly. The result is a feeling that industrial policy has not been clearly thought out in its own right, implying that many projects have been suggested that are neither relevant nor realistic.

The question of entitlements suggests that this causal linkage is being broken to some extent. If this continues, then in the future it may well mean that oil policy would dance to the tune of industrial policy. Because of the key role of Saudi oil policy in the world economy, this would have very wide-ranging implications. It could also presage a serious rethinking of Saudi industrial policy although where this would lead is difficult to say. One possible avenue that is already being explored is a much greater degree of economic cooperation and integration in the Gulf region.[38] The political and economic consequences, if such moves were successful, would be enormous.

Notes

1. For details, see P.J. Stevens, *Joint Ventures in Middle East Oil, 1957–1975* (Beirut: Middle East Economic Consultants, 1976).

2. See "Petromin" in the series of OPEC publications on national oil companies, February 1980.

3. Ibid.

4. *Saudi Arabia Newsletter,* January 1980.

5. British Petroleum Company Limited (BP), *BP Statistical Review of the Oil Industry, 1979* (London: BP, 1980).

6. Ibid. and *Aramco Review, 1978.*

7. From a study by Dr. O. Aburdene, details published in *Middle East Economic Survey,* vol. 23, no. 21 (Hereafter *Middle East Economic Survey* will be cited as *MEES*).

8. For further details, see P. Stevens, *Saudi Arabia's Oil Policy in the Seventies: Its Origins, Implementation and Implications* (University of Exeter, Centre for Arab Gulf Studies, forthcoming).

9. For example, M. Adelman, "The World Oil Cartel—Scarcity, Economics and Politics," *The Quarterly Review of Business,* vol. 16, no. 2, and M. Adelman, "Is the Oil Shortage Real?" *Foreign Policy,* Winter 1972-1973.

10. M.A. Adelman, "The World Oil Cartel," p. 15.

11. *MEES,* vol. 22, no. 6.

12. *An Nahar Report and Memo,* April 30, 1979.

13. Interview with *As Siyasah,* April 16, 1977.

14. *MEES,* vol. 21, no. 20.

15. *Saudi Arabia Newsletter,* May 1980.

16. *International Currency Review,* vol. 9, no. 2.

17. *MEES,* vol. 17, no. 23.

18. Ibid., vol. 21, no. 19.

19. For example, see the recent statement by the Deputy Minister of Oil 'Abd al-'Aziz al Turki, *MEES,* vol. 23, no. 50.

20. A. Sampson, *The Seven Sisters* (London: Hodder and Stoughton, 1975).

21. *Arab Report and Record,* September 1974.

22. *MEES,* vol. 18, no. 33.

23. Ibid., vol. 20, no. 2.

24. *Saudi Arabia Newsletter,* February 1980.

25. *MEES,* vol. 23, no. 16.

26. Kingdom of Saudi Arabia, *Saudi Arabia: Developmental Aspects* (Ministry of Information, 1978).

27. "Petromin."

28. Kingdom of Saudi Arabia, Saudi Arabian Monetary Agency (SAMA), *Annual Report, 1979.*

29. *Saudi Arabia Newsletter,* February 1980.

30. See P. Odell, *An Economic Geography of Oil* (Bell, 1963); Middle East Economic Consultants (MEEC), *Refining in the Middle East until 1985* (MEEC Oil Report No. 27, August 1976).

31. For details, see L. Turner and J. Bedore, *Middle East Industrialization* (London: The Royal Institute of International Affairs, 1979).

32. For example, see *European Chemical News,* March 31, 1980, and *The Oil and Gas Journal,* July 23, 1979.

33. For example, see J.S. Birks and C.A. Sinclair, *Economic and Social Implications of Current Development in the Arab Gulf,* in *Social and Economic Development in the Arab Gulf,* ed. T. Niblock (London: Croom Helm, 1980).

34. *Materials Engineering,* January 1980.

35. Ibid., May 1980.

36. *Saudi Arabia Newsletter,* January 1980.

37. *Saudi Arabia Newsletter,* February–March 1980.

38. Turner and Bedore, *Middle East Industrialization.*

5 Oil and Gas: Industrial Implementation

Saud Ounallah

In this chapter, I will try to give you an idea of Saudi Arabian activities in the field of oil and gas and how these activities are contributing to the national objectives of industrialization and economic development.

While rapid economic development and industrialization is taking place, both domestic and world demand for energy is increasing. Upon the successful implementation of the second five-year development plan, major growth was achieved in the nonenergy sectors. This growth has stimulated the domestic demand for energy throughout Saudi Arabia. Demand for energy is expected to reach 1 to 1.2 million barrels per day by 1990. A large share of it will be met by natural gasoline and LPG (liquefied petroleum gas).

At present, we have 615,000 barrels per day refining capacity. To meet the ever-increasing demand in the Kingdom, decisions have been made to expand and add to the present refining capacity. Jeddah Oil Refinery has been expanded to 100,000 barrels per day. Riyadh Oil Refinery will reach 120,000 barrels per day. A new domestic refinery is under construction in Yanbu with 170,000 barrels per day capacity and scheduled to start operation in 1983. Another domestic refinery will be erected at Juayman with a 250,000-barrel-per-day capacity; it is expected to be on stream by 1986.

Nine distribution bulk plants are either under construction or planned to be implemented in the next few years. Thousands of kilometers of product pipelines are now under construction. These bulk plants and product pipelines are part of an updated distribution system that will serve the Kingdom and make products available where needed.

Two parallel transpeninsula—east-west—pipelines are under construction. The first one is a crude pipeline with 1.85-million-barrel-per-day capacity and 1,215 kilometers long. The other is a NGL (natural gas liquids)/ethane pipeline with 270,000-barrels-per-day capacity; this one is 1,160 kilometers long. Both pipeline capacities could be expanded in the future by almost 50 percent. These two pipelines will serve the Yanbu industrial complex, in addition to other purposes, by supplying it with energy and feedstock.

The Saudi economy has long been overwhelmingly dependent on oil and the oil industry and will continue to depend to a large extent on the oil-

and gas-based industries for some time in the future. Also, with respect to the fact that oil and gas are depletable resources, with our realization of our international responsibility, and in order to achieve our national objectives, several projects have been undertaken. By far the largest project is the Master Gas Gathering System. It is one of the largest in the world, and it will make Saudi Arabia by far the largest NGL exporter in the world. Phase 1 of this project is expected to be completed by 1982. At present Saudi Arabia has facilities to process 360,000 barrels per day of NGL; the Kingdom is the largest exporter of NGL in the world. When completed, the master gas system will have a processing capacity of 3 billion cubic feet of gas per day. It will produce 15 million metric tons of propane and butane and 5 million metric tons of natural gasoline per year.

This system will enable Saudi Arabia to carry out its third ambitious five-year development plan and its industrialization projects by making available low-cost energy and low-cost feedstock from associated gases. It will also help in the development of hydrocarbon-based industries in new geographical areas like Jubail and Yanbu.

The master gas system will contribute to alleviating the international energy problem by adding the equivalent of 700,000 barrels per day of oil to the world's energy supply. A large portion of production will be exported; the output also will meet a large share of local energy demand. Thus more quantities of crude oil will be available for export. Moreover, to cushion and ease the international gas market's fluctuations, an underground-storage facility has been constructed as part of the system.

Experience has shown that crude products and NGL should be made within the easy reach of customers. For this reason, two export terminals are being built: one on the Arabian Gulf and the other on the Red Sea at Yanbu. The latter will be served by the east-west pipelines mentioned earlier. These two terminals, in addition to the existing ones, will ensure a stable and continuous supply year-round. Furthermore, Yanbu is 3,500 miles closer to the United States and Europe than the existing terminals in the Arabian Gulf.

Three export refineries will be constructed in the next few years, each with a 250,000-barrel-per-day capacity at Jubail, Yanbu, and Rabigh. The Jubail and Yanbu refineries are expected to be on stream by 1983 and 1986, respectively. With the emergence of these export refineries, exports of crude oil will be proportionately replaced by the export of products.

Of course, there are many other projects based on oil and gas approved for construction during the third five-year plan, including the lube refinery, which will be one of the largest in the world at Jubail. Lube-blending plants, as well as ethylene, methanol, ammonia, and urea plants all are expected to be on stream between 1983 and 1985. These projects are part of the industrialization of the Kingdom and will provide an added value to the economy.

In spite of the fact that Saudi Arabia has 26 percent of the world's reserves, large amounts of money continue to be spent on exploration. Many new oil fields are being discovered every year. Additionally, exploration efforts are now under way to find and develop nonassociated gas. The latest and most advanced methods will be used in such activities. Side by side, new oil fields as well as existing ones will continue to be developed within a framework of first-class oil-field practices, which is guided by maximizing the oil to be recovered from these fields.

In view of the depletable nature of oil and gas reserves, Saudi Arabia is gradually attributing increasing importance to the development of alternative sources of energy such as solar-energy projects. Steps to develop the use of nuclear energy have been taken as well. Any oil for which alternative sources of energy can be substituted means improved availability of petroleum for export to the world market. This applies not only for the Kingdom but also to the rest of the world, especially the industrialized world.

For the same reason, the government of Saudi Arabia is taking major steps to diversify its economy and thus reduce the dependence on oil. To partially achieve this, two industrial complexes are being built in Yanbu and Jubail. The master gas system will supply low-cost fuel and feedstock to the various projects and plants now under construction or planned at these two sites. Besides Petromin's projects in these two areas, which were mentioned earlier, there are other plants and industries to be built under the auspices of the Royal Commission for Jubail and Yanbu and the Saudi Basic Industries Corporation, such as petrochemical plants, fertilizer plants, a steel mill, and a host of complementary secondary industries and supporting businesses.

With close coordination between the various authorities and organizations, the construction of these two industrial complexes has already begun.

Finally, no opportunity should be allowed to pass without repetition of the call for energy conservation. Saudi Arabia's goal is to urge all countries, especially the industrialized nations, to actively become involved in developing other alternatives and sources of energy, thereby aiding themselves and the developing nations and enabling the oil-exporting countries like Saudi Arabia to make oil available for a longer period.

6 The Saudi Petrochemical Industry in the 1980s

Hugh George Hambleton

Saudi Arabia has by far the largest reserves of crude oil in the world; natural gas is also abundant. Yet these resources are finite. It is estimated that the output of oil will start to decline toward the middle of the next century. The Kingdom could use the natural gas, which is largely flared, and the crude oil, which is largely exported, to form the basis of a petrochemical industry.

In 1960 the Saudi government was already negotiating with foreign oil companies concerning the development of a petrochemical industry. Since these companies showed little interest, other ways had to be found to attract investment. In 1962 the General Petroleum and Mineral Organization (Petromin) was established precisely to undertake hydrocarbon projects that did not attract private investors. State support for industrialization increased when Faisal Ibn Abd al-Aziz Al-Saud ascended the throne in 1964. The desire of the government to press forward with the development of the petrochemical industry was underlined in 1976 when the Saudi Arabian Basic Industries Corporation (SABIC) was created with Dr. Ghazi A. Algosaibi (the Minister of Industry and Electricity) as chairman of the board, and Abdulaziz A. Al-Zamil as chief executive officer.

This emphasis on the petrochemical industry finds its full expression in the third five-year plan' (1980–1985), which calls for the production of an important volume and variety of petrochemicals as well as fertilizers. However, it will effectively be during the fourth five-year plan that these projects fully come to fruition.

Initially it was decided to establish a plant to produce ammonia-urea—not, strictly speaking, a petrochemical. The governor of Petromin Dr. Abdel Hady Taher interested Dr. Armand Hammer, of the Occidental Petroleum Corporation in this venture. In 1965 the Saudi Arabian Fertilizer Company (SAFCO) was launched. In the beginning the plant was plagued by technical difficulties, management problems, and the falling world price of urea. However, the natural-gas feedstock, the water and the electricity were provided at heavily subsidized prices, and at the same time the government purchased the output for use in its overseas-aid program. Eventually, the price of urea began to rise, and in 1976 SAFCO took over the exclusive management from Occidental Petroleum. Since that time SAFCO has

51

started to show a profit—$35 million in 1979. In the first six months of 1980, 145,084 tons of urea were produced. With the continuing upward movement in the world price of urea and expanding international markets, future prospects look good. SAFCO provided the backdrop for a petrochemical industry. However, an infrastructure first had to be established.

The Jubail and Yanbu Infrastructure

In the early 1970s Petromin saw Jubail as a possible growth pole for petrochemical and other industries because of the proximity of the Berri crude oil and gas field and the deep-water channel that makes that site suitable for international shipping.

In 1973 the Bechtel Corporation was called in to draw up a master plan for Jubail that defined infrastructure requirements, located industries within the site, and set forth land use and community plans, conceptual designs of components, and environmental-control measures. When the master plan was presented to the Saudi government in 1975, it was decided to establish a Royal Commission for Jubail and Yanbu, the latter town being added as the second development pole. In June of 1976 a management contract was signed with Bechtel covering a 20-year period. The subsidiary of Bechtel, the Arabian Bechtel Company Limited, was given the responsibility to map out the infrastructure of the industrial complex and the town and to supervise the granting of contracts after evaluating bids and actual construction. The Royal Commission, however, retained the responsibility for policy.

Jubail's industrial harbor will be the largest in the world. By the year 2000 this "Industrial City" could have 300,000 inhabitants with petrochemical complexes, oil refineries, a steel mill, and over a dozen other industries as well as a port area and an airport. The total investment could reach some $40 billion.

The new "Industrial City" of Yanbu is rising under the direction of Dr. Yousef Ibrahim Al-Suliman Al-Turki, the director of the Yanbu branch of the Royal Commission for Jubail and Yanbu. Saudi Arabian Parsons Limited, which acts as project manager for the Royal Commission, has already something to show for its efforts: storage tanks dot the area; the NGL (natural-gas liquids) facility is preparing for the gas that will arrive by pipeline from the Eastern Province in 1981; and a pier has been built. Under the eight-year initial development program, the port will be divided into nine areas, one being specifically designed for petrochemicals. Thus by 1988 this port should have the capacity to handle 400,000 tons of petrochemicals a year. Possibly by the year 2010 the number of inhabitants in the city will reach 150,000. While Jubail will be the center of the petrochemical industry, Yanbu will not be so far behind. These centers must, however, be in a position to provide this industry with the necessary inputs—feedstock, fuel, water, electricity, manpower, and the like.

The industrialization program calls for large quantities of gas as fuel and feedstock. This has led to Petromin's gigantic gas gathering, treatment, and transmission project—the world's largest engineering project, which will cost some $15 billion. By the early 1980s some 3 billion standard cubic feet of gas a day will be processed to provide gas for industry, power generation, and water desalination. Ethane would be used largely as a feedstock and fuel for petrochemical complexes in Jubail and Yanbu. The propane, butane, and natural gasoline would be exported.

The gas made available to the emerging Saudi petrochemical industry would be furnished at a small fraction of the world price. Thus ethane, the basic feedstock for the petrochemical industry, will apparently be provided at about SR 1.67 ($0.56) per thousand cubic feet. As Abdulaziz A. Al-Zamil, the chief executive officer of SABIC, has observed, the gas available to the petrochemical industry will be much cheaper than anywhere else. This is identified as the principle behind Saudi industrialization: utilizing a primary resource in as many ways as possible.

Water availability is a major constraint in the industrialization of the Kingdom since there are no rivers or lakes and little rainfall. The pools of groundwater, which underlie parts of the country, are diminishing and are largely nonrenewable. This shortage of water leaves the desalination of water a critical aspect. The world's largest desalination project is now being implemented in Jubail. After two stages of this project are completed in 1983, this system will have a capacity of 235 million gallons a day. Connected with the desalination project, the Saudi Consolidated Electric Company, which dominates production in the Eastern Province, will expand its peak load to over 6,000 megawatts by 1983.

The desalination of water also is progressing in the Yanbu area. A desalination plant there, with an eventual capacity of 25 million gallons of fresh water per day, was activated in August of 1980. The plant's generating output of 500 million kilowatts of electricity will come on stream in 1981.

The price of fresh water fixed by the Council of Ministers in 1980 is SR 0.25 (about $0.08) per cubic meter. Yet the real cost of this water is probably about SR 7.5 ($2.50)—some thirty times greater. Electricity is provided to industrial concerns at about SR 0.07 (about $0.025) per kilowatt-hour about the price in the United States.

In the latter half of this decade over 5,000 engineers, technicians, and workers will be needed for the emerging petrochemical industry. Saudis should be able to play a predominant role in staffing the petrochemical complexes. The Ministry of Higher Education expects that in 1980 some 3,000 Saudis will graduate from Saudi and foreign universities; this number should increase as the years pass. Many of these graduates will go into the hydrocarbon sector since Saudi university graduates must serve the state for the same length of time as their education was financed by the government. Again, it is to be recalled that the hydrocarbon industry has had considerable success in attracting Saudi manpower.

While Saudis will be able to fill an important and increasing proportion of the positions in the petrochemical industry, those with experience as managers or engineers are still scarce. The cost of specialized labor is about twice the level in the United States or Europe. Thus the median annual salary for scientists and engineers in the United States is about $30,000, while in Saudi Arabia it is about $60,000 a year.

Capital costs are exceptionally high in Saudi Arabia. In Western Europe a 500,000-ton-per-year ethylene cracker together with the units to make derivatives cost about $2.6 billion in 1979. This same complex would cost about $4.0 billion in the Middle East—some 50 percent more. The difference of the two areas is estimated in table 6-1.

A study made by Shell International Chemical Company in 1979 compared the capital cost of a chemical plant constructed in Europe with one built in the Gulf. It was shown that the location alone would make capital costs 35 percent higher in the Gulf, whereas, if the need for additional infrastructure was taken into consideration, the costs then would be 67 percent higher.

Joint Ventures with American Corporations

The technological leadership of the United States in the petrochemical and indeed in the whole chemical field is now paramount. This lead is particularly evident in process innovation. The latest ammonia plants designed by Pullman-Kellogg reduce energy consumption by a third. Again, Union Carbide's new Unipol process for low-density polyethylene gives not only a significant saving in energy use and capital cost but also increased safety and reduced plant space. The United States also leads the world in providing the latest state of the art in process computer-control technology. The control room of a modern petrochemical plant with its interactive color-graphics terminals is a most impressive sight.

Corporations holding proprietary rights to technology are normally prepared to license their technology to other firms with which they have a close working relationship. However, they are not anxious to sell the technology. An executive vice-president of Dow Chemicals, Robert W. Lundeen, has noted that in so-called outward licensing, his firm will not license anyone unless Dow Chemicals has a substantial share of management participation in the enterprise using the technology. This position is seen as allowing the shareholders to get the maximum return on the licens-

Table 6–1
Comparison of Capital Costs: Europe and Middle East
(in million of dollars)

	Europe	Middle East
Materials	$1,500	$2,000
Labor	900	1,500–1,900
Other	200	300
Total	$2,600	$4,000

ing of their property. Moreover, to bring a new petrochemical plant on stream demands highly specialized skill, perfect coordination, and faultless timing. To sell the final product requires a good marketing system. It is thus not surprising that Saudi Arabia has opted for joint ventures with some of the world's leading corporations.

Saudi Arabia has moved to the first place as a supplier of foreign oil to the United States. In 1979 some 1.4 million barrels a day of oil were shipped to the United States, and LNG is starting to move to the same market. The value of these exports, which reached $4.9 billion in 1979, are expected to rise to $6 billion in 1980. This dependence on Saudi oil can be expected to continue. Thus, although U.S. demand for oil may decline by nearly 6 percent between 1979 and 1990, American gross oil imports (crude and refined products) are expected to decline from 8.2 million barrels a day in 1979 to 7.6 million barrels a day in 1990. At the same time, U.S. imports of LNG are expected to increase significantly to 1.2 trillion cubic feet (TCF) in 1990.

Apart from crude oil and LNG, Saudi Arabia could well find a market in the United States for its petrochemicals. In the United States, then in Europe, Japan, and an increasing number of other countries, there has been a revolution in materials: polyester clothing and polypropylene furniture, plastic automobile parts, milk bottles, toys, and synthetic carpets—a virtually endless list of replacements for natural materials. In the 1960s and 1970s the production of the petrochemical industry grew at about three times the rate of the gross national product until it has become a $150-billion industry worldwide. The future is, however, expected to see somewhat slower growth rates—in the 1980s and 1990s about 1.5 to 1.8 times the rate of GNP increase. In the United States demand for petrochemicals is expected to grow at an average annual rate of 4 percent in the 1980s.

Plastics, one of the principal products of the petrochemical industry, illustrates this growth. In the United States in 1940, production stood at 114,000 tons, rising to 19 million tons in 1978. The Organization for

Economic Corporation and Development (OECD) estimates U.S. plastic production to reach between 22 and 26 million tons in 1990.

The ethylene supply growth rate between 1980 and 1983 will be only 2.3 percent a year, while overall demand should grow at nearly 6 percent a year. Thus ethylene demand will strain capacity. An OECD study indicated that the rate of capacity utilization will increase appreciably between 1980 and 1985. Another study by the marketing-research firm of DeWitt and Company (Houston) reported that after 1986 the demand for ethylene in the United States could well begin to exceed capacity.

With unsettled conditions prevailing in the Middle East and other parts of the world, the major U.S. oil and chemical corporations are looking for assured supplies at competitive prices. Even if an investment in a joint venture by a foreign corporation in Saudi Arabia does not appear to have an acceptable rate of return, the broader picture should be taken into consideration. If the rate of return on a specific venture is low, it can be compensated by supplies of oil or other hydrocarbons at a specially attractive price or even simply an assured level of supply. Under these conditions a large corporation may be prepared to lose in one venture if this leads to an assurance of greater profitability in other activities. This strategy of oil entitlements as an incentive to invest was clearly underlined by Saudi Oil Minister Ahmed Zaki Yamani in February of 1980 when he stated that in the future Saudi Arabia will grant oil contracts only to customers willing to help build up industry in Saudi Arabia.

Saudi Arabia has long had close working relationships with some of the major world oil corporations. Standard Oil Company of California first secured a concession in Saudi Arabia in 1933, which was assigned to the Arabian American Oil Company (Aramco) in 1944. In order to secure additional investment capital and marketing outlets, Aramco brought in Texaco, Exxon, (then Standard Oil Company of New Jersey), and Mobil as partners. Although Aramco is being taken over by the Saudi government, relatively secure supplies and favorable prices—the so-called "Saudi advantage"—continues for the moment to be accorded these majors.

Shortly after SABIC was established in 1976, Dr. Algosaibi approached some of the leading oil and chemical corporations to interest them in establishing joint-venture petrochemical complexes. These corporations had great misgivings. Doubts existed concerning the adequacy of the rate of return, as to whether satisfactory markets could be found for the petrochemical products and whether or not the political risk in the Gulf area did not preclude any massive commitment. After negotiations in Riyadh, Houston, and other world centers, five major U.S. corporations showed serious interest: Mobil Oil, Shell Oil, Exxon, Dow Chemicals, and Celanese-Texas Eastern. It has been tentatively agreed with the five U.S. corporations to produce for the present the petrochemicals noted in table 6–2.

These joint ventures are not easily or quickly put together. Even up to the actual signing of a contract, a great deal of negotiation must take place:

Table 6–2
Joint-Venture Petrochemical Production
(in metric tons per year)

Product	SABIC- Mobil	SABIC- Shell	SABIC- Exxon	SABIC- Dow	SABIC- Celanese/ Texas
Ethylene	450,000	656,000	—	500,000	—
Low-density poly- ethylene	200,000	—	240,000	68,000	—
High-density poly- ethylene	91,000	—	—	105,000	—
Ethylene glycol	200,000	—	—	300,000	—
Ethylene dichloride	—	454,000	—	—	—
Caustic soda	—	377,000	—	—	—
Styrene	—	295,000	—	—	—
Ethanol	—	281,000	—	—	—
Chlorine	—	330,000	—	—	—
Ethyl benzene	—	327,000	—	—	—
Methanol	—	—	—	—	730,000

the petrochemical products and the volume of output must be decided upon; the various processes to make these products have to be reviewed and selected; contractors to design and construct the complex have to be surveyed and chosen; bidding documents have to be issued and bids received; the bids have to be reviewed with the bidder's justifying the process; finally, the contract has to be drawn up, including the financial arrangements. All this takes time.

SABIC/Mobil Complex

The Mobil Oil Corporation is an old and loyal friend of Saudi Arabia. As far back as 1946 Mobil came to the Kingdom to produce and distribute oil under the aegis of Aramco. By 1974 Mobil was already examining with Saudi authorities the possibility of establishing a petrochemical industry in the Kingdom. In August of 1976 an interim agreement was signed between Mobil and SABIC calling for a feasibility study, an economic assessment of the project, and for negotiations for the establishment of a joint-venture company. Since those days, some $31 million has been spent on different studies related to the complex. Finally, on April 19, 1980, the final agreement was signed by W. Jack Butler, chairman of Mobil Saudi Arabia (the wholly owned subsidiary of Mobil Oil Corporation), and SABIC. At this time, Industry Minister Dr. Algosaibi identified this agreement as a major landmark in the Kingdom's industrial development history.

The 725-mile East-West natural-gas liquids (NGL) pipeline, linking

Shedgun in the Eastern Province with Yanbu, should start carrying 270,000 barrels per day of NGL in December of 1981. The liquids would be separated in Yanbu into ethane, butane, isopentane, propane, and natural gasoline. The ethane would be sold to the SABIC/Mobil complex for both feedstock and fuel at about one-fifth of the world-market price. The ethane would be used to produce: 450,000 tons annually of ethylene using the Mobil process and Bechtel engineering; 200,000 tons of low-density polyethylene (LDPE) using the Union Carbide process; 200,000 tons of ethylene glycol again using the Mobil process; and 91,000 tons of high-density polyethylene (HDPE) once again using the Mobil process.

The capital cost of this project would be about SR 7,000 million ($2,000 million). Mobil Saudi Arabia and SABIC would be partners, each holding 50 percent of the equity. Each partner is expected to provide 15 percent of the capital cost in cash. The remaining 70 percent is to be provided by the Public Investment Fund of Saudi Arabia (60 percent) and by private banks (10 percent). A crude-oil entitlement is also being made available by Saudi Arabia to Mobil as an added inducement to invest.

The director of Shell International Chemical, W.C. Thomson, believes these ventures will be successful both for the host government and for their partners. A Shell study dealing with the production costs for ethylene glycol and low-density polyethylene in the Gulf and in Europe determined that if the price of ethane was about 35 cents per million BTU in the Gulf and of naphta, about $250 per ton in Europe and with due consideration given to the cost of feedstock and fuel, other manufacturing, capital, freight and duty, then these two petrochemicals had a considerably lower production cost in the Gulf.

The SABIC-Mobil plant is expected to come on stream in early 1985. About 3,000 people will be needed to staff this complex. Initially, 40 percent of the employees will be Saudis and 60 percent expatriates; by 1990 it is hoped that these percentages will be reversed. The complex at Yanbu would market their products in Europe, along the eastern seaboard of the United States, in the Arab world, in Africa, and in Saudi Arabia itself. Three-quarters of the sales would be handled by Mobil. When the plant was at full capacity, this would mean that Mobil would increase its petrochemical production by one-third. In fact, Mr. Butler has indicated that Mobil is now taking steps to expand its marketing distribution in anticipation of when this project comes on stream in order to handle all the production.

SABIC/Shell Complex

SABIC and the Shell Oil Company are pooling their capabilities to build one of the largest petrochemical complexes in the world—a "mega project." An interim agreement between SABIC and Pecten Arabian Limited of the Shell Oil Company goes back to 1976.

Using ethane and methane, this complex annually would produce: 656,000 tons of ethylene using the C.F. Braun of California process and engineering; 295,000 tons of styrene using the Mobile-Badger process and and Badger engineering; 454,000 tons of ethylene dichloride using the Stauffer process and Dravo Corporation engineering; 281,000 tons of crude industrial ethanol using the Shell Development Company process and C.F. Braun engineering; 377,000 tons of caustic soda and 330,000 tons of chlorine using the Diamong Shamrock process and Davro for the engineering; and finally, 327,000 tons of ethyl benzene. Some of the firms doing engineering and other work in Saudi Arabia are joining with Saudi entrepreneurs to establish local subsidiaries. Thus the Badger Company Incorporated of Cambridge, United States, is going with the Rezayat Trading Company Limited to form the Arabian Badger Company Limited.

The capital cost of this complex is expected to reach the astounding figure of some $3,000 million. Nonetheless, it is to be recalled that the investment required to produce a ton of ethylene has more than tripled over the last decade. The cost of the ethane cracker, some $900 million, would be shared, it is hoped, by the SABIC/Exxon complex in return for part of the ethylene. SABIC and Pecten would each invest $400 million in this venture. The balance would be funded by the Public Investment Fund of the Saudi Ministry of Finance, which would be prepared to make available 60 percent of the total cost of the complex with a grace period of five years and at a rate of interest between 3 and 6 percent. Commercial banks are being brought into the financing as well.

It is also expected that the Shell Oil Company would secure an oil entitlement. This could be some 500 barrels per day for every million dollars invested. However, the Supreme Petroleum Council still has to arrive at a final decision.

The hoped-for return on equity for this complex, as with others, would be some 15 to 20 percent. This return would depend in part on the price of such inputs as feedstock, fuel, electricity, and water as well as the world price of the products and the volume of sales. It can be confidently expected that the costs of the feedstock and the fuel will be much lower than in the industrialized countries and that the other variable costs will be at least comparable. In view of the importance of feedstock and energy costs in the gross production cost—sometimes placed as high as 75 percent—this complex should be a viable venture.

Much naturally depends on finding a market for these products. It is indicative, however, that a recent study by the Briefing Service of the Shell International Petroleum Company Limited predicts that the growth prospects for petrochemicals in Western Europe will probably be sustained by the tendency to substitute and innovate. This should lead to a growth of 1.5 percent above that of industrial production through the 1980s. Much the same increase can be expected in the United States, as already indicated, and in Asia.

The products that the SABIC/Shell complex proposes to place on the market should find a ready outlet. According to a study by Roger Williams Technical and Economic Services Incorporated, the annual worldwide output of fuel-grade should increase from 1 billion gallons in 1980 to 10 billion gallons by 1990. This would call for a great increase in capacity starting in 1985, which might be achieved by Shell's reactivation of its Deer Park facility or the importation by Saudi production. This latter projection was contained in a report by Frost and Sullivan Incorporated of New York.

SABIC/Exxon Complex

Exxon, the world's largest company, first came to Saudi Arabia in 1946 as a partner with Aramco. The Kingdom soon became a major source of oil for Exxon. In the 1970s the possibility was raised by SABIC of a joint venture in Saudi Arabia to produce low-density polyethylene (LDPE). After an agreement was signed in March of 1977, a number of feasibility studies were undertaken. A final agreement to proceed with the LDPE complex was signed on April 26, 1980, between SABIC and Howard Kauffman (the president of the Exxon Corporation) and Ed Homer (the president of Exxon Chemical Company, United States).

This complex, to be known as Saudex, would use ethylene as a feedstock, which would come from a cracker to be shared with the Saudi Pecten Petrochemical Company. Probably using Union Carbide's new Unipol process, some 260,000 tons of LDPE would be produced annually. The engineering would be done by the Fluor Corporation. The cost of this project has been put as $1,100 million, with the equity being shared equally. As an additional incentive, Exxon will probably receive a commitment from Saudi Arabia to provide 500 barrels a day of crude oil for each million. dollars invested in the Saudex complex.

The total personnel of this plant should be about 350. When the plant starts up, between one-third and one-half of the personnel is expected to be Saudi. A number of Saudis are now with Exxon in the United States for training, and their number will gradually increase. The plans for the plant have now been approved, and it is scheduled for a 1984 startup.

Some nine-tenths of the 240,000 tons per annum of LDPE would be marketed by Exxon. Abdulaziz Al-Zamil has emphasized that the transfer of technology and management expertise is important; what he deems critical is the responsibility for marketing the products. Feeding the plants' production into Exxon's marketing network is the most significant portion of the agreement. The output of Saudex will be channeled into world markets, presumably including Europe. Thus Essochem Europe, with headquarters near Brussels and with some 6,000 employees, undoubtedly will place at least some of the LDPE in Europe. SABIC, which is establishing a marketing department, will initially market the remaining one-tenth of the LDPE in Saudi Arabia and abroad. The proportion marketed by SABIC will gradually increase. Saudex should also give preference to Saudi shipping when exporting. While the exports of LDPE will undoubtedly face some competition abroad, it should be marketed successfully. It is not anticipated that these sales will create any glut on world markets.

SABIC/Dow Complex

The giant American chemical corporation, Dow Chemical, is a relative newcomer to Saudi Arabia. That company is, nevertheless, showing great interest in developing relations with the Kingdom. After an interim agreement signed in February of 1977, a number of economic and financial studies were carried out; a major feasibility study was completed in January of 1980.

The basic feedstock to be used would be ethane. Using the Dow Chemical processes, SABIC/Dow complex annually would produce 500,000 tons of ethylene, 68,000 tons of low-density polyethylene, 300,000 tons of ethylene glycol, and 105,000 tons of high-density polyethylene. Dow Chemical also could carry out the engineering. This plant should be virtually identical with one recently completed in Canada. The cost is estimated at $1,300 million. Approval by Dow Chemical was forthcoming in May 1981; it is hoped that this complex would go on stream by 1985.

SABIC/Celanese-Texas Eastern Complex

The Celanese Corporation and Texas Eastern Arabian (a subsidiary of Texas Eastern) have been negotiating with SABIC to launch a joint-venture methanol plant in Jubail. On February 24, 1978, it was agreed to make a detailed feasibility study, start preliminary engineering design, and negotiate agreements for a joint-venture company.

Considerable progress has been made since that time. It has been decided to establish a world-scale complex—one that would use local methane to produce 730,000 tons of methanol a year employing the Imperial Chemical Industries process. The engineering would be done by C.F. Braun and Company.

The cost of this plant is now estimated at $350 million, which may be compared with the $215 million that Celanese is to spend for another complex to be built in Canada with an annual capacity of 235 million gallons of methanol. Celanese expects to hold 25 percent of the equity in the Jubail complex, with SABIC as a partner. This plant is now expected to go on stream in late 1984.

This venture would seem to have particularly good prospects. Methanol is becoming a key product for Celanese. Total demand in the United States is expected by Celanese to triple over the next decade. In the United States and indeed throughout the world, the big new outlet will be as a fuel, being blended with gasoline or alcohol. Use for this purpose in the United States could well increase a hundredfold, from 23 million gallons in 1980 to 2,300 million gallons in 1990. While U.S. nameplate capacity would probably triple during this period, imports would move as seen in table 6–3. The 230 million gallons produced by the plant in Saudi Arabia could undoubtedly be absorbed in the United States. However, there is also the Western European market, where demand will considerably exceed supply.

Joint Ventures with Asian Corporations

Asia, rapidly becoming a major economic region in the world, accounts for many of the most dynamic economies today: Taiwan, Japan, and South Korea. With their lack of natural resources, these countries have made outward-looking policies central to their overall economic strategy.

While these Asian nations are, with the exception of Indonesia, net importers of oil and gas, they are developing an appreciable petrochemical capacity. Even the ASEAN countries—Indonesia, Malasia, Thailand, the Philippines, and Singapore—will be self-sufficient in petrochemical products or possibly exporters by 1985. These Asian states can play a key role in Saudi Arabia's budding petrochemical industry. Japan, the most industrially advanced, can provide technology and markets. Taiwan and South Korea can provide technicians and markets. Even Mainland China might prove to be an interesting market in a few years. Of all the Asian countries, possibly the closest to the Saudi heart is Taiwan.

SABIC has now arranged three joint-venture agreements with Asiatic corporations, one of which is Taiwanese and the other, Japanese. Table 6–4 outlines the agreed-upon production.

Republic of China

Taiwan has virtually no oil and very little coal. Some 80 percent of energy products are imported, including about 120 million barrels of oil a year. The most important source of this oil is Saudi Arabia, followed by Kuwait and Indonesia. In 1979 Saudi Arabia exported crude- and refined-oil products to a value of $2.44 million; in 1980 the value of these exports are pro-

Table 6–3
Projected U.S. Imports of Methanol, 1980–1990

Year	Imports (in Million Gallons)
1980	33
1982	132
1985	241
1987	622
1990	690

Table 6–4
SABIC-Asian Company Joint-Venture Production
(in metric tons per year)

Product	SABIC-Taiwan Fertilizer	SABIC-Mitsubishi Corporation	SABIC-Mitsubishi Gas
Ethylene	—	450,000	—
Low-density poly-ethylene	—	250,000	—
High-density poly-ethylene	—	80,000	—
Ethylene glycol	—	80,000	—
Methanol	—	—	730,000
Urea	500,000	—	—

jected to reach $5.5 billion. This dependence on oil can be expected to increase. Under the new ten-year oil-import plan, Taiwan expects oil imports to grow at an annual average rate of 5.3 percent. Imports of liquefied natural gas (LNG) from Saudi Arabia will develop as well.

It is the expertise of Taiwan in market penetration that could be a valuable asset to Saudi Arabia. Taiwan could use Saudi petrochemicals to manufacture synthetic textiles, plastics, and other products that could be marketed not only in Asia but worldwide. It is indicative that synthetic textiles made in Taiwan are already entering Fujian and other provinces of Mainland China via Hong Kong.

The Al-Jubail Fertilizer Company

The close links between Saudi Arabia and Taiwan have found a concrete expression in an agreement signed on December 4, 1979, between SABIC and the Taiwan Fertilizer Company Limited to establish the Al-Jubail Fertilizer Company to be located in the industrial complex of Jubail. This joint venture would use methane to produce 1,000 metric tons per day of ammonia and 1,600 metric tons per day (500,000 tons a year) of urea.

While Taiwan has highly skilled engineers, technicians, and labor, they must rely on U.S., European, and Japanese technology in petrochemicals. Thus, with the Al-Jubail Fertilizer Company, the Pullman Kellogg and Stamicarbon BV processes are being used while the construction-management services are the responsibility of Bakhsh-Pullman Kellogg Saudi Arabia Limited (located in Al-Khobar). Design and engineering is partly carried out in the Houston offices of Pullman Kellogg. The actual construction on the site in Jubail started in June of 1980, and the plant is now expected to go on stream in 1984.

The total investment is estimated at $357 million. SABIC and the Taiwan Fertilizer Company will each subscribe 50 percent of the shares of the Al-Jubail Fertilizer Company, putting up $100 million now, with the balance being loaned by the Saudi Public Investment Fund.

Some 60 percent of the output will be marketed by the Taiwan Fertilizer Company in Taiwan and other places in the Far East. The other 40 percent will be marketed jointly by the Taiwan Fertilizer Company and SABIC elsewhere. No serious difficulty should be experienced in marketing the ammonia-urea. Ammonia, being a source of nitrogen fertilizer, is closely linked to agricultural production. The world population is expected to double over the next thirty-five years, which would mean that, just to maintain subsistence level, the output of fertilizer would have to triple. In the developing countries, output would have to increase fivefold. By 1990 the projected global demand for ammonia-urea should be about 80 million additional tons. In order to meet this demand, a new plant with a capacity of 1,000 tons would have to go on stream every month. However, in certain regions such as South West Asia, a glut might appear. Thus, the U.S. Department of Agriculture predicts a urea surplus of 1,250,000 tons in that specific region by 1985.

Japan

Economic relations with Japan developed rapidly after 1973. In August of that year a Japan-Saudi Arabia cooperation organization was set up under private auspices. A few months later the more all-embracing Japan Cooperation Center for the Middle East was established with government support. Next, in December of 1973 the then-International Trade and Industry Minister, Yasuhiro Miko, visited the Kingdom. These steps led to the signing in 1975 of a Japan-Saudi Arabia economic and technological agreement, consisting of five articles: promotion of economic and technological cooperation; establishment of joint ventures and the contents of technological cooperation; supply of required services and facilities; encouragement of economic and technological cooperation between the peoples of the two nations; and encouragement of Japanese capital investment. The following year, joint committee offices were established in Riyadh.

Saudi Arabia and Japan have much to gain from a close association. The vice chairman of the Mitsubishi Corporation, Keizaturo Yamada, has observed that the Kingdom is interested in securing technology and complete turnkey projects in exchange for the export of Saudi oil. The Japanese technology for the petrochemical industry is almost on a par with the best in the United States and Europe. If Japan is not the innovator of a process, as is frequently the case, it can frequently be secured through licensing or other arrangements. Again, Japanese engineering firms do have a great deal of experience with overseas projects.

Japan is also becoming an important outlet for investments by Saudi Arabia and other OPEC countries. Large commercial-banking institutions and investment firms in Britain and Switzerland are moving petrodollars from the United States and Britain to Japan and West Germany. It has been estimated that by the end of 1980 the OPEC countries will have placed some $25 billion in Japanese blue-chip bonds and convertible debentures, high-technology stocks and top-ranking industrial shares with favorable long-term outlooks.

To secure Japanese technology and the much-needed channels, Saudi Arabia has recourse to the "sogo shosha" (general trading companies). These giant business conglomerates, without counterpart abroad, owe their strength to close business connections. They are active in marketing, distribution, financing, and organizing large-scale plant construction. They can marshal the industrial and technical might of Japan behind megaprojects.

Yet oil is Japan's Achilles heel. Virtually all oil must be imported. Of these imports about 30 percent comes from Saudi Arabia. This dependence became painfully evident in 1973 when oil stopped flowing for three weeks. The yen plunged on the foreign-exchange markets. Stocks collapsed. People began to stockpile and prices rose. The value of oil imported, which stood at $35 billion in 1979, is expected to reach $59 billion in 1980. In the first half of 1980, imports from Saudi Arabia reached $8.9 billion, twice the level in the same period of 1979. Saudi Arabia also provides 50 percent of Japan's imports of LPG (liquefied petroleum gas).

The Japanese were quick to recognize the full extent of their dependence, a dependence expected to persist. Thus in 1990 Japan will probably be importing some 8 million barrels of oil per day. Ethylene and derivatives are also expected to be in strong demand before the middle of the 1980s, forcing Japan to import. The president of Mitsui and Company, Toshikuni Yahiro, has noted that the Middle East is now important to

Japan not only as a supplier of oil but also as one of the most important markets for Japanese manufactures, second only to Japan's exports to the United States.

Relations in the petrochemical field between Saudi Arabia and Japan stretch back over many years. In the late 1960s a number of possible joint ventures were under discussion. In February of 1969 a Japanese delegation visited the Kingdom and submitted several proposals for such ventures with Petromin. In the summer of the following year, the Minister of Oil and Mineral Resources Ahmad Zaki Yamani visited Tokyo. This was followed up by a trip by the governor of Petromin Abdul-Hady Taher, who held talks with Japanese industrialists concerning joint ventures in oils and petrochemicals.

At this time Petromin developed a close relationship with the largest of all the "sogo shosha"—Mitsubishi. The top three in this group, the Mitsubishi Corporation, the Mitsubishi Heavy Industry, and the Mitsubishi Bank, are combined with twenty-eight other Mitsubishi member companies. In addition, Mitsubishi has a tradition of cautious management, skillful judgment, and a vast financial empire.

Mitsubishi has played a key role in Japanese-Saudi relations. Following Taher's visit to Japan, it was agreed that Mitsubishi should construct a refinery in Riyadh and increase the capacity of the one in Jeddah. While Petromin was to pay for these plants, Mitsubishi agreed to buy oil equal in value to the cost of the refineries.

After 1973, relations between Saudi Arabia and Japan were greatly strengthened. The Japanese government through the Overseas Economic Cooperation Fund (OECF) was to throw its support behind closer relations with Saudi Arabia, working in conjunction with Mitsubishi.

Mitsubishi soon realized that a chemical company's success in the 1980s would depend almost entirely on whether it had a solid link with a major feedstock supplier. This was an important point for Mitsubishi and other Japanese firms, which were particularly anxious to assure long-term stable supplies of crude oil and products such as methanol, ethylene, and ammonia. Sharply rising feedstock prices resulting from events in Iran, and the Iran-Iraq conflict induced them to seek closer economic ties with Saudi Arabia. This has led Mitsubishi and various other Japanese firms to look with increasing favor on joint ventures with Saudi organizations in the Kingdom. Saudi Arabia, through SABIC, and Mitsubishi both have strong mutual interests in strengthening cooperation in the development of the petrochemical industry in Saudi Arabia.

SABIC/Mitsubishi Gas Complex

It is not surprising therefore that a consortium of Japanese companies, headed by the Mitsubishi Gas and Chemical Company Incorporated and supported by the OECF, decided with SABIC to establish a complex in Jubail, using natural gas as a feedstock to produce chemical-grade methanol. On April 14, 1980, Kisako Hori, the general manager of the Mitsubishi Heavy Industries Limited, signed the final agreement with SABIC to build the Saudi Arabian Methanol Company (SAMC). This would be the first venture by Japanese firms in methanol production outside of Japan.

The 500,000-square-meter tract of land in Jubail SAMC is leasing from the Royal Commission for Jubail and Yanbu is being obtained under the national industry protection and encouragement laws. The site will be provided with electricity, water, sewage, and communications, in addition, seawater will be used for cooling.

This is to be a relatively modest complex, with a capacity of 600,000 tons of methanol a year. In producing this methyl alcohol, the Mitsubishi Gas Chemical Low Pressure Process will be used. The engineering is to be done by the Mitsubishi staff and the actual construction by the Mitsubishi Heavy Industries Limited. A rather unusual aspect of the engineering is that the modular system will be used. Mitsubishi Heavy Industries will make about a hundred modules in Japan, ranging from 30 to 1,200 tons, and these will be sent by sea to Jubail where they will be assembled.

The capital investment in this plant is expected to be some $268 million. The Saudi Public Investment Fund is to put up 60 percent of this amount and another 10 percent by commercial banks. The remaining 30 percent is to be shared by SABIC and the consortium consisting of the Mitsubishi Gas and Chemical Company Inc., Sumitomo Chemicals, Mitsui-Toatsu Chemicals, the Kyowa Gas Chemical Industry, and C. Itoh. The Overseas Economic Cooperation Fund (OECF) of Japan has insured SAMC against possible financial loss. SAMAC is scheduled to go on stream in 1983. Being a relatively modest undertaking, it would require only about 180 employees, from guards to the general manager.

The Japanese consortium would be responsible for marketing 80 percent of the methanol—some 480,000 tons a year. Of this amount, 300,000 tons would be placed on the Japanese market itself, to be used in the manufacture of hormalin for urea resin and manmade fibers. While Japan has a considerable domestic production of methanol, it should be able to absorb this Saudi output. The other 180,000 tons of methanol would be marketed by the Japanese in the other countries of the Far East. The balance of 120,000 tons would be placed on the market by SABIC.

SABIC/Mitsubishi Corporation Complex

By far the most important joint venture with the Japanese is a giant petrochemical complex to be located in Jubail. Using ethane as a feedstock, the plant would have an annual capacity of 450,000 tons of ethylene,

250,000 tons of low-density polyethylene (LDPE), 150,000 tons of ethylene glycol, and 80,000 tons of high-density polyethylene (HDPE), according to tentative agreements.

A great deal of capital would be required—possibly some $2 billion. Funding would be by SABIC and a consortium of fifty-four Japanese firms, grouped in the Saudi Petrochemical Development Corporation (SPDC), which was formed in 1979. The consortium is led by the Mitsubishi Corporation and fourteen other Mitsubishi companies as well as thirteen oil companies, nine power companies, eleven petrochemical companies, four banks, and two gas companies. The Japanese corporate commitment is 7.5 percent of the capital investment. Another 7.5 percent will come from the OECF, which classifies the complex as "national." In fact, Tazio Wanatabe of the Japanese Foreign Ministry has observed that this undertaking is the largest economic cooperation agreement yet between Japan and Saudi Arabia and that the Japanese government holds the realization of this project is of vital importance.

A preliminary feasibility study was made several years ago that was rather pessimistic. It indicated that the complex would not break even for a decade. Yet, as the price of feedstock continued to rise and as oil entitlements grew in importance, some of the basic assumptions had to be revised. In April of 1980, Mitsubishi agreed with SABIC that a new feasibility study had to be made. Chiyoda Chemical Engineering and Construction Company has undertaken this study, with the $10 million cost being divided equally between SABIC and Mitsubishi.

The Japanese consortium attaches great importance to the oil entitlements. The managing director of SABIC has indicated that these entitlements depend on such factors as: (a) the equity contributed by the partner; (b) the commitment of the partner to the project; (c) the contribution to marketing the product; and (d) the technology transferred. The special oil bonus to be accorded to SPDC was still under negotiation in 1980; it has been suggested that it could reach 200,000 barrels a day of crude petroleum.

From planning to plant operation, a number of years can elapse. This project is now targeted to go on stream in 1985. When SPDC effectively does go on stream, the Japanese consortium would undoubtedly be interested in marketing the output in Japan and other Asian countries. Yosiharo Hongo, the general manager of business development for the chemical department of Mitsubishi, asserted early in 1980 that Japan will be obliged to import ethylene and derivatives from the United States, Canada, and Singapore until SPDC comes on stream.

Faced with steadily increasing difficulties in securing supplies of oil and gas as well as the continuing upward pressure on prices, leading members of the Japanese administration and industry recognize that the domestic petrochemical industry will have to be restructured or it will be doomed to stagnate or even decline. The Minister of International Trade and Industry, Masumi Esaki, declared in July of 1979 that this policy will be continued even if two or three domestic petrochemical plants go bankrupt.

A number of highly competent and forward-looking industrialists seek a change of emphasis in the petrochemical industry. One of these, Takeshi Hijikata, the president of Sumitomo Chemical Company Limited, has advanced three new attitudes toward his own industry. (a) Given the oil price increases of the 1970s and the decision in developing countries to move into the petrochemical industries, the expansion of basic and general-purpose products output, such as polyethylene and methanol, is less economically justifiable in Japan. (b) The next logical position would be to actively cooperate with oil-producing nations in the development of their petrochemical projects geared toward output of such basic products. (c) Simultaneously, Hijikata urges Japan's chemical industry to orient its research-and-development efforts toward high value-added specialty products that require more sophisticated technology as, for example, engineering plastics. These three policy suggestions are seen responding to the need for international division of labor in an era of global economic interdependence. They do not necessarily advocate a departure from primary petrochemical products toward engineering plastics in Japan per se or a competition with oil-producing countries.

The Saudi Polymer-Processing Industry

A vital part of the Saudi industrialization policy is to move from the production of crude oil and gas to the manufacture of polymers and then, further downstream, to the processing of these polymers. As one moves from the original feedstock to the final consumer—that is, moving downstream—the more value is added. Thus the principle thermoplastics such as high- and low-density polyethylene, polyvinyl chloride (PVC), polypropylene, and polystyrene, increase in value between two and five times. The price of these thermoplastics ranges near $1,000 a ton.

Strong support is given by Saudi authorities to private entrepreneurs who are prepared to establish enterprises if they qualify under the Protection and Encouragement of National Industries Statute. Various incentives are offered. Exemption is accorded on customs duties on imported machinery and equipment, spare parts, raw or semiprocessed materials, and packing materials; there are protective tariffs or quotas on competing imports; there is long-term leasing of industrial sites—called "Industrial Cities"—at a nominal rent; there is preferential treatment locally manufactured goods in government procurement; there is assistance in the identification of viable projects through market research and feasibility studies; and, above all, there is the assistance provided by the Saudi Industrial Development Fund (SIDF), which grants interest-free medium- and long-term loans to industrial firms. While loans are interest free in accordance with Islamic strictures, a 2-percent administrative fee is charged. The SIDF can finance up to 50 percent of the capital requirements of a project or the Saudi equity, if it is less in a joint venture. Virtually all lending has been for amounts of over SR 2 million ($600,000). The only problem is the time taken before a commitment can be secured—up to a year.

A considerable number of entrepreneurs have been taking advantage of these generous incentives. This is reflected in the imports of artificial resins and plastic materials, cellulose esters, rubber, and synthetic rubber, which increased from a value of SR 114 million in 1972 to SR 1,496 million in 1978. In real terms this would mean a tripling of imports.

By 1979 there were some eighty plastics, chemical and allied products plants in the Kingdom. These are usually relatively modest undertakings, using a few thousand tons of raw material a year, with an equity of a little over a million dollars and employing a few dozen employees. Many of these employees are expatriates, frequently Jordanians, Syrians, or other Arab nationals. The enterprises tend to be concentrated in the larger cities such Riyadh, Jeddah, Mecca, Medina, and Dammam. The newer firms normally take advantage of the industrial parks established on the outskirts of these centers.

One of the leading producers of plastics in Riyadh is the Saudi Plastic Products Company (SAPPCO), established almost a decade ago to manufacture plastic pipes and fittings. The British firm Chemidus was brought in to provide the technology and part of the equity. The output and the profitability of SAPPCO, under its managing director Omar A. Aggad, has grown steadily. Today there are eleven extruders and two molding machines which use 22,000 tons of PVC a year and 350 workers with an office staff of fifty. In order to enter into the field of polyurethane (PU) insulation panelboard—which is particularly suitable for roofing insulation on institutional, commercial, industrial, and even private residences—SAPPCO linked up with Texaco Saudi Investment Incorporated (a wholly owned subsidiary of Texaco Incorporated) to set up the firm SAPPCO-Texaco Insulation Products (SAPTEX) to be located in Riyadh. This partnership is seen as providing Saudi Arabia with manufacturing technology for products that previously have been available only through imports. One of the main reasons for Texaco's entering into this venture is its profitability since benzene, readily available in Saudi Arabia, accounts for some 40 percent of the cost of the raw materials going into PU. When this plant goes into production near the end of 1981, it will have a capacity of 100 million square feet of PU insulation panelboard. The cost of the enterprise is estimated at $30 million. Sixty percent of the equity would be held by SAPPCO and the other 40 percent by Texaco Saudi Investments Incorporated. While SAPTEX is only interested in the domestic market at present, exports could eventually be considered. World demand for PU in 1980, now estimated at 6.7 billion pounds, is expected to grow at 7 percent a year, bringing demand to 9.4 billion pounds in 1985 and to 13.1 billion pounds in 1990.

Another of the larger enterprises is the Modern Industries Companies, established in Dammam in 1980, to manufacture and sell detergents. The capital is $10.8 million, half of the equity being subscribed by the Swiss firm Detergent Products and the other half by Saudis.

Much more typical of the downstream enterprises is the Dammam-based Babtain Polyurethane which went on stream in 1980 with the manufacture of polyurethane furniture. The capital of $1.3 million is subscribed by the Josef Egli Company of Switzerland, which provides the technology, and by members of the Saud Al-Babtain family.

Cooperation by the Arab Gulf States

If Saudi Arabia is showing great ability in drawing on foreign technology and in developing export markets for its petrochemicals, the Kingdom is at the same time attempting to develop the petrochemical industry within a Gulf and even in an Arab context. Despite the political divisions of the Peninsula, a free flow of manpower, capital, and goods has been maintained over the years. Indeed, a cornerstone of Saudi policy is to advance unity throughout the region. Iraq, as a Gulf and Arab state, is now drawing closer to the other Arab nations of the Gulf.

Close relations are maintained between the heads of state, principal officials, and leading personalities of the Arab Gulf states. In 1973 and 1974 the foreign ministers discussed political and economic cooperation between the Arab Gulf states. The drawing up of a single economic plan for the area was even envisaged. Later, in 1976, the ministers of industry of Saudi Arabia, Kuwait, Bahrain, Qatar, the United Arab Emirates, Oman, and Iraq gathered in Doha, Qatar, and called for greater industrial coordination and cooperation. The possibility of joint ventures was proposed.

One of the practical results of these meetings was the creation of the Gulf Organization for Industrial Consulting (GOIC) in 1977. The GOIC was given the responsibility for: collecting and publishing documentation dealing with industrial development policies and projects; examining possible joint projects; proposing measures to coordinate projects; coordinating and promoting technical and economic cooperation between companies and corporations; providing technical assistance in the preparation and evaluation of projects; and preparing data and studies related to industry. Dr. Ali

Al Khalaf was appointed Secretary General of GOIC, and a staff of some seventy employees was established in Doha. Since that time the Secretariat has done a number of studies dealing with the petrochemical and other industries. In some cases consulting firms have been called in to assist the Secretariat as, for example, the Chem Systems International Limited study for GOIC entitled "Petrochemical Marketing Strategies."

A seminar dealing with the marketing of Gulf petrochemicals was held in Doha under the auspices of GOIC in May of 1979 using the Chem Systems report as a basis for discussions. Among the conclusions drawn from the seminar was that due to the availability of raw materials in the Gulf, the states of this area will have a large and increasing advantage relative to the production costs, especially for synthesis gas-based derivatives such as ammonia, urea, and methanol. The possibility of a common pipeline for ethylene in the region was considered. An aggressive marketing strategy was suggested that should be implemented in consultation with such other major producers as Algeria and Libya. Many of the conclusions of the Doha meeting were reexamined by the ministers of industry of the Gulf when they met in Riyadh in June of 1979. The ministers agreed that certain products should be marketed jointly in the more promising regions. The funding of joint ventures was also considered. Such activities, it was felt, would further the long-term objective of greater economic, social, and political unity in the Peninsula and Arab Gulf.

When the planning ministers met in May of 1980, they once again pressed for greater cooperation and coordination and suggested joint marketing of specific products. This time, however, they went one step further. Saudi Arabia renounced plans to establish an aluminum smelter in Jubail so as not to be in competition with one in Bahrain. Saudi Arabia, Kuwait, and Bahrain decided to launch a joint venture in Bahrain.

This joint venture, as it is now envisaged, accepts the recommendation of the GOIC that it is advantageous to reproduce synthesis gas-based derivatives (ammonia, urea, and methanol) in the Arab Gulf states. The venture now calls for the production of 1,000 tons a day of methanol and 1,000 tons of ammonia. The total investment is estimated at $400 million, with the capital for the venture to be 60 million Bahrian dinars ($159 million) shared equally among the three parties. The products would be marketed in the United States, Western Europe, Japan and other Asian countries, Africa, and the Arabian Peninsula itself.

This venture, in the view of Saudi Industry Minister, Dr. Algosaibi, is a turning point in the Gulf's economic integration, moving from planning to implementation and taking a positive step in reducing duplication in industry, which can lead to excessive and wasteful competition.

The issue of duplication raises some questions. Iraq, Kuwait, and Qatar all have relatively important petrochemical projects. The Basrah Petrochemical Complex No. 1 built for the Ministry of Industry and

Minerals of Iraq by C.E. Lummus and Thyssen Rheinstahl Tecknik, using Lummus, Stauffer, and other processes, was to have gone on stream in 1980. However, after the severe damage inflicted during the Iran-Iraq conflict, this date will undoubtedly have to be put forward. The complex will have a capacity of 130,000 tons per year of ethylene, 60,000 tons of polyvinyl chloride (PVC), 66 tons of vinyl chloride, 70,000 tons of low-density polyethylene, 30,000 tons of high-density polyethylene as well as 43,200 tons of caustic chlorine and 42,000 tons of flake caustic soda. This same ministry has had another plant put up in Khor al Zubair to produce 1,400 tons per day of carbon-dioxide remove and 1,000 tons of ammonia.

In Kuwait, the Petrochemical Industries Companies is planning to establish a plant in Shuaiba to produce 1,000 metric tons per day of ammonia, and an annual output of 280,000 tons of benzene, 350,000 tons of ethylene, 135,000 tons of ethylene glycol, 340,000 tons of styrene, 60,000 tons of orthoxylene, 86,000 tons of paraxylene, and 130,000 tons of low-density polyethylene. The complex is expected to go on stream in 1983 and 1984.

Qatar has possibly one of the largest gas fields in the world—the North West Dome field with perhaps 100 billion cubic feet. With expansion, the Qatar Fertilizer Company (QAFCO) will soon be producing 1,800 tons a day of ammonia and 2,000 tons a day of urea. The output will be going largely to Asia—India, Pakistan, and China—as well as to the United States and Latin America.

Spurred on by the relative success of QAFCO, the partly nationalized Qatar Petrochemical Company (QAPCO) has been launched. Using associated gas, QAPCO annually will use 400,000 tons of ethane to produce 280,000 tons of ethylene. This will allow 140,000 tons of low-density polyethylene to be produced a year as well as 200 tons per day of sulphur. Technip of France, Coppee-Rust of Belgium, Turbotecnica of Italy, and Japan Gasoline are all participating in this project. The cost of this venture is estimated at QR 2,400 million ($641 million). The state would own 84 percent of QAPCO and the balance by CDE Chimie of France. A marketing agreement has been signed with CDE Chimie, which will largely export the products to the Middle East and the Indian Ocean area. An entry to the European market might also be gained through a petrochemical company in Dunkirk, Copenor, established by the Qatar General Petroleum Corporation and CDF Chimie. This plant should go on stream in 1981. QAPCO has decided to expand its activity in Umm Said by erecting a plant to produce 70,000 tons a year of high-density polyethylene. The cost of this plant is estimated at between $48 and $58 million. The process to be used and the engineering work are under negotiation.

In the United Arab Emirates, the Abu Dhabi National Oil Company is planning to put up a plant in Ruwais with a daily output of 1,000 tons of ammonia and 1,500 tons of urea.

Resolute and forceful measures are needed to rationalize the production and marketing of petrochemicals of the Arab Gulf states. The main potential markets for these petrochemicals—the Far East, Western Europe, and the United States—all have appreciable domestic production or have alternative sources of supply. However, Saudi Arabia, Kuwait, and Iraq do enjoy a considerable power of negotiation since they can link crude-oil sales with the distribution of petrochemical products. Qatar and certain other Arab Gulf states can offer little crude oil as an incentive to stimulate sales.

Conclusion

As the different joint ventures come on stream in 1984, 1985, 1986, and possibly even later, Saudi Arabia will have gradually increasing amounts of petrochemicals and urea to place on world markets. Taking into consideration that actual output will initially be considerably below nameplate capacity, by 1985 about 1 million tons of methanol should be produced. This would represent about 8 percent of world methanol output. Given the cost advantage of producing methanol with cheap feedstock, the sharp increase that can be expected in demand and the fact that much of the marketing will be handled by Mitsubishi and by Celanese—two particularly well-entrenched corporations—this product is almost a "sure winner." Much the same can be said for ethylene glycol, with about half a million tons, and for ethanol, with about a quarter of a million tons. A somewhat greater marketing effort may be required for both high- and low-density polyethylene and some of the other products, but the difficulties should not be insurmountable.

   To supplement marketing agreements, as they are now being drawn up, it is suggested that Taiwan and South Korea serve as springboards for bulk petrochemicals from Saudi Arabia, giving them more value-added and then marketing them throughout the world.

   At the same time the emerging petrochemical industry has to be placed in perspective. The production of the major petrochemicals, ethylene, propylene, buta diene, benzene, toluene, and xylenes, in the free-market world is 86 million tons a year. The Saudi production of a few million tons of petrochemicals would thus represent a relatively insignificant proportion of the world total.

   Even in Saudi Arabia itself the output of petrochemicals would play a minor role for at least the next decade. The total value of the production of petrochemicals in the mid-1980s would not exceed some $3 billion a year. This may be compared with a gross domestic product of close to $160 billion and gross export earnings of just over $100 million in 1980.

   Yet there is the danger of succumbing to the all too human desire of having the latest and biggest. The most recent process and other technologies may be more cost efficient, and the larger plants may show economies of scale. Though Arab countries once led the world in science and technology, they now tend to be on the margin of scientific advances. This is particularly true for Saudi Arabia, where the industrial and technological base has been weak. While the latest in the state of the art might be applied with relative success in the Texas "spaghetti bowl," if applied in Saudi Arabia it could cause serious problems. Difficulties with one unit could bring the operation of a whole complex to a halt. Thus, at times it is preferable to forgo a technology that is still largely experimental. With respect to the desire for the "biggest," there is now a move in the petrochemical industry away from large-volume commodity petrochemicals toward such higher technology and value-added products as additives, catalysts, pharmaceuticals, and agrochemicals.

In conclusion, one cannot but be struck by how a small dynamic group of technocrats from the Saudi Ministry of Industry and Electricity, SABIC, the Royal Commission for Jubail and Yanbu, and other entities as well as executives from Mitsubishi, Mobil, Shell, Exxon, Dow, Celanese, and other corporations have, despite basically divergent interests, pooled their abilities to create a great new industry. These efforts, backed up by a host of engineers and other professionals in the United States, Japan, and elsewhere, virtually assure the viability of these ventures, thereby laying a firm basis for future industrial development.

7 Technology Transfer to the Developing Nations: The Case of Saudi Arabia

Talal K. Hafiz

Introduction

Few countries in the world have experienced the accelerated economic growth and business development that is now occurring in Saudi Arabia. Saudi Arabia no longer requires what had become its traditional dependency on foreign aid. With its capital surplus and established oil reserves, the Kingdom supplies a logical and balanced model of supply and demand for competitors from technologically advanced countries.

Foreign planners, consultants, and workers are being challenged to adapt their professional services and goods to the Saudi Islamic culture. Thus the Saudi situation presents a unique opportunity for a developing country to interact on an equal basis with the industrialized world while maintaining its traditional values.

However, domestic planners are facing a different challenge: reducing the Kingdom's dependence on foreign manpower while maintaining a steady modernization program. Such a challenge requires that the Kingdom pool all available training resources to develop Saudi manpower for the jobs foreigners now are doing.

To complete this huge task while oil revenues remain a viable financial resource, Saudi planners have carefully organized the development process into a series of five-year plans. The Kingdom's first and second five-year plans emphasized the steady expansion of the economy, particularly for infrastructure. Now that the majority of the infrastructure is in place, the main emphasis is on training the Saudi work force to operate and maintain the infrastructure.

The Kingdom's long-term objective of human-resources development is being fulfilled on both the domestic and international levels. Domestically, thirteen universities and four girls' colleges have been established to train and educate Saudi manpower in disciplines ranging from agriculture to industrial management. On the international level, Saudi students are attending universities and colleges throughout Europe and North America to receive the specialized-skills training not available in the Kingdom.

77

Still, the effort for human-resources development on the domestic level is growing rapidly. It is estimated that training and educating Saudis in the various fields of industrial technology, according to the third five-year plan (1980–1985), will require several more years. In the meantime every possible manpower gap left by the foreign work force will be filled by a Saudi who has training in the specific area.

An analysis of funds allocated for human-resource development shows a steady increase since the first plan. The first plan, which encompassed the years 1970–1975, allocated some $3 billion for this purpose. The enormous leaps in infrastructure expansion that took place under the first plan made it more evident that human-resource development should be expanded rapidly.

The second plan, covering the years from 1975–1980, allocated $22.76 billion for human-resource development. The allocation was almost eight times the amount provided under the first plan.

The third plan offers a detailed analysis of the advances made under the first and second plans. Some areas are recommended for more attention than others such as the sciences and engineering, and other programs will be implemented for more thorough manpower training within the Kingdom. The third plan allocates $36 billion in the human-resources area.

Such attention to technology transfer and human-resources development is becoming a budgetary requirement for most developing nations. The diverse perspectives offered by social, cultural/religious and business specialists emphasize the complex concerns that arise from this phenomenon. Economic planners, for example, emphasize that, to develop needed human capital, education must be easily accessible to all citizens, which means that the bulk of training and education should occur inside the country, not abroad.

Social scientists, on the other hand, view society itself as a major tool for development, but they recommend that planning should include awareness of the individual factor. Organizational developers caution that organizations must be able to change with the society in transformation. They also stress the need to adapt organizational structures to better serve the public.

Traditionalists resist modernization for its unmeasurable effect on society and culture. Foreign advisers and consultants working with the developing nations often are puzzled when the Western approach to modernization fails. They note that attempts to develop a nation without concern for the religious and moral values of the country can have an opposite effect of what is desired: the developing nation will reject modernization because of its apparent link to the different moral standards of the West.

Communication experts suggest that one way to remedy this problem is to create a climate favorable to modernization through an informed and participating citizenry. An involved public assures that the society's values and moral standards will be incorporated into any changes that occur. Educational technologists believe that a major factor in this concern is extensive use of the broadcast media to extend human-resources development.

One common denominator in all processes of technology transfer and development is qualified human resources able to implement and coordinate the complex job of modernization. Using this common denominator, the next most important step is to identify the possible variables affecting the process of technology transfer and human-resources development in the context of Saudi Arabia as well as other developing nations.

The Transfer of Resources

In the traditional role model, developing nations count on the more technologically advanced states to help provide the resources necessary for modernization. Logically this approach allows the developing countries to take advantage of modern technology without undergoing the time-consuming, trial-and-error processes that the advanced nations had to undergo in order to develop the technology. Wilbur Schramm of Stanford University explains this trend:

> Why should these [developing] countries have to follow the long, painful path of the older countries from agricultural society? Why should they not jump directly from the oxcart to the airplane, from the town crier to television? Why can they not make use of the experience of Japan and the West, instead of learning by their own trials and errors?[1]

However, an important consideration in viewing modernization this way is that the advanced nations experienced a slow, gradual change as they adopted new technologies. Developing nations, on the other hand, face a comparably rapid evolution that may present unforeseen problems. Therefore, the most important aspect in the development process is to maintain good lines of communication from the beginning.

Several popular misconceptions arise when communication is inadequate. One misconception is that modernization implies westernization. This misconception, although inaccurate, prevents the synthesis from the old to the new in adaptation to the changing environment.

Another misconception is that modernization is always good for a developing nation. Modernization perpetually brings change, which can produce benefits but relative disadvantages as well.[2] The introduction of highly sophisticated technology into developing nations is likely to have social, political, and cultural repercussions difficult to predict, let alone control.

Observers from developing countries often perceive modernization as a threat to the structure and function of their established societies. They express concern about the double-edged price of rapid development, as reflected in the following remarks by participants of the Agency for International Development:

> While introducing the improved technology of agriculture and industry, they [developing nations] fear they will also set in motion destructive forces leading to the breakdown of the extended family group, a rise in crime and divorce rates, and many other aspects of American life they perceive as highly undesirable. Modernization means, therefore, adapting new ways of life, the consequences of which do not necessarily lead to a "better" life for all individuals involved.[3]

These consequences can be kept at a minimum, however, if planners use all existing human resources in the developing nation who can serve as "buffers" between the West and the developing nation. In the case of Saudi Arabia, whenever possible, Saudi planners who are trained and experienced in modern Western technology are used in place of foreign planners.

Saudi Arabia emphasizes, above all else, the protection of religious and cultural values within the process of rapid economic growth. In fact, the number-one priority of the Kingdom's long-term modernization goal is to "maintain the religious and moral values of Islam."

Being a very traditional Islamic society, the Kingdom finds the most crucial problem arising from its massive need for foreign manpower is the social impact such an alien labor force might have on the country. While the first and second plans emphasized high growth in all sectors, which required the relatively free import of foreign labor, the third plan (entering its second year) aims to consolidate rather than expand the foreign labor force.

By using domestic manpower whenever possible and by making the most efficient use of the foreign skilled manpower, the Kingdom has harnessed the influx of expatriates. Thus Saudi planners hope the country's social system, based on a strict following of Islamic principles, will resist undesirable Western influences.

It is a primary concern that, until the time comes when massive foreign manpower is no longer required, Saudi nationals should learn to accept, absorb, and perceive the necessary measures for development of their country while maintaining their distinctive Islamic social order.

Development of Human Capital

The highly complex process of education and modernization in developing nations requires that extensive research, planning, and resources be harnessed to achieve constructive change. The desired constructive changes, as suggested by Everett M. Rogers and Lynne Svenning of Michigan State University, include higher per-capita incomes and levels of living through more modern production methods.[4]

Developing countries particularly confront the difficult problem of adapting human and natural resources to parallel the requirements of contemporary development plans. Because of the lack of qualified human resources, managing the process of modernization and technology transfer becomes a highly complex problem that entails not just the desired goal but all intermediate steps needed to reach that goal.

A critical factor in the modernization process is the relative availability of manpower qualified to draw and implement development plans. Economists Harbison and Myers define human-resources development as:

> the process of increasing the knowledge, the skills, and the capacities of all the people in a society. In economic terms, it would be described as the accumulation of human capital and its effective investment in the development of an economy.[5]

The principal resources for upgrading human development are made available through educational systems. In a developing nation, these resources provide the teaching of skills and the means to introduce and cope with change. To be effective, education must cut across all sectors of the society, upgrading literacy, training methods, mechanical skills, health care, and the overall standard of living.[6] In effect, educational systems serve as the blueprint by which human-resources development occurs.

But education should not be viewed by educational planners as confined by the walls surrounding classrooms and laboratories. Educational technologists and economists identify five main sources through which human resources can be developed by the educational process: (1) formal education; (2) ''on-the-job'' training; (3) self-development, by which individuals seek to acquire greater knowledge through personal initiative; (4) better medical and public health facilities; and (5) improvement in nutrition increases the working capacity and working life of the people.[7]

Education, formal or informal, is an integral yet far-reaching part of the process of technology transfer for national development, making it impossible and unwise to limit its boundaries. Whatever capacity a society has for increasing its access to technology, every avenue should be utilized for maximum benefit.

In Saudi Arabia one such resource for technology transfer is derived from petroleum and its by-products. Saudi universities utilize the wealth of expertise available in the Kingdom to train and educate Saudis to take a more dominant part in oil production, petrochemicals, and refining. Then the universities take the process one step further by applying the technology already available to the environment and society within the Kingdom.

Whether inside the classroom or on the job, the educational process hinges on consideration of the individual, for without the individual consideration, technology transfer on the societal level becomes only a temporary and artificial advancement. Schramm identifies the interdependency between the individual and societal levels:

> A social transformation is basically a set of human transformations—people to be educated and informed, attitudes and values to be changed, human relationships, customs, social behavior to be reviewed and rethought .... Farms should be made more productive so that part of the human resources can be moved from agriculture into industry.[8]

Modernization is dependent on the ability of individuals to accept and adopt innovative behaviors and roles, consistent with the demands of a changing environment. Significant societal transformation generally occurs when the processes of education and modernization motivate citizens to accept rather than resist change. In a full-employment economy, "the individual has greater freedom of choice and greater potential mobility. Outstanding workers are hard to find and difficult to keep."[9]

When considering plans for social and developmental change, it must be remembered that organizational role models in developing countries are not necessarily similar or applicable to the models used in industrialized nations. A tested and proved organizational model used in a developed state often will differ from that used in another nation—developed or undeveloped. Therefore, the organizational model selected for any one nation should parallel the established social structure in the country.

Development of organizational structure and training in developing countries also differs from that of industrialized nations because it requires the creation of new jobs and roles. Management in developing nations has been accustomed to different styles of individual work and contribution. Industry brings problems of interrelated and interdependent working groups requiring precision and the use of a variety of instruments and machines. The individuality of work becomes no longer an extension of family or community control, as usually is the case in lesser-developed societies. The control now shifts to the system adopted by the organization.

The Role of Educational Media in Saudi Arabia

The potential use of the educational media for information flow in education and human-resources development has become a central issue in modernization planning for developing nations. While the use of media cannot automatically answer all development requirements, its power to cohesively integrate education and social change is substantial. Media can help create an atmosphere for innovative education but must do so with consideration for the culture it intends to serve.

In Saudi Arabia, where education is subverted by acute shortages of faculties and facilities, mass media—particularly television—enters as a catalyst to multiply these scarce educational resources. Perhaps just as important, mass media allows for education and training in a cultural environment that discourages mixing of the sexes in a classroom setting. By using television in the classroom, an all-female group can receive instruction from a male instructor without his physical presence in the room. Thus, using the available technology, the Saudi culture is adapting to the critical shortage of female instructors, yet it still is maintaining its religious and traditional cultural standards.

Educational mass media achieves power as a stimulant for development because it serves as an educational multiplier and because it can promote identification with new roles. The rising expectations of people in developing countries coupled with the ability of broadcasting to personalize experience make the media a viable force for change. *Empathy,* the ability of individuals to project themselves into the roles of others,[10] enables individuals to make use of experience lived by others. The power of broadcasting lies partly in its power to facilitate this process of identification.

But the necessary communication flow is not a simple process originating only from those working at government levels or private institutions. Therefore, successful planning relies on the input of the community concerning the understanding of programs and the assessment of needs:

> Information must flow not only to them, but also from them, so that their needs can be known and so that they may participate in the acts and decisions of nation building; and information must also flow vertically so that decisions must be made, work organized, and skills learned at all the levels of society.[11]

Conclusion

One way to facilitate the transfer of technology in a culturally sensitive situation, such as that obtaining in Saudi Arabia, is to have the transfer occur within the developing nation itself. A very large part of the Saudi manpower-training program takes place within the Kingdom because of the various advantages home-country training offers. In the World Conference on the International Transfer of Management Skills, Jan Tinbergen, a Nobel Prize winner, expressed the possibility that this transfer can be effected by a training institution, particularly those institutions in the developing countries themselves, for

> despite the fact that there are in developed countries some very specialized abilities, . . . at a medium level, and at a lower level, it is certainly better if people are not separated from their environment.[12]

The main benefit of manpower training on the domestic level is that the resulting technology is much better adapted to the developing country's environment and culture. Furthermore, new ideas and new technologies introduced by one's own countrymen are generally much more acceptable than those introduced by foreigners.

It must be remembered that in the transfer of skills or other resources between industrialized and developing countries, emphasis cannot be placed solely on specialization. Managers in developing nations require sophisticated training; yet they also need to achieve a larger perspective for engineering social and developmental change. With the need for experts, training has become so involved and so specialized that very few are educated to see the whole picture. And the ability to see the whole picture is the key to a lasting success in modernization.

The example served by Saudi Arabia shows how the complete overview of development supplements the specialized manpower training now in progress. The best evidence of how the Kingdom looks at the big picture, as well as the more minute details, is the Kingdom's series of five-year development plans. Each five-year plan has covered every section of the economy in which development has been planned. The plans also document the carefully drawn and implemented development projects initiated with the big picture in mind: to diversify the Saudi economy and reduce its dependence on petroleum exports and foreign labor.

Thus the Kingdom's development structure and its complete program to train and employ the domestic work force serves as a model other developing nations could follow. Not only has this program produced phenomenal results to improve the standard of life for the entire Kingdom, the program also has ensured that the distinct social and cultural values of Saudi Arabia will be maintained. And this perhaps is the Kingdom's greatest success as it faces the challenges ahead.

Notes

1. Wilbur Schramm, *Big Media, Little Media* (Washington, D.C.: Information Center on Instructional Technology, Academy for Educational Development, 1973), p. 8.

2. Everett M. Rogers and Lynne Svenning, *Modernization Among Peasants: The Impact of Communication* (New York: Holt, Rinehart and Winston, 1969), p. 15.

3. Ibid.

4. Ibid., p. 14.

5. Frederick Harbison and Charles A. Myers, *Education, Manpower, and Economic Growth: Strategies of Human Resource Development* (New York: McGraw-Hill, 1964), p. 2.

6. Wilbur Schramm, *Mass Media and National Development: The Role of Information in the Developing Countries* (Stanford, Calif.: Stanford University Press, 1964), p. 25.

7. Harbison and Myers, *Education, Manpower, and Economic Growth,* p. 2.

8. Schramm, *Mass Media,* p. 9.

9. Fred Tickner, *Training in Modern Society: An International Review of Training Practices and Procedures in Government and Industry* (Albany: Graduate School of Public Affairs, State University of New York at Albany, 1966), p. 158.

10. Daniel Lerner, "International Cooperation and Communication in National Development," in *Communication and Change in the Developing Countries,* eds. Daniel Lerner and Wilbur Schramm (Honolulu: East-West Center Press, 1967), p. 117.

11. Schramm, *Mass Media,* p. 246.

12. Jan Tinbergen, "The Industrialization of Developing Countries: Guidelines and Problems," *Prospect* 4 (Winter 1969):11.

8 The Saudi Arabian National Center for Science and Technology (SANCST)

Fahad Sultan Huraib

General Overview of SANCST Role and Activities

The Saudi Arabian National Center for Science and Technology (SANCST), established by Royal Decree in November of 1977, is charged with the responsibility of promoting and encouraging applied scientific research and coordinating the activities of scientific research organizations and centers in accordance with the Kingdom's development requirements.

In its first four years of activity, several major programs were initiated or expanded, each of which is expected to make a significant contribution to the scientific and technological development of the Kingdom. In science and technology infrastructural development, the design and establishment of a national science and technology information system consisting of nine data bases and on-line search capabilities is complete. In other areas, SANCST has supported on-going and proposed research at the Kingdom's universities through its Applied Research Grants Program (AR). During the last two years, thirty-two research grants were awarded under the first AR program, and still more grants are to be made.

In the field of solar energy, several major procurements were awarded in cooperation with the United States. Among these is a contract for the construction of a 350 kilowatt photovoltaic electrical-power generation facility in Saudi Arabia; the long-range goal of this project is the installation of a solar system capable of delivering 1 megawatt of electrical power to two remote Saudi villages. Additionally, a contract was awarded for a series of solar-cooling engineering field tests in the United States and a solar data-collection project in Saudi Arabia. Approval was also given for construction of solar-cooling test laboratories at four of the Kingdom's universities. A solar-energy water-desalination study and a closed-environment agriculture study were approved.

Functions and Objectives of SANCST

SANCST was established as an independent legal entity administratively attached to the prime minister. In accordance with its bylaws, the center is

87

entrusted with the responsibility of formulating a national science and technology policy directed toward and consistent with the social and economic development of the Kingdom. To achieve this objective, but also without limiting its functions, the center is to undertake the following: (1) conduct applied scientific-research programs in the fields that serve the economic- and social-development objectives of the Kingdom; (2) formulate a scientific-research plan that will specify national objectives for achieving scientific advancement; (3) establish and operate laboratories for applied scientific research in areas of importance to the Kingdom; (4) establish and manage an information center that collects and disseminates data on the scientific and technological manpower resources in the Kingdom; (5) establish and manage an information center maintaining data on national and international scientific institutions; (6) award scholarships to develop the necessary skills for conducting research work; (7) award grants to individuals and scientific organizations to undertake applied-research work; (8) coordinate with government agencies, scientific organizations, and research centers in the Kingdom to enhance research, information and expertise exchange and to avoid duplication of effort; (9) provide assistance to the private sector in the development of productive agricultural and industrial research that will help increase the gross national product; (10) support joint-research programs between the Kingdom and international scientific foundations; and (11) support joint-research programs between the Kingdom and international scientific foundations in an effort to keep pace with scientific developments in the world by awarding research grants and undertaking joint-research projects.

Organizational Structure

SANCST is administered by an executive director who serves as the chairman of the board and is assisted by his deputy. An autonomous board of directors is responsible for, among other things, developing and recommending national scientific and technical policies; for fully reviewing SANCT's research plans on an annual basis; and for periodically reviewing and approving budgetary requirements.

The key technical organization elements of SANCST are embodied in four directorates: (a) Directorate for Science and Technology Infrastructure; (b) Directorate for Scientific Research; (c) Directorate for National Research Institutes; and (d) Directorate for Manpower Development and Science Education.

The Directorate for Science and Technology Infrastructure is responsible for the development and implementation of a national science and technology information system and a scientific instrumentation facility which is considered critical to the overall development of science and technology in the Kingdom as well as to the establishment of SANCST's own research activities and policy-planning process.

The Directorate for Scientific Research consists of three divisions: engineering sciences, mathematical and natural sciences, and life sciences. It is responsible for working with universities and research institutions (other than SANCST's own agencies) and providing support needed to make the most of existing research potential. The main efforts of this directorate initially involve the implementation and administration of a grants program for the creation or application of new science and technology in order to further the development objectives of the Kingdom.

SANCST will establish a number of research institutes that will be staffed by scientists and engineers from a variety of disciplines with common objectives; this program falls under the Directorate for National Research Institutes. The institutes that are planned initially include: Arid Land Research Institute, Energy Research Institute, Petroleum and Petrochemical Research Institute, Natural Resources and Environmental Research Institute, Industrial Research Institute, and Applied Interdisciplinary Social Research Institute. A plan is to be developed to identify the relationship among these institutes, Saudi Arabian universities, and other research institutions.

The Directorate for Manpower Development and Science Education has the responsibility for the development of scientific and technical manpower for SANCST and, through interaction with other government agencies, for the Kingdom as a whole. Implementation will involve supporting and improving the education and training of Saudi engineers and scientists at the university and lower levels.

Activities Performed under the Auspices of International Cooperative Agreements

Although oil is Saudi Arabia's primary energy resource, the government is interested in research and development of solar energy, a nondepletable energy source also in plentiful supply. In May of 1977, Crown Prince Fahad expressed the Kingdom's interest in initiating a cooperative technical research program with the United States for development of solar energy (SOLERAS). In October of that year, a bilateral agreement setting up a $100 million joint trust fund was signed for the purpose of supporting efforts to cooperate in the field of solar energy for the mutual benefit of the two countries; to advance the development of solar technology; and to facilitate the transfer of technology developed through the program.

The SOLERAS program to date is involved in five areas. First, the villages of Al-Jubailah and Al-Uyaynah have been selected as the site for installation of the world's largest photovoltaic system that will be capable of delivering 1 megawatt of electrical power. To meet the target, the project will be implemented in phases, the first of which would provide for 350 kilowatts to be installed and operational with storage capacity by 1981.

Second, the objective of the solar controlled-environment agriculture project is to integrate controlled-environment agriculture with solar energy to demonstrate the technical and economic feasibility of commercially viable solar controlled-environment agriculture facilities in hot arid zones. To accomplish the objective of this project, a two-phase activity is planned. Phase 1 is for preliminary system design and cost analysis, and phase 2 is for detailed design, construction, operation, and evaluation of an engineering field test, and for personnel training.

The third SOLERAS program is the solar-energy water-desalination project. In 1980, five system studies were started for a solar-energy water-desalination project. The objective of the project is to advance the technical and economic feasibility of large-scale, solar-powered desalination of brackish water and seawater. In 1981 the system studies will be concluded, and two of the most promising concepts will be selected for further development through construction and operation of pilot plants. The system studies will be completed in August of 1981 and selection of concepts for pilot plant construction is expected in November of 1981.

The three objectives of the resource-development activities program are to provide training of Saudi Arabia/U.S. personnel for the monitoring, operation, maintenance, and repair of all solar-powered demonstration equipment to be installed in Saudi Arabia and in the United States; to expand professional communities in the field of solar-energy technologies; and to develop educational programs to establish self-sufficiency in professional training.

The fifth SOLERAS program involves urban applications. The objective of this program is to improve the quality of life for inhabitants of urban areas in hot climates, both arid and humid, by providing domestic solar cooling. In 1980, two separate cooling projects were initiated: engineering field tests for a solar active cooling system and Saudi Arabian university solar-cooling laboratories.

In February of 1979 the Project Agreement for Technical Cooperation in Science and Technology was signed by the Saudi government and the U.S. National Science Foundation (NSF). The agreement sets forth the terms for an understanding to work in close cooperation during the period of program planning, implementation, and operation of SANCST. Another project agreement is that with the Canadian National Research Council for the National Observatory Project. SANCST has been entrusted with the development of the Kingdom's national observatory project, and in cooperation with the Canadian council, tremendous progress has been made toward the selection of a site for the Kingdom's national observatory. Finally, as a result of a survey conducted in March of 1979 by a team of scientists from the Republic of China and in accordance with the "memorandum of cooperation in the field of science and technology," two areas for cooperative projects have been identified. These projects will involve cooperation in the field of single-cell protein manufacture and aquaculturing.

SANCST and Society

SANCST's operations are directly and indirectly related to society. It cooperates and coordinates with the various universities, agencies, and institutions concerned with research and technology; it encourages Saudi experts to undertake research that will help promote society's development and evolution. SANCST plans to organize research grant competitions that will promote the objectives of social and economic development. Thus it participates in enhancing society's evaluation and appreciation of science and technology.

Furthermore, there are several channels of communication between the center and the various organizations, agencies, and scientific institutions for the exchange of data and information pertaining to research fields. SANCST has participated in numerous scientific and technological symposia and conferences held during 1978 and 1979, which provided a favorable arena to become acquainted with the development of trends, fields, apparatus, and studies related to scientific research and modern technology. Moreover, SANCST's cooperation with certain world institutions and scientific organizations is a clear indication of the Kingdom's interest in research, science, and technology.

The center follows up on and evaluates all domestic and global scientific and technological literature as well as advanced and specialized research and makes the results available to Saudi researchers, thus providing a favorable environment for conducting advanced Saudi studies and research. Similarly, SANCST makes use of experts employed by the Kingdom's universities, providing them with the opportunity to introduce innovations and to promote research and studies required by the country.

The center also functions to provide advice to several official agencies in the Kingdom and hence contributes to the rationalization of decision making regarding science and technology. Last, the center donates scholarships and research grants to Saudi students in various universities to support a new generation of experts and researchers capable of keeping pace with the rapid development in the fields of science and technology.

9 Saudi Arabia: From Tribal Society to Nation-State

John Duke Anthony

In any discussion of economic development in Saudi Arabia, the matter of linkages to social and political variables is often raised. In the present context, this is not only natural but realistic and appropriate, serving as it does to underscore the interdependent universe in which development is proceeding. Whether one is examining five-year plans or such technically complex phenomena as absorptive capacity and industrialization, the utility of sociological perspectives would seem to be self-evident. In considering the circumstances of the people affected by the development process, some brief comments on the Kingdom's basic social units—in this instance, tribes— may therefore be of value.

This focus on a traditional "interest" group is admittedly limited. It clearly highlights but one kind of voluntary association among many others involved in the development equation. Depending on perspective, there may be other limitations in this approach as well: more than a few critics who grapple with the amorphous concept of social change in Saudi Arabia, for example, consider contemporary concern with such phenomena as distinctly unmodern, if not anachronistic. Yet, in terms of examining the impact of development in the Kingdom, the tribe qualifies as well as any other grouping as a useful unit of analysis.

The Tribe's Established Role

A consideration of particular relevance in this regard is the fact that tribes were the basic social and political units to which many Saudi Arabians looked for centuries for the preservation of order and the resolution of conflict. More than that, in pre-oil Arabia they were the repositories of both the means and actual process of a substantial proportion of what limited production occurred in the nonurban areas.

To be sure, the functions of maintaining order and administering justice are nowadays attended to by somewhat newer political structures associated with the central, regional, and local governments. Even so, there remain hundreds of tribes and subtribes scattered across the Kingdom, as in the two Yemens and Oman. And while the numbers of tribes are not nearly as great outside those four countries, the same phenomenon persists throughout all Arabia. Indeed, despite a half-century's official campaign against tribalism in the name of encouraging national and Islamic solidarity, clan and lineage links remain a potent force in Saudi Arabian society. The ongoing manifestation of such forces has long been especially pronounced in terms of the innermost circle of the Ruler's entourage, the Ahl Al Sheikh, the Ahl al-'Aqd wa al-Hal, and even the Council of Ministers.

Among the most important tribes in the Kingdom over the years have been the following: 'Anaza, Harb, Utaybah, Al Murrah, Shammar, Mutayr, and Qahtan, to name perhaps the seven largest in terms of members. Hardly less significant have been the Ruwala, Dawasir, Manasir, Munjaha, Yam, Ghamid, Shah Ran, Al Jahadilah, Juhaynah, Balt, Huwaytat, Bani Hajir, Bani Khalid, Quraysh, Al Rashid, 'Ajman, and Awazim. For much of Arabian history—indeed, until well into this century—most of these tribes existed as independent political entities in microcosm. As such, they were capable, like other groups (for example, the *ulama* or religious leaders, the merchants, and members of important families) of uniting for common action. At the same time, however, they more often than not acted as divisive forces in any larger societal context.

It was this latter characteristic as much as any other attribute that prompted the late King Abdul Aziz, the founder of modern Saudi Arabia, to seek a number of means by which he could integrate the various tribes into the new national political structure of the Kingdom. The religious content of Abdul Aziz's message as he set about knitting Arabia into a single state proved to be his greatest source of strength. He was able to direct and control a strict adherence to Islamic doctrines and, in this manner, affect a significant modification of the tribal distinctions which formerly had divided the realm.

Besides military conquest and spreading the discipline of the Hanbali school of Islamic law, Abdul Aziz employed to great effect one other means of unification—the institution of marriage. Through this device he was able to fuse further the interests and destinies of the tribes. In his own case, he married into many of the most important tribes and, through this device, produced a far more numerous progeny than ordinarily would have been possible. Many of Adbul Aziz's numerous sons (plus more than one hundred grandsons and more than five hundred great grandsons) and daughters have continued the broadening of the base of support for the ruling family by marrying, in their turn, the members of families of different tribes. As a result, it is now difficult to find major tribes in the Kingdom without some close family link to the ruling household. Both his efforts and those of his successors necessitated the creative ingenuity of compromise. The accommodations produced, however, have resulted in new patterns of order in a national context.

To be sure, the compromises required and the adjustments achieved could hardly be expected to have been entirely satisfactory to either the tribal sheikhs or the country's development leaders. Yet the process itself, half a century old, is much further along than in several neighboring countries. And, as the 1980s began, there was little doubt that countrywide there had been a definite shift in the direction of public sentiments and outlook. In essence, the shift was away from the more traditional and local orientations of the past to more general affiliations.

Even so, for most of the population born before World War II, tribal affiliation has remained an important symbol identifying their membership in the wider Saudi Arabian society. Such affiliation in the contemporary era has been a significant link between a great many individuals and the regime in Riyadh, providing them with prima facie evidence of a claim to the rights, duties, and privileges of citizenship. The point is hardly an insignificant one: such documentation has frequently constituted the all-important admission ticket for the positions of employment available to Saudi Arabians. Equally, in the absence of any other form of documentation for purpose of identification, it has made possible the entrance of countless Saudi Arabians into one of the local school systems, gained them access to the government's health facilities, and, for those who sought to travel abroad, warranted the issuance of a passport in their name.

Distinguishing Tribal Factors

In the early years of this century, a number of tribes proved politically decisive both to the ongoing acceptance of Al Saud rule in the Najd and, no less important, to the extension of the ruling family's writ to areas previously under different administrative control. Among the more highly regarded tribal groupings in this regard were the Qahtan, the Mutayr, Utayban, Dawasir, the Shammar, the Al Murrah and, of course the 'Anaza, from which the Al Saud themselves claim to originate (as do their dynastic counterparts in Bahrain and Kuwait).

The importance of these and other tribes derived more often than not from a combination of one or more of the following factors: size, military power, geographic location, form of livelihood, character and orientation of leadership and progeny, and/or religious outlook. In earlier times, another factor was often identification with one side or the other in a fundamental genealogical (not necessarily ethnic) distinction between the Adnani and Qahtani elements among the tribal population whose roots predate the Islamic era.

That the size of a given tribe has not always been directly related to its influence, however, has been exemplified historically by the Quraysh, the tribe of the Prophet Muhammad. Several tribes are larger. Similarly, the importance of other tribes in earlier days stemmed less from their numbers than their military power and—of crucial importance in determining their influence over time—their reputation of being among the most consistently loyal to the central government. In recognition of these two traits, it is of considerable contemporary significance that members of such tribes form to this day a substantial segment among the country's National Guardsmen, headed by Emir Abdallah.

The Manasir, Al Murrah, the Shammar, the 'Anaza, Ruwala, and the Huwaytat, among others, have long been of special importance strategically, owing to their location near (and often extending beyond) the country's borders and to their traditional ties with neighboring states. A number of these tribesmen at times have made the conduct of relations between the Riyadh government and such states as Iraq, Kuwait, Jordan, Abu Dhabi (United Arab Emirates), and Oman much more complicated than would have been the case had they been positioned instead deep within the interior of Arabia.

Other tribes have been influential for reasons having little to do with their numbers, military prowess, or territorial position. Due to their origins, substantial segments of some tribes, for example, remain distinguished by their long–standing cultural orientation toward areas other than Riyadh: the coastal communities of the Gulf or the Red Sea in some instances, the east Arabian areas beyond the Rub' al-Khali Desert in others, and now and again one or the other of the Yemens. One tribe, the Shammar—whose members extend into Syria and as far into Iraq as Mosul—is of added significance owing to the fact that the mother of the previously mentioned Emir Abdallah, a key leader in the ruling family, was one of its more important members.

The notion of "tribe" has not in every instance involved a social or political entity. Indeed, at times some groups have been considered tribes even though they may not have been known or prone to act as a single unit. For these and other groups, the term *tribe* has become associated more and more with the idea of a loosely knit membership unit. Such groups are typically devoid of any past or present implications of sovereignty or even autonomy. Yet they manifest such unifying characteristics as ethnic homogeneity, cultural continuity, linguistic similarity, and/or a common, deep-seated attachment to a given geographical area. In the past the close identification of many tribes with the last-mentioned trait gave rise to much strife and internicine tension between neighboring tribes, causing in turn the creation of competing coalitions of tribal groupings from different descent groups.

No less affected by the changes of the past half-century have been the tribal sheikhs. The tribal sheikhs have traditionally played a role that goes far beyond merely enhancing tribal identification in the Kingdom. The influence of tribal leaders for many years derived largely from their role as a major channel of communication between the authorities in Riyadh and the country's hundreds of thousands of tribesmen. Yet there were always well-defined limits to the manifestation of their influence. Whether the tribe was settled or nomadic and whether its lands were strategically important or not, their influence seldom extended beyond the geographic locus of the tribe itself.

The Family Unit in Saudi Society

Finally, with respect to all the tribes in the Kingdom, it is impossible to gain an adequate picture of their social and political organization without an examination of family structure. The impact of the family as an extended unit on government has, of course, been immense in the formation of past and present political structures in Arabia. Yet its paramountcy in the initial formation of the tribes themselves has often been overlooked along with the predominant role of one or more families in the determination of the political functions expected of the tribal sheikh. Most important of all, perhaps, is the fact that tribal roles were usually the roles of a particular family writ large. This certainly appears to have been the case with respect to the Al Saud, which over time eclipsed the political role of its tribal progenitors.

As the core unit within the overall system of political activity in the Kingdom, the government knows it is on firm sociological and doctrinal ground in emphasizing, as it has repeatedly done, the ongoing importance of familial solidarity as a fundamental value. In its view, the family—far more so than the tribe or other kinds of societal groupings—remains the structural foundation on which, ultimately, the edifice of the Saudi Arabian state will stand or fall. Indeed, much is made of the fact that this one unit remains at the center of the process through which the procreation and perpetuation of all the other social units in the Kingdom is manifested. Of no less significance, it remains the key unit through which lineage (read individual and group identity) is maintained, social cohesiveness is reinforced and nourished, and, by extension, structural integrity up through the highest levels of the national government is enhanced. By contrast, the overall degree of influence wielded by tribal leaders as a whole has been diminished considerably as a result of numerous forces of change, which they find increasingly difficult to control or influence in their favor.

Tribal Units and the Future

The growing impact of the central authority on traditional tribal autonomy and the effect of a rapidly expanding national economy continue to affect the influence of all the Kingdom's tribal leaders. The first factor has been manifested by the ambitious development programs and administrative machinery of Riyadh and the individual governates that have drawn the tribal population and its leaders ever closer into the government's orbit. The second has long been evidenced by the growing numbers of Saudi Arabian citizens migrating away from the Kingdom's villages—and in the process, of course, from the authority of the tribal sheikhs—to the urban centers of Riyadh, Dhahran, Abha, Jeddah, and elsewhere, where opportunities for wage and salaried employment abound.

Although it may yet be too early to discern the ultimate impact of these phenomena on the roles of individual tribes and their sheikhs within the national political structure, there is evidence enough to indicate some of the consequences of the trend to date. There is little doubt, for example, that the previous rather marked polarity between the interior-based capital and some of the country's more remote areas—indeed, among the coastal, mountainous, and desert regions in general, not to mention more intricate polarities between and within these regions—has become more and more blurred with each passing year. In its place there is no question that new links between and within these areas have emerged. The tribal sheikhs, moreover, have long since been unable or unwilling to reverse this trend that has relegated more and more of them to a lower echelon within the overall political structure.

To conclude, it is clear that the process of modernizing and diversifying the economy and other sectors of national life has brought vast changes to the position and role of the Kingdom's tribes. Looking to the future, the process seems certain to continue, given the government's ongoing commitment to promoting economic growth, industrialization, and numerous other changes along a broad societal front. Equally assured will be the continuing challenge to development planners, economists, and many other Saudi Arabian leaders of managing some of the basic kinds of conflict—especially those associated with psychological stress and moral unease—which often become manifest in such a process, and of working these conflicts out between the central and local authorities.

10 The Transition from a Tribal Society to a Nation-State

Abdulrahman H. Al-Said

It is perhaps useful to indicate at the outset what this chapter is not. It is, despite the assuming title, not written in order to (and does not even aspire or claim to) fully trace the development of Saudi Arabia from its humble beginnings to the present times. Rather, the intent is to put in sharper focus some of the events and developments leading to the country's emergence from a tribally organized and dominated entity to one in which authority and significant decision making are increasingly assumed by a central source of power.

Of particular interest to this effort are certain changes taking place in the various cultural, economic, and social bonds lending context and credibility to a process of national integration. Thus, in our attempt to formulate a clearer notion of Saudi Arabia's transition from an essentially tribal society to a nation-state, we shall briefly examine the changes occurring in the following areas: (1) The decline of traditional tribal modes of existence and (2) the process of institution building and the consolidation of authority.

Since this effort is geared toward an understanding of a transitional process, it would seem that a concise delineation of its historical framework is a desirable prerequisite. For analytical purposes, as well as convenience, this framework shall extend from the formation of the contemporary Saudi state (1932) until the end of the decade of the sixties. This designation focuses on the dissolution of certain modes of socioeconomic organization and the appearance in their place of alternative ones. Saudi Arabia's successful unification and the country's remarkable stability is a testimony to the manner in which this transitional process has evolved. Many experts predicted a far different outcome from the one being experienced at present. D.G. Hogarth, a noted expert on the Arabian Peninsula, wrote in 1925:

> I see nothing in the circumstances or constituents of the present Wahhabite expansion to promise it a longer life than has been enjoyed by early Nejdean ebullitions. These, to take only one test, have prevailed in Mecca for ten years, on the average. . . . I prophecize, therefore, that Arabia is not in for more than a decade, at the most, of Wahhabite domination outside Nejd.[1]

Mr. Hogarth's prophecy reflected the conventional-wisdom approach of the experts. The question then becomes: What combination of forces and circumstances has altered the course of events in this part of the world? That the Arabian Peninsula and particularly Saudi Arabia have opted for an alternative mode of existence and that socioeconomic organization is the central theme of the following discussion.

Decline of Traditional Tribal Modes

Perhaps the most decisive and least understood of the transformations taking place in the Arabian Peninsula is the massive and continuous movement of people from the desert to the urban and rural centers. That this detribalization process has troubled most observers and the experts is due in no small part to the prevailing state of conceptual confusion regarding such elementary questions as, Who can we call a Bedouin? Unfortunately, even the "experts" have tended to perceive the Bedouins in unidimensional terms. In other words, to be Bedouin is to be totally nomadic with next to no ties to the surrounding environment. Such a view finds expression even in specialized journals and volumes such as the *Encyclopedia of Islam,* which defined the Bedouins as "pastoral nomads of Arabian blood, speech, and culture who are found in the Arabian Peninsula proper and in parts of Iran, Soviet Turkestan, North Africa, and the Sudan."[2]

This view of Bedouin life, however innocent, is as incorrect as it is unfair. The complexity of the city-desert interaction has often eluded the scholars who have dwelled on the surface manifestations—raiding, hostility, and so on—and ignored the ecological and economic underpinnings of this relationship. The scholars' attitude was undoubtedly influenced by the ideas of no less an authority than Ibn Khaldun who conceived of the desert-town relationship as a vicious cycle of ebb and flow. But to his credit, Ibn Khaldun was speaking of a different era with a different set of circumstances. Unfortunately, this state of confusion can be detrimental to such efforts as the proper classification and enumeration of the whole populace. A clear example is provided by the 1970 United Nations *Yearbook,* which described the Saudi population as 85 to 95 percent Bedouin.[3] On the other hand, a recently published study suggests that as the 1980s open, perhaps 5 percent of the Saudi population remains wholly nomadic.[4] The conceptual rigidity regarding the classification of the Bedouins is undoubtedly spurred by the romantic and antiquated notion that insists on viewing them as totally nomadic and completely isolated from the sedentary population. Bedouin life, of course, has never been as static as the romanticists insist on recounting. And the demarcation line between sedentary and nomadic populations is not a hard-and-fast one.

Central to such problems as what percent of the population can be considered Bedouin is a serious lack of understanding of the process of settlement. This process through which the Bedouins move gradually from one life style into the other—often combining the two before they are absorbed into the sedentary mold—has only lately begun to receive the kind of scrutiny it deserves. Both M. Katakura, in her study of the Wadi Fatima settlements, and D.P. Cole, in his brilliant book on the Al Murrah Bedouins provide the kind of insight needed for a proper understanding of this process.[5] Both cases, though representing different groups, document a willingness to settle in response to changing economic circumstances.

As a result of these and other lesser-known efforts, three patterns of Bedouin settlement have been identified. At the risk of oversimplification, these can be seen as: (a) nomadic Bedouins; (b) the seminomadic Bedouins; and (c) settled Bedouins. The first classification includes nomadic tribespeople who will "generally move around in a familiar territory," taking into consideration the state of pasture and the accessibility of a market. They live off the sale of sheep and goat fat, dried-milk cakes, sheep, goat and camel hair, and their livestock of camels, sheep, and goats. The seminomadic Bedouins are half-settled communities that may eventually establish themselves in one place permanently or they may return to the nomadic life at any time. The third group of settled Bedouins lives, by and large, in huts or houses forming a village or hamlet. Some of the settled Bedouins work as agricultural laborers, others find employment in the cities, and some engage in small-scale artisan manufacturing.

Naturally, Bedouin social organization tended to change and rearrange its rules and mechanisms—and eventually some of its values—in a manner that is compatible with the adopted pattern.

In more recent times the natural ubiquity of the process of settlement has been greatly enhanced by two external factors: oil and droughts. The simultaneous occurrence of a prolonged drought (1958–1965) with the escalating position of economic predominance assumed by oil has confronted the Saudi Bedouin with an offer he cannot refuse. As it happened, the increasingly attractive pull of the urban economy was sharpened by the increasingly inhospitable state of dry pastures. Whether it was the result of settling in new towns near Aramco (Arabian American Oil Company) water wells, joining the National Guard or the army, entering the labor force of large companies, or owning taxis in the cities, the national economy's ability to absorb the tribal economy has been manifest. In a study commissioned by Aramco, the writers observed:

Even among Bedouins, we are told, the older tribal and sub-tribal allegiances are being replaced by the idea that the center and not the tribal head or his subordinate is seen as the source of effective power and the place for submitting petitions and bringing requests. Wealth has loosened the connection between tribal leaders and the common man, and the rise of a wealthy central government has, together with this, promoted a more direct relationship between the people and the top.[6]

Institution Building and Consolidation of Authority

The erosion of the social, economic, and cultural bases of the Bedouin social system was accompanied by a similarly significant phenomenon. The emergence of strong and central institutions hailed a new era and paved the way for significant changes in all areas of national life. The cornerstone for much of this change was the Council of Ministers, which was created in the final days of King Abdul Aziz's reign (1953). Of special interest in this connection was the implicit recognition of the need to identify areas of responsibility, to separate them, and to delegate authority in accordance with a more formal set of rules and procedures. This mushrooming of governmental institutions represented an attempt to cope with a condition of "rising expectations." As the citizens heard of the building of new schools and municipalities in neighboring towns and cities, delegations would go to the capital and demand similar privileges. As a result, limited and understaffed ministries of yesterday were giving way to larger and more numerous ministries and bureaus.

The steady growth of the central government and its bureaucratic apparatus has tended to weaken local power centers in the cities and provinces. This process seems to have proceeded in two stages. First, a considerable weakening of the powers of the city "notables" greatly enhanced the role of the bureaucracy. The notables, a residue of tribal strength, were unofficial representatives of the various tribes and families residing in an area and collectively sharing in the decisions affecting the other residents. In most cases they were joined by a representative(s) of the religious establishment and occasionally by others famous for their wisdom and influence. Second, this was followed by a visible reduction and minimization of the powers and prerogatives of provincial governors (Emirs). These two centers of local power were, since the inception of the Kingdom, able to retain a great deal of influence over governmental plans and projects designed for their respective areas. In the case of the notables, this power was manifested in their ability to suggest to the central government the desirability of a certain project or to point out the lack of such desirability. The central government never felt that this was more than a mere privilege to suggest, and when it deemed it necessary, its plans and projects were carried out despite the notables' objections. The governors, on the other hand, were representatives of the central authority with vast administrative and executive powers over their respective provinces.

The decline of the notables as a viable social force was a gradual and almost invisible process. As the bureaucracy expanded and became less inclined to heed their advice and as the ranks of their elders thinned, due to death, old age, or mere inertia, this institution faded and was relegated to perform mere ceremonial tasks. In the city of Buraydah—about 470 kilometers northwest of Riyadh—for example, the notables exhibited opposition to many government projects. In the early 1960s the government decided to establish a girls' school in Buraydah. The notables "sent a delegation 200 miles across the desert to protest. . . . When the school was about to open, however, the townfolk threatened to tear it down. Faisal sent armed guards to protect the school."[7] Encouraged by the King's steadfastness, another delegation representing bureaucrats and school teachers, asked for and got more schools. This, according to the city's mayor, "considerably weakened the notables." A general feeling of "lack of irrelevance" to new situations developed even "among some members of the council." Councils of notables varied in terms of their significance due, among other things, to the region's particular tribal configuration. The eclipse of traditional centers of power as represented by the town notables and Bedouin sheikhs, in favor of a centralized authority, has further curbed provincial particularism and eased the transitional process.

Unlike the decline of the institution of the notables, the reduction of the governors' power was not a response to the state's need for asserting its authority nor the removal of obstacles for the implementation of its plans and projects. It was a natural outcome of the tendency to confer more power on the central government, due in no small measure to the Council of Ministers' emergence as a viable source of authority. Ministries such as Health, Education, and Finance created provincial offices, and "these have represented a great inroad into the former sphere of authority of the local Amirate [governorship]. . . . The institition he [the governor] so long embodied has seen new functions grow up beyond its sphere of competence and old ones removed from its control."[8]

The governor, originally intended to be the personal representative of the King and his principal agent in the area, was expected to oversee and direct all governmental activity in his area of jurisdiction. The simple nature of many of the projects started in the 1930s through the 1950s did not require any significant alteration of this formula. However, the mushrooming of agencies and the explosion of the civil service in the 1960s (the government doubled the number of its employees between 1962 and 1967) radically changed this situation. At present the governor is still responsible for the preservation of public order, an area over which he exercises direct control. Overall his leadership in other spheres of government, however, has greatly diminished. Some exceptions exist. The emergence in the last few years of dynamic and technically competent governors such as Prince Khaled Al-Faisal (governor of Asir) has restored to that office a considerable degree of influence and vitality.

Thus both the decline of the institution of notables and the reduction of the governors' power ushered in an era of increased national integration and decreased fragmentation and provincialism. Measures that were originally applied to some provinces were now applied nationally. All over the country people came to look to Riyadh and to the government's budget for information regarding projects and expenditures in their area. Instead of going to the provincial governor with requests for more schools and hospitals, delegations flocked to Riyadh in order to lobby ministers and bureaucrats. This might be judged a classical case of moving from a traditional to a rational basis of authority, and in the narrow sense of the concept, such would be correct.[9]

Another significant development was taking place in the educational sphere. The establishment of a unified educational system catering to students from all parts of the Kingdom was significant in at least one respect: students for the first time were reading the same curriculum and were thus being socialized along the same lines. This aspect of the socialization process represented a radical departure from that to which their parents were exposed and can be seen as a catalyst leading to the emergence of a new national consciousness. The government's extensive scholarship programs have allowed thousands of students (some of them leaving their home town for the first time) to live and study as colleagues and roommates, exposing them to each other and enabling them, at a crucial stage in their lives, to draw on shared experiences. In a land where people were identified either through their tribes or their towns and villages, the forging of a new identity superceding the old and familiar one is a matter of high priority on the road to national homogenization and nation-statehood. Professor A. Mazrui asserted the significance of this catalyst: "It can therefore be seen that a process of cultural fusion—leading to an enlarged empathy . . . of a shared life style—is a contribution toward the integrative process."[10]

The process of national integration has been accelerated by the revolution in communications. In this regard, the state's ability to introduce visible and significant economic changes is augmented by its access to powerful and persuasive means of communication such as radio and television. The widespread use of radio, especially, has introduced the nomad and the farmer to the larger society. Their limited picture of their milieu and their needs was changed as a result. Katakura found during her stay among the Wadi Fatima nomads and farmers that, "When I asked a group of them what they might call a new settlement, they answered jokingly 'Toshiba!' for most of the villages had transistor radios."[11] Cognitive frontiers were extended, and the reluctance to be a part of a larger unit was to a considerable degree curbed and neutralized. Earlier, as is well known, isolationism and provincialism were not characteristic only of the Bedouins and farmers. In fact, the whole area was governed by a compartmentalized mentality, due, to a large degree, to the prevailing state of geographical insulation. According to George Rentz, previously "isolated from one another, people thought of themselves as citizens of the Hijaz or of Najd rather than of a larger entity."[12] The de facto reversal of this situation came as a result of the unification of the country in the 1930s, but its *de jure* realization came on the heels of the great changes of the 1960s. As Tachau has pointed out:

> The resources which have become available to the whole provide a clear and immediate means and motive for avoiding the fragmentation into the older component parts which might leave some of these parts without sufficient resources for their own development or an increased standard of living.[13]

Notes

1. D.G. Hogarth, *The Wandering Scholar* (London and New York: H. Milford and Oxford University Press, 1925), p. 77.

2. *Encyclopaedia of Islam* (Leiden: Brill Publishers, 1960), p. 872.

3. United Nations, *Yearbook of the United Nations,* 1970 (New York: United Nations, 1970).

4. Fouad Al-Farsy, *Saudi Arabia: A Case Study in Development,* 2nd ed. (London: Stacey International, 1980), p. 78.

5. Motoko Katakura, *Bedouin Village* (Tokyo: University of Tokyo Press, 1977) and Donald P. Cole, *Nomads of the Nomads* (Arlington Heights, Ill.: AHM Publishing, 1975).

6. Aramco Special Study Group, Thomas O'Dea, ed., "Social Change in Saudi Arabia: Problems and Prospects," Dhahran, Arabian American Oil Company (Aramco), 1963, p. 70 (mimeographed). This unpublished report is cited in A.H. Said, "Saudi Arabia: The Transition From a Tribal Society to a Nation-State" (Ph.D. dissertation, University of Missouri, Columbia, 1979), bibliography.

7. *Reader's Digest,* January 1967, p. 118.

8. Aramco Special Study Group, "Social Change in Saudi Arabia," pp. 71-73.

9. As, for example, Max Weber, *Economic and Society: An Outline of Interpretative Sociology,* ed. Guenther Roth and Claus Wittich (New York: Bedminster Press, 1968).

10. Ali Mazrui, *Cultural Engineering and Nation-Building in East Africa* (Evanston, Ill.: Northwestern University Press, 1972), p. 278.

11. Katakura, *Bedouin Village,* p. 27.

12. George Rentz, "Saudi Arabia: The Islamic Island," in *Modernization of the Arab World,* ed. J.H. Thompson and R.C. Reischauer (Princeton: Van Nostrand, 1966), p. 188.

13. Frank Tachau, ed., *Political Elites and Political Development in the Middle East* (Cambridge, Mass.: Schenkman, 1975), p. 182.

11 Saudi Arabia's Role in International Finance and Development Assistance

Yusuf A. Nimatallah

Saudi Arabia's growing contribution to international finance has occurred at a rapid rate because of the Kingdom's cooperative response to alleviate the energy shortage facing the world. This process has been without historical precedent. The industrial countries obtained growing foreign assets through increased production from a sustainable and growing base of production. Moreover, the differential growth of the financial-reserve component of their external assets was accrued in large part because of the lack of coordination of their economic policies. But in the case of Saudi Arabia, it is the exchange of limited oil reserves for financial resources that has resulted in increasing monetary balances. This has occurred for two major reasons: (1) Saudi Arabia has produced oil in excess of its current domestic financial requirements in a cooperative response to meet international energy needs; and (2) financial balances with time have increased in nominal value but not in real terms.

Saudi Arabia's goal is to transform its oil into tangible domestic productive assets with which to produce real income for this and for all future generations.

The Need for Economic Diversification

Domestically the need to diversify away from oil is necessary given the special characteristics of the oil sector. First, the oil sector, unlike much of the industry in other countries, is not integrated into the rest of the economy through various backward and forward linkages. A change in the level of oil production has a limited impact on domestic inputs of materials, capital, equipment, and labor. While this may be seen as generally undesirable from a development perspective, it does have the benefit of limiting reallocation of resources between the oil and nonoil sectors as output fluctuates. Second, the oil industry provides employment opportunities that are limited in number and are restricted to a narrow range of skills and professions that may not match overall aspirations and domestic supplies. Third, the gov-

107

ernment, by owning oil resources, receives the revenues from oil exports. While this theoretically affords the government unusual control over expenditure rates and resource allocation between sectors, it does not provide a mechanism for distributing income. Government ownership of oil reserves presents additional difficulties. The government is given the task of determining major investment projects and thus the specifics of economic diversification, without the benefit of receiving indications through the market mechanisms that are present in a more gradual process of industrialization through the private sector.

The necessary domestic transformation of the Saudi economy presents a very difficult challenge. The rapid absorption of oil revenues, by dramatically increasing domestic incomes, can result in noticeable and immediate difficulties. A quantum increase in incomes can occur over a short span of time, while the development of infrastructure and a domestic productive base require a longer gestation period. Thus as incomes increase, expenditures on all goods increase—tradeables (importables) and nontradeables (housing, health, and the like). Initially inflation is all pervasive because infrastructural bottlenecks cannot accommodate the large increase in imports. In the case of nontradeables, inflation is more noticeable as imports by definition can do little to augment domestic supply, and domestic supply is highly inelastic. After the expansion of basic infrastructure, the input of tradeable goods can be accommodated. But in the case of nontradeables, much more time is required for the productive structure to adjust to the higher and changing composition of demand. The most noticeable areas of excess demand tend to be housing and social services.

The government has very little leeway in arresting these affects. Taxes and similar measures are not sufficiently developed to selectively discourage the consumption of nontradeable goods and services. Thus a general reduction in government expenditures and demand is called for. This is, however, socially and politically difficult to implement. Moreover, such a policy would result in higher external surpluses, which is, on the one hand, a cause of international recriminations and, on the other hand, it results in the further accumulation of external assets. In essence, the oil-exporting countries find themselves in a vicious circle, which unlike the traditional form of the vicious circle in development literature, is not caused by too little current revenue but by too much current revenue from a nonsustainable source coupled with limited domestic investment opportunities.

It is clear from this brief discussion that the transformation of the Saudi Arabian economy, though imperative, cannot take place as quickly as its oil is depleted because of domestic economic constraints and realities. Specifically, the necessary domestic factors of production must be developed with which to diversify the economy in an efficient manner. The necessary factors of production include professional and vocational skills, the institutional framework, infrastructure, water resources, and so on. In some of these areas, the gestation period is long and cannot be short-circuited. As a result, in the interim, the Kingdom will have to accumulate foreign assets with which to finance its future development.

Utilization of Accumulated Foreign Assets

During this necessary interim period, Saudi planners are resigned to acquiring diversified external assets, including real assets abroad. But the acquisition of real assets abroad has not been easy given the availability of domestic professionals and the limitations of institutional and legal frameworks. Moreover, such an endeavor also is limited by institutional and legal impediments in the countries where the assets are to be acquired. Saudi Arabia can endeavor, however, to proceed on this course more aggressively in the future. But for the immediate future, the concentration will be on investing in financial assets abroad. In acquiring such assets, three important criteria should be kept in mind: (1) to guarantee the principal, (2) to earn a positive yield, and (3) to support the international financial system in a cooperative manner.

Within this framework, there are various opportunities open to Saudi Arabia: (a) bank deposits in dollars, in other currencies, and/or in a basket of currencies such as the SDR (special drawing right) of the International Monetary Fund; (b) acquisition of treasury bills and similar papers from other governments; (c) bonds of foreign governments or companies; (d) lending to international institutions in various currencies or baskets to ameliorate recycling; and (e) direct lending on concessional and nonconcessional terms.

For Saudi Arabia to achieve even these immediate financial goals, the cooperation of its partners is needed. The developed countries can help by: (a) controlling inflation; (b) reducing fluctuations in exchange rates; and (c) allowing for the free movement of our capital.

The developing countries could help themselves and potential lenders by: (a) adopting sound and realistic programs; and (b) utilizing funds more efficiently.

The international financial institutions could assist these endeavors by: (a) playing a more active role, especially in recycling; (b) giving legal and economic guarantees; and (c) adjusting their structure to new realities and requirements—by giving appropriate weight to financial contributions of other countries and limiting the total control of the institutions by a few industrial countries.

It is evident that Saudi Arabia's cooperative response to meet the world's energy need has resulted in growing financial assets, which in turn has given the country added problems and responsibilities. This challenge has been taken up by the Kingdom in a cooperative manner. The trading and investment partners of Saudi Arabia can help in several areas for both the medium and long terms: (1) a meaningful program to reduce energy consumption and to conserve the world's rapidly depleting supply of oil; (2) a commitment to promote our internal development in a true partnership, especially through the transfer of appropriate technologies; (3) policies to preserve the real value of our oil; and (4) appropriate legislation and legal framework to guarantee a real yield on our foreign assets and to guarantee its availability.

Cooperative Approach Required

The two latter areas of cooperation from industrial countries deserve more discussion. There are two broad approaches that could be helpful. One such solution would be the floating of bonds (off market) bilaterally by the strong currency countries—Germany, Japan, Switzerland, and possibly other industrial countries. Germany and Japan have initiated such a policy on a small scale; it is questionable whether the yield is still sufficiently attractive relative to preserving Saudi Arabia's oil wealth. Such initiatives at least offer a beginning for a process of orderly financial-reserve diversification; they could be increased in volume and diversity of offering.

The other initiative should be based on the fact that countries such as Saudi Arabia are exporting oil, beyond the level needed for their own financial needs, in order to satisfy international requirements. At the same time the capital surplus of oil exporters represents an increase in world savings, which could be used to finance necessary capital expenditures in many nations. A large increase in investment is needed to increase productivity growth and to reverse the continuing deterioration of the international economic structure. Thus a broad global effort to create an asset with appropriate characteristics would be helpful both to capital-surplus oil exporters and to ameliorating the financial needs of the international community. Such a proposal could be adopted by the industrial countries in proportion to their oil imports or by the entire international community through the IMF (International Monetary Fund). If this proposal and if a larger and more diversified floating of bilateral off-market bonds were forthcoming, then oil-production decisions would be more immune to domestic investment opportunities, and the energy and financial needs of the international community would be met on an orderly basis.

Finally, in line with the Kingdom's cooperative approach in the oil and financial market, a thrust has been made to promote the economic goals of developing nations. The developing bloc, while representing over 80 percent of the world's population, has enjoyed only a small share of the world's output and has had little say in reforming the outdated international economic structure and its implied relations. These unrealistic historical relationships have been further sanctified in institutions such as the IMF, where around 120 developing countries out of a total membership of 141 have less than 40 percent of its quota and its vote.

Saudi Arabia has endeavored to play a positive role in these areas. As a developing country, the Kingdom has not only supported the reform of the international economic system but has taken an active role by advocating appropriate changes and supporting the financial needs of other developing nations. Whereas in the past developing countries had very little to bargain with vis-à-vis the industrial countries, Saudi support has given the developing bloc hope in achieving a new international economic order.

Saudi Arabia's support has been important from a financial standpoint. Over the five years from 1975 to 1979, the OECD (Organization for Economic Cooperation and Development) estimates that Saudi Arabia gave over $10 billion in official development assistance. The official development assistance (ODA) represented an average 4.3 percent of the Kingdom's GNP. In 1977 Saudi Arabia had become the second largest source of ODA after the United States. Its assistance has been institutionalized in part through the Saudi Fund for Development. From its establishment in 1975 to 1978, the activities of the fund covered more than fifty countries in Asia, Africa, and Latin America. To these nations the Saudi fund extended 130 loans amounting to 10.3 billion Saudi riyals. It is noteworthy that commitments of the fund during the financial year 1397/1398 A.H. (1977/1978 A.D.) alone exceeded 32 loans amounting to more than about 3 billion Saudi riyals. During this same fiscal year, 26 loan agreements were signed, which amounted to about 2.36 billion Saudi riyals. Thus, over a span of four years, the Kingdom had become a major contributor of concessional assistance to developing countries. These financial contributions become even more impressive when it is noted that during these years the Kingdom's per-capita income was less than that of the OECD states. Moreover, in assessing Saudi aid contributions, the nature of the respective economies of the aid extenders should be kept in mind.

Moreover, Saudi Arabia has contributed to nonconcessional assistance to developing countries. One important channel for this has been the IMF. In 1974 and 1975 Saudi Arabia entered into an agreement to lend the IMF SDR 2.25 billion for that body's oil facility. In 1979, SDR 1.934 billion was committed by Saudi Arabia to the Supplementary Financing Facility. In both of these arrangements, the Kingdom was the single largest contributor. This extraordinary level of contribution has been partially recognized through the appointment of an executive directorship at the IMF because, on average, Saudi Arabia has been one of the two largest creditors to the

IMF since 1976. This is only one example of the Kingdom's contribution in this area and why the country has clearly become an important factor in nonconcessional financing.

Saudi Arabia will continue to carry out its policies in a cooperative and responsive manner; the Kingdom looks toward its partners for their cooperation and support.

12 Monetary Sources of Inflation in Saudi Arabia

Michael W. Keran and
Ahmed Abdullah Al-Malik

Saudi Arabia's great oil wealth has provided the country with a unique opportunity to help its citizens achieve a better life. However, along with this opportunity, oil wealth has created some problems. Specifically, it has contributed to a substantial rate of domestic inflation. Some Saudi Arabians believe that, at the current price of oil, the country's reasonable investment and consumption needs could be met with the revenue from no more than 4 million barrels per day of oil production. As this level of output is less than half the current level of output, it could lead to a substantial increase in the price of oil. This presents the country with a dilemma. A more prudent and efficient level of spending which would match its absorptive capacity would require considerably less oil revenue than is currently being earned. On the other hand, a lower level of oil production would be disruptive to the world economy in which Saudi Arabia has an important stake.

Conceptually, revenues in excess of spending should not be a problem. The excess revenue can be invested in foreign assets whose risk is low and on which interest is paid. The decision as to how much oil to produce and how much excess revenue to acquire should depend on whether the interest rate on holding foreign assets gives a better or worse rate of return than holding oil in the ground, i.e., the decision should depend on whether the future price of oil will change by more than the current level of interest.[1]

At the practical level, however, the excess of revenue over spending creates major problems. All oil revenues accrue directly to the government, and the only way that individual citizens can benefit is through the government's budget-spending decisions.[2] When the budget is in substantial

The authors wish to thank the officials of the Saudi Arabian Ministry of Finance and the Saudi Arabian Monetary Agency (SAMA), and in particular, Dr. Omar Chapra, for their assistance in understanding the issues. Any errors, however, are the sole responsibility of the authors. The views expressed in this article are those of the writers and do not necessarily reflect the views of the Federal Reserve System, the Saudi Arabian Ministry of Defense or SAMA. This chapter was originally published as a supplement, winter 1979 issue of Federal Reserve Bank of San Francisco, *Economic Review*. It is reprinted by permission of the Federal Reserve Bank of San Francisco.

surplus there is, as in most countries, a strong incentive to increase spending. As a result, the number of projects proposed in the budget can easily exceed the number which can be carefully planned, and projects may tend to be more elaborate and costly than would otherwise be the case. At the same time, the resulting increase in aggregate demand leads to a higher inflation rate. This article will analyze the causes of inflation in the unique Saudi Arabian context where:

1. Real income is dependent (at this point in time) upon the ability to import goods and services, rather than the ability to produce goods and services (other than oil);
2. Government spending, even with a budget surplus, can still imply stimulative fiscal policy because most government revenue comes from abroad; and
3. Stimulative fiscal policy leads directly to an increase in the money supply because of the underdeveloped state of the financial markets.

The first section briefly reviews the monetary theory of inflation, which argues that the dominant cause of inflation is the growth in the nominal money supply in excess of the real money demand. The second section considers the proper definition of money in the institutional setting of Saudi Arabia. It concludes that currency has the most stable demand function and, therefore, is the best measure of money for central-bank control. The third section looks at the empirical relationship between money and prices, and shows that currency provides the best empirical explanation of inflation. The fourth section analyzes the balance sheet of the Saudi Arabian Monetary Agency (SAMA), and shows the unique relation which exists between government spending (not the budget surplus or deficit) and the growth in currency because of (1) the foreign source of most government revenue and (2) the absence of a well-developed financial market. The fifth section continues the analysis of the SAMA balance sheet, and suggests several ways in which the growth in money can be controlled. The sixth section provides a detailed summary and conclusion. The non-specialist may wish to go directly to the sixth section.

Theoretical Link between Money and Price

In the last few years, the central banks of a number of industrial countries have been setting targets for the growth rate of the money supply. In general, the targets are set over a period of a year or more. The rationale for targeting the money supply is based on the following arguments: (1) central banks have considerable control over the money supply, in the long run, through the use of a standard set of central-bank monetary tools; (2) the use of interest rates as a policy guide is unsatisfactory in the current period of high inflation because a change in interest rates may be more related to changes in inflation expectations than to current actions of the central bank.

In its simplest form the link between money and prices can be stated in the following equation:

$$\dot{P} = \dot{M}S - \dot{m}d^*$$

Where the rate of inflation ($\dot{P}$) is equal to the difference between the growth in *nominal* money supply ($\dot{M}S$) and the real demand money ($\dot{m}d^*$). When the growth in nominal money supply equals that in real money demand, prices are stable.

In most theoretical models, the money supply is assumed to be determined by the central bank. The real demand for money, on the other hand, depends on the behavior of the public. When the central bank permits the nominal money supply to grow faster than the public's real demand for money, an excess supply of money is created. This is eliminated by an increase in nominal demand for money through a rise in the general price level, that is, inflation.

Conceptually, the real demand for money is made up of two elements: (1) a transactions demand associated with real income, and (2) a financial demand associated with developments in financial markets, interest rates and perhaps changes in financial regulations.

If it is assumed that the transactions demand for money is equal to unity—i.e., a 1-percent change in real income leads to a 1-percent change in real demand for money—then the structural changes in the real demand for money will be associated with the financial motive rather than the transactions motive.[3] A period of rapid financial innovation or financial growth can lead to a major change in financial demand for money. Also, changes in the government's regulatory environment can have unexpected effects on the demand for money.[4] This suggests that the best measure of money is one which is dominated by the transactions motive rather than the financial motive, because without such a stable and predictable demand, the consequences of the money supply on inflation become uncertain. (This will be discussed further in the following section.)

The other issue to be considered is the degree to which the central bank can actually control the nominal money supply. *Ceteris paribus,* this is directly proportional to the central bank's ability to control its balance sheet. When it purchases an asset, it pays for it by issuing liabilities, which are in effect costless to the monetary authorities. This is because of the central bank's government-mandated right to print money, which is costless except for a very modest printing charge. The process operates directly when the central bank pays for assets with currency. The process is indirect when the central bank pays for assets by writing a check against itself, thereby creating a deposit which can only be withdrawn in the form of currency. The degree of central-bank control of money depends upon the degree to which the central bank can determine the amount of its purchases and sales of assets. To the extent that other institutions determine the size of changes in central-bank assets and liabilities, monetary control is transferred to those institutions. (This will be discussed further under the heading "Controlling the Money Supply.")

To summarize, the role of the money supply in determining inflation is now well accepted in the economics profession: the link operates through the differences between *nominal* money supply and *real* money demand. Money demand depends upon the behavior of the public; money supply depends upon the behavior of the central bank. In choosing a monetary target, the central bank attempts to determine (a) which measure of money has the most stable demand function, and (b) which measure it can most easily control.[5]

We will deal with the stability of money demand in the next section, and with controlling the money supply in a later section.

Which Money to Target?—A Stable Demand Function

International Monetary Fund statistics present three alternative measures of the money stock in Saudi Arabia: currency in the hands of the non-bank public (M_0), currency plus demand deposits of the public at commercial banks (M_1), and currency plus all deposits of the public commercial banks (M_2)[6]

U.S. readers may find the distinction between M_0 and M_1 artificial. However, in Saudi context the distinction between currency and demand deposits is significant. Salaries are paid in currency; virtually all household spending is transacted in currency; small businesses pay for their supplies in currency. Interest payments on deposits are legally prohibited.[7] Many citizens will hold demand deposits for their convenience and security, but will not hold time and savings deposits because such deposits imply an association with interest payments. As a result, demand and savings deposits are held for similar reasons, which are quite different from the transactions motive associated with holding currency.

In principle, the central banks should target the monetary aggregate with the most stable or predictable demand function. There are two elements which make up the real demand for money:

1. Transactions demand for money, determined by growth in real income; and
2. Asset demand for money, determined by (a) financial developments,

and (b) interest rates, which measure the opportunity costs of holding non-interest-earning money balances relative to holding interest-earning financial assets or income-earning real assets.

A rise in real income would clearly *increase,* while a rise in the interest rate would clearly *decrease,* the real demand for money. Financial innovations could have an uncertain effect on demand for money. Innovations which increase the demand for currency or deposits would lead to an increase in money demand, while innovations which lead to an increase in the demand for other types of financial instruments could work in the opposite direction. In the U.S., financial developments have tended to reduce the demand for money. In Saudi Arabia, however, financial developments have tended to increase the demand for money because they have primarily benefited deposit-accepting financial institutions.

The standard way to test the stability in the real demand for alternative measures of money is to estimate a money-demand equation. This would be done by constructing a data set with an empirical proxy for each of the theoretical sources of demand described above, and then estimating the appropriate equations. The analysis of the statistical properties of the estimated equations would provide a basis for judging which definition of money is most stable.

In the present case, data limitations make the standard approach unfeasible. Therefore, money demand will be analyzed qualitatively rather than quantitatively.[8] Transactions demand provides the centerpiece in the demand for money in a rapidly growing economy such as Saudi Arabia. As a first approximation, transactions demand is assumed to be directly proportional to the volume of private transactions as measured by real non-oil GDP. For every 1-percent increase in GDP, the real transactions demand for money will increase by 1 percent (see footnote 3). In Saudi Arabia, where oil income accrues directly to the government and is a significant portion of GDP, the private transactions demand for money is more appropriately measured by the level of non-oil income. This is the income which accrues to the private sector directly through payments of wages and other income sources. This income obviously is strongly influenced by the government spending.

Actual money balance may not always equal desired money balances because of the lag in the adjustments between money and income. This lag can be especially important when both money and income values are accelerating at a rapid rate. Saudi Arabia provides a good example of this relationship (table 12-1). Between Hijra years 1390 and 1397—approximately equal to the Gregorian years 1970 and 1977—currency/income ratio increased only 8 percent when measured with a one-year lag between the increase in currency and the adjustment in income.

Considerable empirical work, covering both developed and developing countries, suggests that changes in desired money balances generally adjust

Table 12–1
Ratio of Money to Nonoil Income

	Hijra	M_0/Y	M_1/Y	M_2/Y
Ratio	1390 (1970)	.27	.42	.57
	1397 (1977)	.44	1.02	1.23
Percent change				
(1390–97)		63%	143%	116%
Ratio (lagged				
one year)	1390 (1970)	.26	.41	.53
	1397 (1977)	.28	.63	.81.
Percent change				
(1390–97)		8%	54%	53%

to changes in actual money balances with a one-year lag. Table 12–1 and figure 12–1 indicate that, with this one-year lag, the demand for *currency* is very close to unity and thus is almost entirely associated with transactions motives, while the demand for M_1 and M_2 is much greater than unity and thus is strongly influenced by financial developments. As the data show, the currency-income ratio increased very little over the past seven years, while the other two money-income ratios both increased more than 50 percent.

While the stability of the currency/income ratio suggests a pure transactions motive, its high level suggests the presence also of some non-transactions motive. Holding more than 25 percent of annual income in the form of currency seems excessive, especially in view of the fact that the currency/income ratio is stable at around 10 percent in most other countries—both developed and developing. Whatever the non-transactions motive for holding currency, however, it appears to be proportional to the transactions motive and unrelated to changes in financial institutions. Thus as a practical matter, we can treat currency as if it were dominated by a pure transactions motive.

Dr. Omar Chapra, Economic Advisor to the Saudi Arabian Monetary Agency (SAMA), also argues that the demand for currency has been strongly influenced by non-transactions factors. In his view, currency is held for its own sake as a store of value in a period when the Saudi Arabian economy is growing rapidly. The currency supply rises in response to increased government spending, partially because salaries—which rise almost every year—are paid in currency. According to this argument, the public responds by passively increasing the share of assets held in the form of currency—as is seen from the 120-percent increase, from 15.5 riyals to 34.0 riyals, in the average denomination of currency in circulation in the decade ending in Hijra year 1395 (approximately 1975).

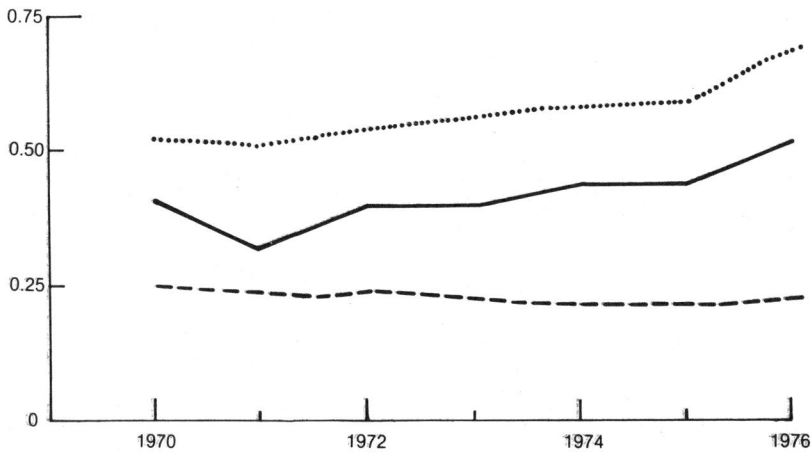

Figure 12-1. Ratio of Money to Nonoil Income

While acknowledging that there is a nontransactions element to currency demand, we believe it is not passive. Rather, it is proportional to the transactions demand. For support, we may point to two pieces of evidence which tend to disprove the existence of an independent nontransactions component to currency. First, the ratio of currency to non-oil income has remained remarkable stable in the face of a very rapid rise in currency. Second, the average currency denomination has increased only 120 percent, in comparison to a 190-percent increase in the price level, over the past decade. The fact that the denomination went up less rapidly than the rate of inflation suggests that households are not hoarding currency at any greater rate—relative to income—than in the past. Thus any currency hoarding is apt to be only temporary, as reflected in the one-year lag between currency and income shown in table 12-1. As soon as households find more profitable alternative uses of funds, they shift their demand to such alternative uses.

Most studies of currency hoarding done elsewhere suggest that the primary non-transactions demand for currency relates to avoidance of taxes and other Government restrictions on private exchange. But the Saudi economy has no significant taxes and is extremely open and free with respect to private transactions. So this incentive to hold a significant portion of wealth in the form of currency does not exist.

The same type of evidence, however, would suggest that there is a strong non-transactions motive in the demand for M_1 and M_2. As we have seen, the growth rate for both monetary aggregates was more than 50 percent greater than the growth rate of nominal income over the past seven years. The growth of those aggregates apparently was related to increased demand for financial assets in excess of the growth of real income, i.e., financial deepening. Othewise, the inflation-stimulated growth of nominal income would have been larger than actually observed, so that the ratio of money to income would have remained relatively stable as in the case of currency. The sharp rise in M_1 and M_2 balances relative to income, or to put it another way, the fall in velocity, suggests that the demand for deposits rose substantially faster than transaction needs would suggest in the last seven years.

Additional evidence can be found in the movements of the currency ratio, which reflects the relative demand by households and firms for currency and deposits. In 1964 the average private Saudi held approximately 1.3 riyals of currency for every riyal of deposit, but this ratio declined by half by 1976. This suggests a strong shift in the preferences of Saudis towards holding financial assets relative to currency. This is a natural consequence of financial deepening, as households increase their proportion of savings in the form of financial deposits rather than as currency.

Nonetheless, the relative importance of financial and transactions demands for money does not help us select an appropriate measure of money. That choice does not depend on the array of motives which influence the demand for money, but rather on our ability to forecast its movement over time.

The financial demand for money has been growing much more rapidly than the transactions demand because of a major change in the perceptions of the average Saudi regarding financial institutions. Along with the recent rapid growth in wealth, there has been a remarkable change in the desired composition of wealth holdings. The traditional forms of wealth—gold, silver and jewelry—are being supplemented with financial wealth in form of domestic deposits and foreign securities.[9]

The average rate of growth in real financial assets (that is, deposits) has been very rapid, and has also varied considerably over time. For example, from 1974 to 1977 the money-income ratio increased between 0 and 36 percent per year for M_1, and between 1 and 24 percent per year for M_2. In absolute terms, bank deposits have grown between 35 and 105 percent per year. This wide variance in the rate at which the private sector acquires financial assets is not surprising for a small country which possesses a rudimentary financial system and which is undergoing a period of major expansion and transformation.

Shifts in government regulation can also affect the rate of growth in the demand for financial assets. For example, a rise in reserve requirements increases the cost to commercial banks of acquiring deposits, so that they

Ratio of currency to deposits.

Figure 12-2. Currency Ratio

tend to offer a lower rate of return (either in services or convenience) to depositors and, thus, discourage the public from investing its savings in this financial form. At the same time, the banks are forced to charge relatively high fees for making loans, which discourages potential investors from using bank services in meeting their needs. Saudi Arabia's dramatic increase in reserve requirements in 1973 (discussed below) slowed financial development for several years. By the same token, the reduction of current high reserve requirements could accelerate financial development in the future.[10]

In summary, this section shows that the real demand for currency (not surprisingly) is dominated by transactions considerations, while the real demand for M_1 and M_2 is dominated by financial considerations. If, as seems likely, Saudi Arabia's financial markets continue to develop rapidly, but at an irregular and unpredictable rate, then the real demand for currency will be more stable and thus more predictable than the real demand for M_1 or M_2. This suggests that currency is the most appropriate central bank target for controlling the rate of inflation.

Estimating the Relation between Money and Prices

In the first section we showed that the relation between money and prices takes the following form:

$$\dot{P} = \dot{MS} - \dot{md}*$$

The inflation rate ($\dot{P}$) is equal to the difference between the growth in the *nominal* money supply ($\dot{MS}$) and *real* money demand ($\dot{md}*$).[11] If the real money demand is unstable, then the relation between $\dot{MS}$ and $\dot{P}$ would be less predictable.

In the second section we showed that the available evidence (although fragmentary and incomplete) suggested that the demand for currency was the most stable of the alternative measures of money. In this section, we will attempt to measure the relation between the growth of currency (M_0) and the inflation rate. In the Appendix, we present similar measures of the link between M_1 and M_2 and inflation.

The data problems which made it difficult to perform standard statistical analysis of the demand for money are not as serious in this case. Money stock and price data for Saudi Arabia are available, on a quarterly basis, for the period 1964 to date, which provides a long enough run of data for statistical regression analysis. The simplest initial test is to compare changes in the nominal stock of currency with changes in the consumer price index. Because it takes some time for the price of goods to adjust to a change in the stock of currency, the equation is estimated with a lag—specifically, a 12-quarter distributed lag, on the basis of the price experience of the U.S. and other countries. (All equations are estimated with a second-degree polynominal distributed lag to conserve degrees of freedom).

$$(\dot{CPI}) = -3.3 + \sum_{}^{12} 0.83 \, (\dot{M_0})$$
$$\qquad\quad (2.4) \qquad\quad (13.4)$$

$$R^2 = .83 \qquad DW = .64$$

$$SE = 5.25 \qquad DF = 37 \qquad\qquad (12.1)$$

[R^2 is the coefficient of determination. The .83 means that 83 percent of the variation in (CPI) is associated with variation in ($\dot{M_0}$) over the past 12 quarters. SE is the standard error, which states that the predicted value of ($\dot{CPI}$) is within 5.25 percentage points of the actual value 66 percent of the time, i.e., plus or minus 1 standard deviation. DW is the Durbin-Watson statistic, which tells whether the error between actual and forecast value is systematic. If the errors are random, the DW statistic would approach 2.0. A value of .64 suggests that these errors are systematic and that some other factor not in the equation systematically effects ($\dot{CPI}$). DF is the degrees of freedom. This equals the number of observations (40) minus the number of degrees of freedom used in estimating the equation (that is, one plus the number of independent variables). If lags are used so that some variable affects the $(C\dot{P}I)$ more than once, more than one degree of freedom is used. The number depends not on the length of the lag (12 quarters) but rather on the degree of the polynominal (2nd degree). In equation 12.1, $DF = 40 - 3 = 37$. The bracketed number ( ) below the coefficient is a t value, which indicates the degree of confidence that the estimated coefficient is significantly different from zero. A t value of 1.95 corresponds to the 95-percent confidence level. A t value of 13.4 is very significant.]

   $(C\dot{P}I)$ is the rate of change of prices, and $(\dot{M}_0)$ is the rate of change of currency. The estimated coefficient linking currency and prices is equal to 0.83 (see box). Thus, for every 1-percent increase in the growth of currency $(\dot{M}_0)$ over the past 12 quarters (3 years), there is approximately an .83-percent increase in the consumer price index $(C\dot{P}I)$.[12] However, the low DW statistic (0.64) suggests that one or more important variables have been omitted in the explanation of inflation. Economic theory suggests two other possible influences: (1) the real transactions demand for money associated with the growth of real income, and (2) the effects of world inflation on domestic inflation.

   Real demand for money. As discussed above, a rise in the money supply associated with an equal proportional rise in real demand for money will have no impact on the domestic inflation rate. The equation as estimated above implicitly allows only for a constant growth in the real demand for money. Given Saudi Arabia's substantial increase in real income since 1973, this is a significant omission. The problem arises because there are no reliable data, other than post-annual data, to measure changes in non-oil real income. Attempts to translate annual data into quarterly approximations have not led to statistically significant results. Thus, the real-demand variables cannot be explicitly introduced into the empirical model at this point. An indirect method of dealing with this problem will be discussed below.

   World inflation. Saudi Arabia is a very open economy with imports (including government imports) representing a significant share of total spending. For that reason, some would suggest that the domestic inflation rate is primarily determined outside the Kingdom. This proposition would seem to be overstated, especially with respect to the consumer price index. Even if all goods were imported, domestic prices would not be completely determined by world prices because imports are a "joint product," of imported goods and domestic services. When an imported good is sold to a Saudi national, he is purchasing not simply that good but also the domestic value added in the form of port deliveries, internal transportation, and wholesale and retail marketing. Thus, the goods component of the CPI represents a weighted average of foreign and domestic value added. This said, it must nevertheless be recognized that the Saudi Arabian economy is strongly influenced by the inflation rate in the rest of the world, especially given the relatively fixed nature of the Saudi Arabian exchange rate with respect to the U.S. dollar.[13]

As one of the authors has shown, the world inflation rate can be measured on the basis of export prices of the major industrial countries from monthly IMF statistics.[14] This index is in dollars, which in the Saudi Arabian context is a reasonable first approximation of world inflation. A second equation was estimated with both the world inflation rate ($P\dot{w}$) and Saudi Arabian currency growth (M_0) as explanatory variables for the domestic inflation rate (CPI). The results are summarized below.

$$CPI = \begin{array}{c} 5.2 \\ (5.6) \end{array} + \sum^{4} \begin{array}{c} 0.51\ (P\dot{w}) \\ (8.0) \end{array} + \sum^{12} \begin{array}{c} 0.70(M_0) \\ (16.0) \end{array}$$

$$R^2 = .94 \qquad DW = 1.62$$
$$SE = 3.24 \qquad DF = 35 \qquad\qquad (12.2)$$

In this equation, every 1.0-percent increase in world inflation over the previous four quarters had approximately a 0.51-percent effect on the Saudi Arabian price level.

The addition of the world inflation variable ($\dot{P}w$) substantially improved the statistical properties of the equation. R^2 which measured the explained variance in ($C\dot{P}I$) increased from 83 percent to 94 percent. The standard error fell from 5.25 percent to 3.24 percent. Most important, the DW statistic increased from 0.64 to 1.62. This substantial fall in systematic error strongly supports the inclusion of ($\dot{P}w$) as an important factor in explaining inflation in Saudi Arabia.

It is interesting to note that while the coefficient value on domestic currency declined somewhat (from 0.83 to 0.70), the statistical significance of that coefficient increased. (The t statistics went from 13.4 to 16.0.) As shown in figure 12-3 the estimated values of $C\dot{P}I$ matched the actual inflation rather closely. The actual inflation rate averaged below 5 percent per year through 1972, but increased sharply in 1973 and 1974 largely because of the rise in $\dot{P}w$. However, it continued high in 1975-1976, in spite of a substantial fall in $\dot{P}w$, because of rapid acceleration in domestic currency (figure 12-6).

These results might be compared with the U.S. 1964-1975 experience, where an equation of the same nature was estimated to explain U.S. ($C\dot{P}I$).[15] (See footnote 14.)

$$C\dot{P}I = -3.6 - \begin{array}{c} 3.3\ DUM \\ (5.8) \end{array} + \sum^{4} \begin{array}{c} 0.16\dot{P}w \\ (5.3) \end{array} + \sum^{12} \begin{array}{c} 1.49(\dot{M}_1) \\ (7.4) \end{array}$$
$$\ \ (3.9)$$

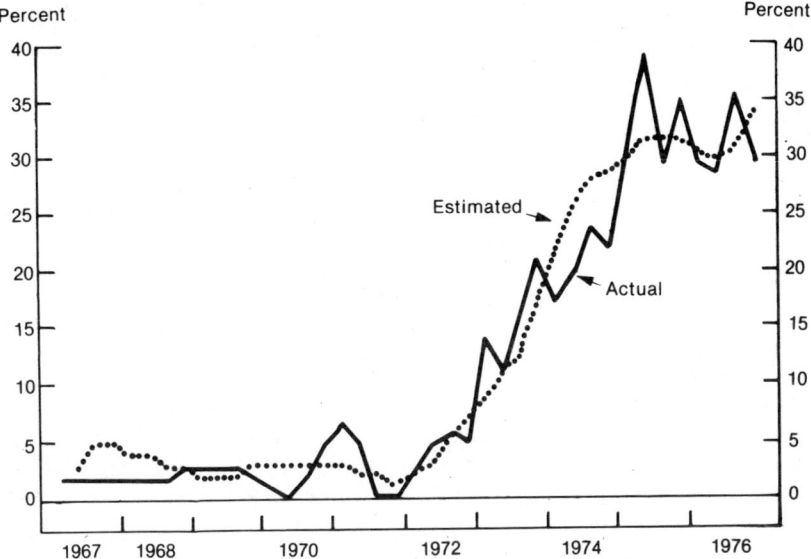

Figure 12-3. Inflation Rate, Actual and Estimated

$$R^2 = .87 \qquad DW = 1.66$$
$$SE = 1.11 \qquad DF = .41 \qquad\qquad (12.3)$$

In this equation, every 1.0-percent increase in world inflation over the previous four quarters had approximately a 0.16-percent effect on the U.S. domestic price level.

As Saudi Arabia is probably one of the most open economies in the world, and the U.S. one of the most closed in terms of ability to provide goods and services from domestic sources—not in terms of protectionism—the range of coefficient values between 0.16 for the U.S. and 0.51 for Saudi Arabia, may suggest the practical range of world-inflation influences for countries generally. The results suggest that the U.S. cannot ignore world monetary influences on its domestic price level, and conversely that Saudi Arabia cannot ignore domestic monetary influences on its price level.

In spite of the generally superior statistical properties of the second equation (including world prices), it clearly suffers from a number of deficiencies because of the lack of an explicit real-income variable. If one were included, we would expect the constant term to have a value of zero rather than its estimated value of minus 5.2; the monetary coefficient would be approximately 1.0 in value rather than its estimated value of 0.70.

Without an explicit income variable, this equation represents only an approximation of the true relationship between world inflation, domestic money and domestic inflation. As such, while it can provide confidence in the importance of the variables being considered, it cannot provide *exact guidance* on setting monetary targets. For example, consider a case where the world inflation rate was zero, and the underlying growth in currency was 50 percent, that is, somewhat below the actual rate of currency growth in 1976. The result would be calculated as follows:

Currency Growth		Coefficient Value		Constant Term		Inflation Rate	Implicit Real Growth
50	×	.70	−	5	=	30	20
20	×	.70	−	5	=	9	11

A 50-percent increase in the currency supply would suggest approximately 30-percent inflation and a real growth rate of 20 percent. A 20-percent growth in the currency supply would suggest an inflation rate of 9 percent and a real growth rate of 11 percent. This positive trade-off between inflation and real growth is reminiscent of the results described in the Phillips curve literature in the U.S. and U.K. The Phillips curve describes the negative relationship between inflation and unemployment, which is consistent with the positive relationship between inflation and real output growth. Whatever the virtues of the Phillips curve in analyzing countries in the industrial world (and considerable controversy surrounds the stability of that relationship), in the case of Saudi Arabia it is clearly a statistical artifact. The results reflect the fact that currency, prices and real income have all accelerated together since 1967, the period covered by this equation. This tends to bias the constant term (the real-income proxy) to a negative value, and the CPI inflation/currency coefficient below 1.0. Thus equation 12.2 cannot be applied "mechanically" to determine the non-inflationary growth in currency.

The discussion to this point would suggest the following conclusions: First, the appropriate monetary aggregate is currency. Second, the non-inflationary growth rate should be established as equal to the growth rate of the real absorptive capacity of Saudi Arabia. That topic is beyond the scope of this chapter. However, casual evidence suggests that the absorption capacity of the country has increased substantially in recent years, and is probably in the rate of 20–30 percent per year in real terms.

Controlling the Money Supply

In this section, we consider what tools the central bank has available to control the monetary aggregates. Money-supply control can be thought of as a two-stage process which is summarized by the following identity:[16]

$$M = m(RM) \qquad (12.4)$$

The money supply (M) is equal to the money multiplier (m), times the level of reserve money (RM). Reserve money is the liabilities of the central bank to the private sector in the form of currency (C) and bank reserves (Rb).

$$RM = C + Rb \qquad (12.5)$$

The money multiplier (m) is simply the ratio of total money (M) to reserve money (RM).

$$m = \frac{M}{RM} \qquad (12.6)$$

The broader measure of the money stock is equal to currency (C) plus deposits (D). For M_1 it includes only demand deposits; for M_2 it includes all deposits at commercial banks.

$$M = C + D \qquad (12.7)$$

By rearranging terms in equations 12.5 through 12.7 and multiplying both the numerator and denominator by (D), we get the following extended definition of the money multiplier:

$$m = \frac{M}{RM} = \frac{C + D}{C + Rb} = \frac{C/D + D/D}{C/D + Rb/D} = \frac{k + 1}{k + r} \qquad (12.8)$$

The currency-deposit ratio (k) describes the behavior of the non-banking public with respect to its desire to hold currency relative to deposits (C/D) (figure 12-2). The currency ratio has declined steadily over time. This reflects the incentive of the public to hold an increasing share of its wealth in deposit form rather than in currency form. This is a symptom of financial deepening. The reserve ratio (r) describes the behavior of the banks with respect to their desire to hold reserves relative to deposits (Rb/D).

The total money supply is simultaneously determined by the behavior of the central bank, the commercial banks and the public. The central bank's behavior is summarized by the movements in reserve money (RM); the behavior of the banks and public is summarized by movements in the money multiplier (m). In Saudi Arabia the dominant element behind the growth in the monetary aggregates is central-bank reserve money.[17] In the second section we concluded that currency was the appropriate measure of money for central-bank control. Thus a direct analysis of the money multiplier is not necessary. However, it is necessary to consider control of reserve money as a precondition for control of currency.

Control of Reserve Money

The specific tools of monetary control differ among central banks for reasons which are related to the institutional circumstances of each country. For example, in the United States, with its large and widely held national debt, the Federal Reserve's dominant tool is buying and selling government securities in the open market (open-market operations). The purchase of government securities adds to Federal Reserve assets and, therefore, increases reserve money. In Japan, with its relative small national debt, the dominant tool is the discount window. The Bank of Japan adds to its assets by extending loans to commercial banks, thereby influencing the level of reserve money. Germany, which has neither a large national debt nor heavy commercial-bank indebtedness to the central bank, uses reserve requirements as its dominant tool.

While central banks differ among themselves with respect to the dominant monetary tool, they agree on a common element in defining the degree of central-bank control—that is, their ability to determine the level of reserve money.[18] To the extent that control of reserve money is in the hands of others, effective control of monetary policy lies outside of the central bank.

A central bank's control can be limited by decisions made outside its jurisdiction in numerous ways. For example, during 1970–73 period, fixed exchange rates imposed such a limitation on the central banks of Western Europe and Japan. A fixed exchange-rate regime requires that the central bank purchase all foreign assets presented to it at a fixed price in domestic currency. During the period in question, these central banks were forced to purchase large numbers of dollars. This increase in foreign assets led to a parallel increase in reserve money. Because the volume of dollars involved was large, it was impossible to offset the impact and, as a result, the domestic money supply in each of the major industrial countries increased at an unprecedented rate. This was a major contribution to the world-wide inflation of 1973–74.[19]

The ability of the Saudi Arabian Monetary Agency (SAMA) to control reserve money is directly proportional to its ability to control the size of its balance sheet. The two dominant elements in SAMA's balance sheet are foreign assets and government deposits. Considered separately, foreign assets add to reserve money while government deposits reduce reserve money. When they increase together, as they typically do in the first instance, there will be no change in reserve money. Given that foreign assets are determined exogenously (by the price and quantity of oil), and that government deposits are determined exogenously by the budget actions of the fiscal authorities, there may be little room for discretionary monetary policy.[20] This is a clear case where fiscal policy and monetary policy are not separate tools but rather a single tool. Fiscal decisions determine the rate of growth of money in Saudi Arabia.

This should not be interpreted to mean that there are no controls on reserve money. In fact, one automatic mechanism—the link between foreign assets and government deposits—provides a substantial amount of control over the growth of reserve money. In addition, SAMA makes effective use of one major policy tool, reserve requirements.

Automatic Controls

There is a very close link between the growth of foreign assets (FA) and the growth of government deposits (GD), which acts as an automatic stabilizer on the growth of reserve money. In effect, the difference between FA and GD determines reserve money. As figure 12-4 shows, three general observations can be made regarding the movement in reserve money over the 1965-76 period: (1) Changes in foreign assets induce parallel changes in government deposits, the series moving closely together on a year-over-year basis; (2) foreign assets almost always increase at a somewhat faster rate than government deposits, accounting for the modest growth in reserve money in the 1965-71 period; and (3) a substantial acceleration in foreign assets (as in 1972-73 and 1975-76) is associated with a slowdown in government-deposit growth in the second year of the expansion, so that reserve money tends to accelerate about one year after a sharp acceleration in foreign assets.

This automatic process can be described as an initial injection of reserve money and its offset in a series of leakages. Assume, for simplicity, an initial condition of a balanced government budget, to which is added 1 million riyals of oil revenue. This will initially flow to SAMA as an increase in both foreign assets and government deposits. At this stage, there is no change in reserve money because the transactions are all within the government. However, SAMA's larger government deposits mean that the budget is now in surplus by 1 million riyals. Give the official policy of balancing expenditures and receipts, an increase in government deposits may induce an increase in spending, which transfers government deposits to the private sector in payment for goods and services. The decline in government deposits will lead to an increase in reserve money in the hands of the public, except to the extent of offsetting leakages. There are three potential leakages associated with (1) purchases of foreign goods and services by the government or private sectors, (2) purchases of foreign assets by the private sector, and (3) purchases of domestic financial assets other than currency by the private sector.

1. *Purchases of foreign goods and services.* To the extent that govern-

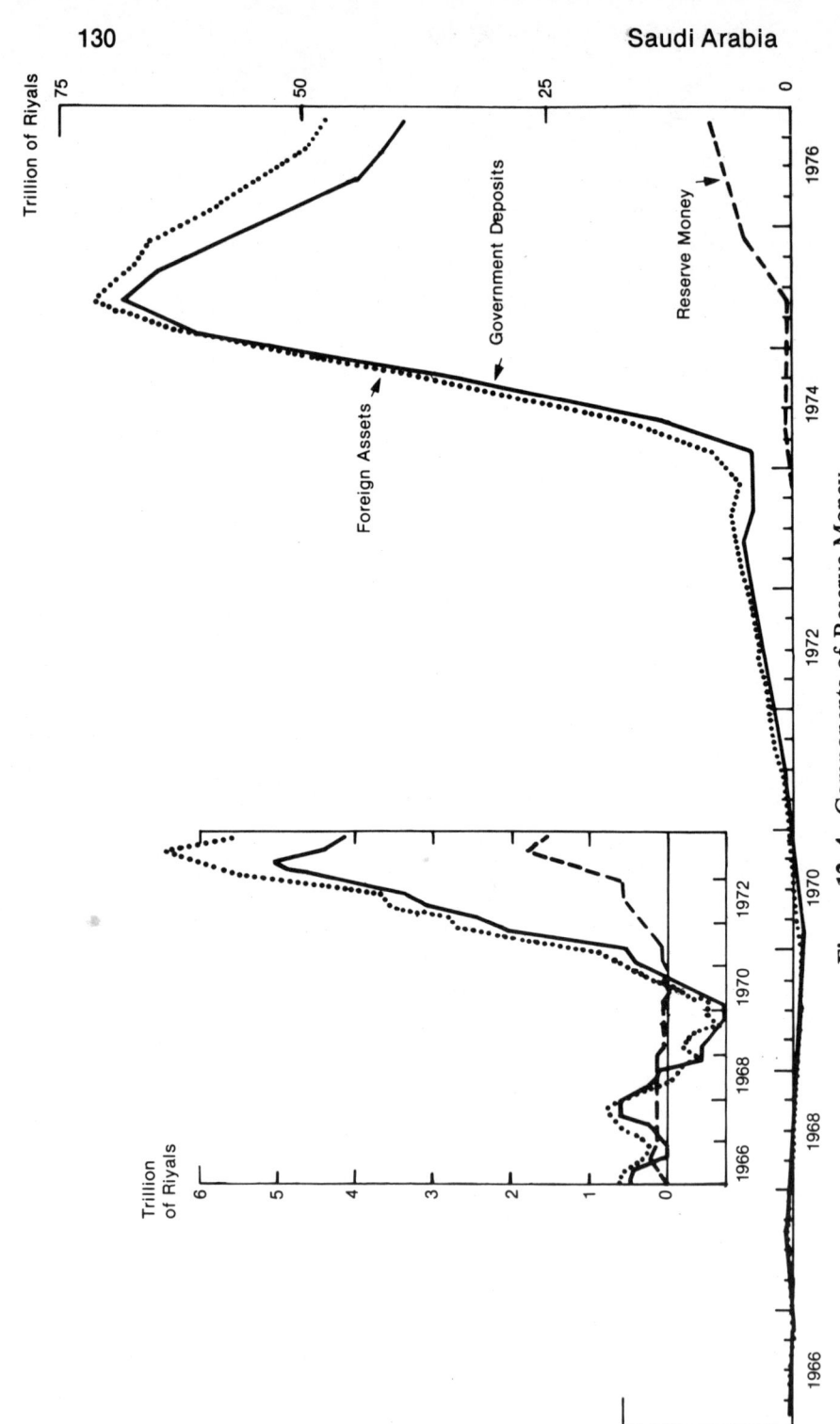

Figure 12-4. Components of Reserve Money

ment spending involves direct purchases of foreign goods or indirect induce-
ment to the private sector to make such purchases, the effect on reserve
money is neutralized because of a parallel reduction in foreign assets. The
major constraint here is the technical capacity of the domestic economy to
absorb imports without creating bottlenecks. An example is the well-
publicized port congestion of 1976, which was successfully eliminated by
early 1977.

2. *Private purchases of foreign assets.* To the extent that government
spending leads to an increase in private savings, and hence to purchases of
real or financial foreign assets, it will neutralize the effect on reserve money
in much the same way as imports. The constraint here is not the technical
absorptive capacity of the economy but, rather, the degree to which private
Saudi Arabian citizens are willing to hold their assets abroad in foreign-
currency form and to accept foreign-exchange risk. This is an especially
important constraint in the current environment of uncertainty regarding
the international value of major foreign currencies, especially the dollar.

3. *Private purchases of domestic financial assets.* To the extent that
government spending induces increased private savings in the form of
domestic financial assets, the decline in government deposits at SAMA will
be matched by an increase in bank reserves to support the new private
deposits, which is the most likely form in which domestic assets will be
held.[21] This would be a leakage only if SAMA acts to control currency—not
if it acts to control M_1 or M_2.

The Saudi Budget: Unique Features

This discussion brings out an important and unique feature of the Saudi
Arabian Government budget and its relation to monetary policy. Most
developing countries with rudimentary financial systems would observe
close links between the government budget and the money supply. A budget
deficit would be financed by borrowing from the central bank, leading to an
increase in the money stock. A budget surplus would have the reverse effect.
The reason for this close association is that, without a well developed financial market, the only source of financing a deficit or disposing of a surplus
is via the central bank's money creating and cancellation process.

Saudi Arabia is similar to other developing countries in terms of its
relatively underdeveloped financial markets. And yet in spite of a substantial budget surplus, Saudi Arabia has experienced a large increase in the
reserve money and currency issue of its central bank. This is contrary to
what would be expected to occur with the large and persistent government
budget surpluses which Saudi Arabia enjoys.

The reason is that Saudi Arabia has been running budget surpluses only in a narrow accounting sense—not in a real economic sense. An "economic" balanced budget can be defined as a condition in which the government demand for resources (spending) is equal to the government-induced reduction in demand for resources by the private sector (receipts). In most countries the accounting and economic balanced budget can be treated as identical. This is because government revenues are almost all acquired by levying taxes on domestic individuals and firms. These, in turn, reduce the private demand for resources. If spending is just equal to tax receipts, the central bank will be free from monetizing the budget deficit, and there will be no change in reserve money from this source.

In Saudi Arabia, the accounting and economic balanced budget are different because so large a proportion of government revenue is paid by non-resident foreigners as oil royalties rather than by domestic Saudis in income or sales taxes. In this special case, economic balance is the equality of government spending with imports of foreign goods, services and financial assets. Government spending in excess of these imports would represent a net fiscal stimulation of the private economy, and therefore, would be exactly analogous to a budget deficit in most other countries. This economic deficit is financed under Saudi conditions by central bank monetization, which leads to the rise in reserve money and currency which contributes to the rate of inflation.

In terms of SAMA balance sheet, government spending appears initially as a decline in government deposits. There would, however, be no increase in reserve money if it were matched by an equal decline in foreign assets of SAMA, i.e., imports of goods, services and foreign assets. Thus, an economic balanced budget in the case of Saudi Arabia would lead to a zero increase in reserve money issued by SAMA. This is precisely the effect of an ordinary balanced budget in most other countries.

Another feature which sets Saudi Arabia apart from other high-income nations, but is common to many developing countries, is the rudimentary nature of its financial system. This has important implications for monetary policy. It means that when Saudi Arabia runs an economic deficit, there are relatively few ways in which that deficit can be financed other than via the Central Bank. The ability of government to finance its "deficits" via sales of its own securities directly or indirectly to the private sector is a key element in distinguishing monetary policy from fiscal policy. To the extent that mobilizing private domestic savings is an alternative to monetizing the government's economic deficit, one can distinguish fiscal policy (the size of the deficit) from monetary policy (growth of money supply).

To summarize, we may make the following observations for the Saudi Arabian case:

1. Because of the absence of a well-developed financial system, the government budget is the most important factor in determining the growth in reserve money and the other measures of money.

2. Because the government revenue comes almost exclusively from abroad rather than from domestic taxes, the appropriate definition of a balanced budget is *not* that spending equals receipts, but rather that spending equals imports of goods, services and foreign assets. Economic consequences exactly analogous to a budget deficit occur in Saudi Arabia when spending is in excess of imports of goods, services and foreign assets.

3. This economic-deficit analogy applies to SAMA. When government spending (decline in government deposits) is greater than imports (decline in foreign assets) there is an increase in reserve money (see figure 12-4). The central bank must monetize government spending in excess of imports.

4. The automatic neutralization of reserve money from government spending via imports is an important source of monetary stability. However, in recent years, the economic deficit has increased as government spending has increased faster than imports. This has led to a significant acceleration in reserve money, currency, and inflation. Thus, it is important for SAMA to have sufficient monetary tools to control the growth in reserve money.

Monetary Tools of SAMA

Monetary control in Saudi Arabia consists of controlling the spread between the growth of foreign assets and government deposits. Therefore, SAMA's monetary tools can be judged on the basis of how they affect this spread.

Actually, SAMA has available only one of the three traditional central-bank tools—reserve requirements. Open-market operations are excluded as a potential tool of policy, partly because the large cumulative government-budget surplus has made it unnecessary to issue government debt, and partly because the legal prohibition of interest payments has prevented the development of a domestic securities market. The discount rate is not a viable tool either, because SAMA's charter does not allow it to lend to commercial banks or to receive interest. That leaves reserve requirements as the primary monetary tool.[22]

SAMA has the statutory authority to vary reserve requirements within a range of 10 to 17½ percent of deposits. It can exceed those limits (1) when it receives permission from the Ministry of Finance and National Economy, or (2) when commercial-bank deposits exceed 15 times the banks' net worth. In the twenty years since SAMA's creation, it has changes the statutory reserve requirement only three times.[23] SAMA's reluctance to pursue an active policy of monetary control via reserve requirements reflects the fact that most domestic money creation results from government spending and loan programs, rather than from lending and investment activities by commercial banks.[24] If most domestic liquidity is created outside the commercial banks, any SAMA action to restrain their activity would contribute to the relative decline of those institutions while only temporarily affecting the total amount of liquidity. In addition, if bank loans were an important source of private investment, then squeezing the banks would also reduce the production capacity of the economy.

On one occasion, however, SAMA apparently used reserve requirements to absorb an excess growth in reserve money. In 1972 and 1973, the worldwide business-cycle boom greatly increased oil revenues, and thus SAMA's foreign assets rose to what were then unprecedented heights (figure 12-4). Government deposits at SAMA also rose proportionately in the first of the expansion (1972), thereby keeping the growth in reserve money only moderately above its average growth rate of the preceding eight-year period. But in 1973, government spending increased in response to the higher level of revenue, and government-deposit growth declined relative to foreign assets. Reserve money, as a consequence, increased by 62 percent in 1973, versus 25 percent in 1972 and the 1- to 13-percent growth range of the preceding eight-year period (figure 12-6).

Commercial banks participated in this domestic boom with a substantial increase in deposits. While SAMA normally sets reserve requirements within a legal range of 10 to 17½ percent, it can raise the requirement to 50

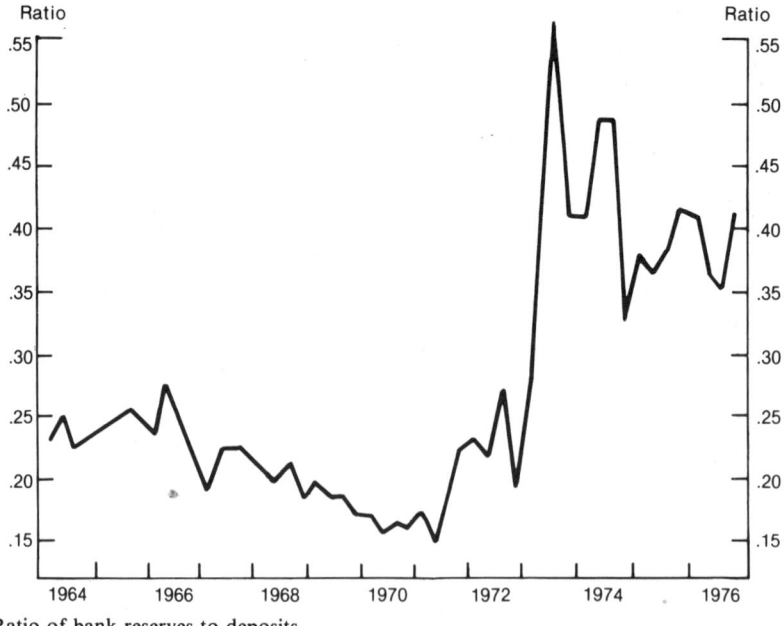

Ratio of bank reserves to deposits.

Figure 12-5. Reserve Ratio

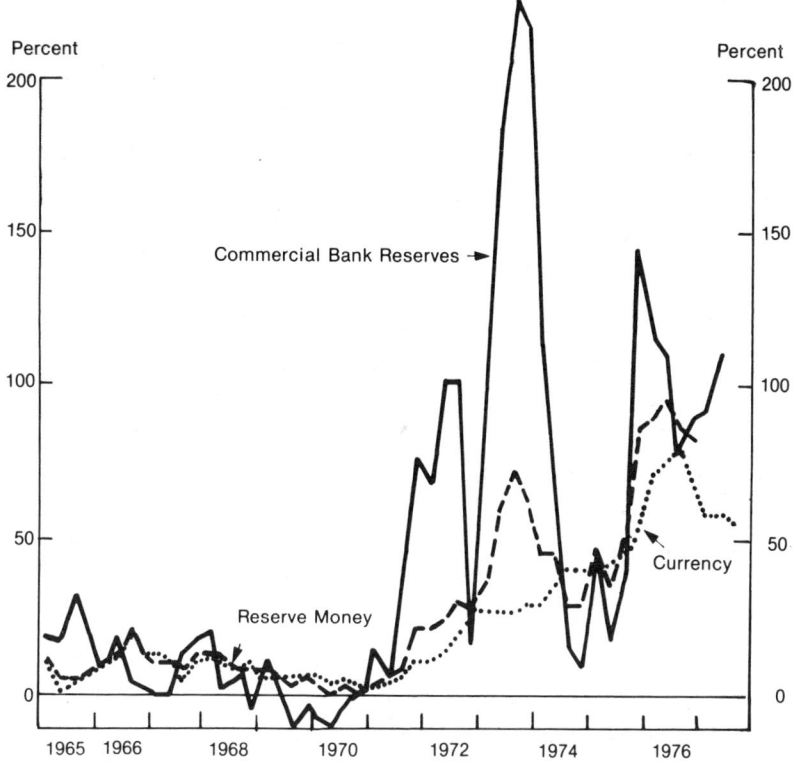

Figure 12-6. Components of Reserve Money, Liabilities to the Public

percent for any bank whose deposits exceed 15 times that bank's net worth. Previously, when deposit growth approached the 15-times-net-worth limit, SAMA under its statutory authority permitted banks to increase their capitalization, so that they could avoid the higher marginal-reserve requirements. It apparently did not follow this path in the 1972–73 period, however, and the ratio of reserves to deposits (r) thus went from an average of .16 in 1971 to .22 in 1972 and to more than 0.50 in the third quarter of 1973 (figure 12–5). SAMA later permitted some banks to increase their capitalization, and the reserve ratio then declined to about 0.40.

The *de facto* increase in reserve requirements increased the demand for reserves by 90 percent in 1972 and by more than 200 percent in 1973 (figure 12–6). This absorbed much of the excess growth in reserve money generated by the increase in government spending, so that the currency increase was held to 15 percent in 1972 and 25 percent in 1973. The growth in M_1 and M_2 was also held below what would be implied by the expansion in reserve money (figure 12–7).

This *de facto* rise in reserve requirements was clearly successful in restraining the potentially inflationary expansion in reserve money from be-

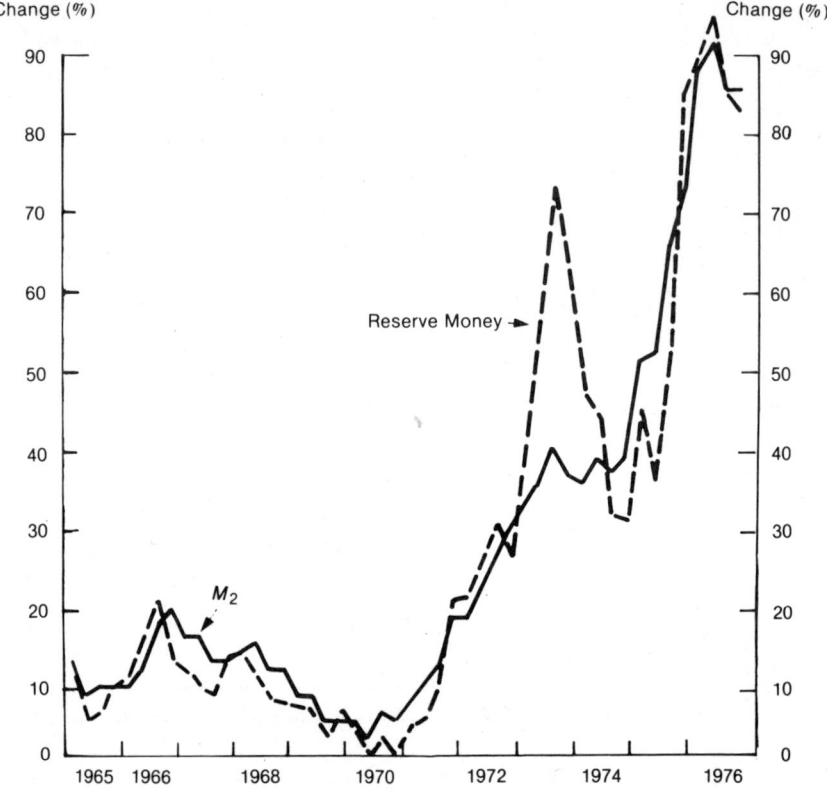

Figure 12-7. Reserve Money and M_2

ing transmitted to the monetary aggregates. However, this action, once taken, is hard to repeat.[25] The theoretical maximum reserve requirement—100 percent—would destroy the banking system, and it would also greatly impede the financial development which is such an important ingredient of the economic-development process. Thus, this powerful monetary tool probably has already been used to the fullest extent practical.

The reluctance of the monetary authorities to repeat the 1973 action in the face of another rise in reserve money is demonstrated by what occurred in 1975-76. This was almost a repeat of the 1972-73 story, except that all the numbers were scaled up by a factor of ten due to a dramatic rise in the price of oil. The large increase in oil revenues which commenced in early 1974 led to an unprecedented rise in SAMA's foreign assets, and this led in 1974 and early 1975 to a proportional unprecedented rise in government deposits (figure 12-4). But after mid-1975, government-deposit growth fell behind the growth of foreign assets, and reserve money accelerated once again. This time, while there was a small rise in *de jure* reserve requirements, there was no change in *de facto* reserve requirements and no exceptional increase in the demand for reserves by commercial banks. As a result, currency, M_1 and M_2 all increased in line with the accelerated growth in reserve money (figures 12–6 and 12–7).

From Reserve Money to Currency

While the discussion above has focused on the control of reserve money, our primary interest is the control of currency. Reserve money equals currency plus bank reserves, so that targeting the growth of currency means that SAMA should accommodate increases in the demand for bank reserves, but not increases in the demand for currency.[26]

Once control of reserve money has been achieved, there are few additional technical problems involved in controlling currency. All that is needed is information on the break-down of reserve money between currency and bank reserves. As reserves play a more important role in supporting financial deepening, they could be allowed to grow unhindered. A currency target could be achieved in the same way as a reserve-money target, i.e., by controlling the spread between foreign assets and government deposits. The growth in bank reserves, treated as a potential leakage, would probably permit a somewhat faster growth in reserve money than in currency. Data on bank reserves are available from commercial-bank reports made to SAMA, with a relative short time lag. Thus currency data could be determined as the difference between reserve money and bank reserves.

Techniques of Control

In the preceding section, we showed that control of reserve money and currency required control of foreign assets, or of government deposits in the SAMA balance sheet. A number of possible control techniques are considered below.

Foreign Assets

Given the importance of oil revenues, the only way that foreign assets can be controlled is by inducing the private sector of the economy to exchange domestic assets for foreign assets of goods. Purchase of foreign goods is constrained *not* by government controls but by the capacity of the economy to absorb additional goods and services. This is the most important limit in the growth of real income, and thus is the main factor in targeting currency growth. The private Saudi purchase of foreign assets is independent of the absorptive capacity of the Saudi economy, but is constrained by the degree of foreign-exchange risk people are willing to take. SAMA could provide various incentives to encourage private Saudis to increase their foreign-asset holdings, and thus reduce proportionately SAMA's own holdings of foreign assets. Specifically, this could be done by denominating government foreign contracts in foreign currency, or by encouraging the development of financial institutions to invest private Saudi funds abroad.

Denominating foreign contracts in both foreign and local currencies. Present practice in Saudi Arabia differs from one ministry to another and from one contractor to another. Since the budget is defined in local currency, it is easier for the government to control its spending if foreign contracts also are defined in local currency. Without this provision, a change in the exchange rate could cause the government's budgeted spending to be in error. Problems could arise from local-currency denomination because payment in riyals would add to private liquidity as government deposits with SAMA are transferred to private ownership. At first blush the problem would seem to be minimal, occurring only if foreign contractors kept their receipts in riyals for an extended period of time. To the extent that most foreign contractors would convert into foreign assets of SAMA, parallel with a decline in government deposits, this would neutralize the effect on reserve money.[27]

But where an appreciation of the riyal is expected, the payment of foreign contractors in riyals could lead to a substantial increase in domestic liquidity as they maintained riyal balances and borrowed foreign exchange to cover their expenses. These considerations suggest the advantages of denominating foreign contracts in foreign currency, especially during periods of intense speculation about riyal appreciation, because its course would provide better control of the domestic money supply and hence of inflation. However, by denominating foreign contracts in foreign currency, any change in the exchange rate would create errors in the government's budget and spending plans. It is difficult to determine whether the advantage of improved control over inflation would outweigh the disadvantages arising from denominating foreign contracts in foreign currencies.[28]

Encouraging foreign investment by Saudi nationals. Private capital outflows, as we have seen in recent years, represent an important way of reducing SAMA's foreign assets. However, the incentive to invest abroad is weakened in any period of exchange-rate uncertainty, such as the present. The government could take several actions to counter this uncertainty, such as absorbing part of the exchange risk involved or developing new institutions to channel funds abroad.

The government could absorb part of the foreign-exchange risk involved in foreign investment by guaranteeing all or part of the domestic-currency value of foreign assets. Such a guarantee could be potentially costly to the government, but perhaps no more so than other transfer payments that are designed to add to the wealth of the public. For example, the government provides a housing subsidy in the form of long-term zero-interest-rate loans in which only 80 percent of the value need be repaid. A foreign-exchange subsidy would have the added advantage of not straining—as a housing subsidy does—the already heavy demand for real goods and services within Saudi Arabia. However, with a foreign-exchange subsidy, the government could be criticized for apparently encouraging investment abroad rather than at home—even though the major hindrance to domestic investment is the lack of ability to import additional real resources. In any event, the proposal for a foreign-exchange subsidy is probably premature at the stage.

Alternatively, the government could provide increased information regarding foreign-investment opportunities, and even support financial institutions which act as conduits for investing private funds abroad. Such a step, without at least partial coverage of foreign-exchange risks, would probably not stimulate increased savings in the form of foreign securities. But any success in transferring private domestic assets into foreign assets would reduce SAMA's foreign-asset holdings.

Increasing the incentive of the private sector to invest abroad could not be considered a "fine-tuning" technique of controlling reserve money, because this approach requires the voluntary cooperation of private persons in controlling the level of foreign assets on a continuing basis. Thus, while foreign-asset control is an important tool, it is also blunt—analogous to the use of reserve requirements to control the money supply in the U.S.

Government Deposits

The control of government deposits represents the only fine-tuning technique for controlling the currency issue of SAMA. The reason is quite simple: the government can unilaterally determine the level of these deposits. Thus, once the Council of Ministers decrees a given currency issue, the decision can be implemented directly via control of government deposits at SAMA. This policy tool is highly flexible, and can be fine-tuned in a way analogous to open-market operations in the U.S. The government can operate in either of two ways: directly, via control of government spending, or indirectly, via mobilization of domestic private assets.

Controlling government spending. One approach would be to develop a "monetary" budget parallel to the normal spending and loan budget. Budget makers would determine the target growth in currency, and would then look at the government spending budget to see if leakages into imports, foreign assets and domestic assets (other than currency) would lead to a growth in currency which is consistent with the target. In the last section we showed that these three leakages between government spending and the currency growth act as an automatic control on the growth of currency. Thus, given a currency target and knowledge of the leakages, one can target government spending to hit a currency target with some small margin of error. If for whatever reason the government-spending target is not realized, the resulting excess growth in currency could be calculated and the consequences for domestic inflation determined.

The necessary institutions for controlling currency growth are already in place. The Council of Ministers currently must approve the size of any SAMA currency issue. At present, if SAMA issues more currency than expected within a given time period, the Council will generally authorize a further issue of currency as a matter of routine. In other words, any error is treated as a simple forecasting error, representing an over- or underestimate of the growth of the economy. But if policy makers perceived that currency growth was not simply a *consequence* of domestic growth, but rather a major *cause* of domestic inflation, they could utilize this same procedural mechanism to make the currency target a matter of high policy.

Mobilizing private savings. A second approach would be to finance government spending by borrowing from the public so that there would be no need to draw down government deposits at SAMA. This is the type of "leakage" used by developed countries to finance government spending. Indeed, this is the very technique used to separate monetary policy (control of money) from fiscal policy (government budget).

In Saudi Arabia, however, there would be several problems with such an approach. First, it might seem strange if a government with a large budget surplus were to "borrow" money to meet its expenditure. The action could be justified on the basis that because government revenue comes from abroad, any government spending which is not directed at foreign purchases will be analogous to running a government deficit in the United States. This "deficit" should be financed by domestic savings if it is to avoid adding to inflation.

A second and more substantial problem would be the government's inability, for legal and religious reasons, to pay interest on its securities. The problem may not be insurmountable, for reasons discussed below. Even if such securities could be made acceptable to the public, they could increase the pressure on the government to raise its spending even further, because the statistical budget surplus would remain large. And with increased government spending, we would be faced again with the original dilemma.

This particular proposal thus is not technically viable, but it does point to an important potential avenue of monetary control, i.e., providing the private sector with a secure and risk-free asset. Such an asset would be in great demand in this financially conservative country. It would also tend to legitimize financial assets generally, in a land where the public suspicion of banks is still strong. All that is needed, as discussed below, is a technically feasible way of mobilizing private savings to achieve the desired monetary-policy goal.

Pass-Through Certificates[29]

A potentially useful method of controlling currency, combining elements of both foreign-asset control and government deposits, would involve the use of "pass-through certificates." These certificates would operate as follows:

1. SAMA would establish a special pass-through account, to which it would transfer a certain share of its foreign assets.

2. SAMA would stand ready to sell riyal-denominated pass-through certificates in an amount equal to the local currency value of the foreign assets in the special account. If these certificates were purchased by the government, they would be paid for by a reduction in government deposits at SAMA, with no initial effect on reserve money or currency. If the certificates were purchased by the public, they would be paid for by both currency and checks, which (via a reduction in bank reserves) would reduce the amount of reserve money and currency in the hands of the public.

3. These certificates would not pay interest directly, but would simply "pass-through" the income received by SAMA on the foreign assets in its special account. In addition, because the certificates are denominated in local currency, there would be foreign-exchange risk to the purchaser.[30] These characteristics would make the pass-through certificates desirable to hold by the public.

4. Government purchases of these certificates would not immediately affect the level of reserve money, because the reduction in government deposits at SAMA would be matched by an equal and opposite increase in the number of pass-through certificates which SAMA would "warehouse" for the government. However, in the event that the government runs a budget deficit at some future time, the pass-through certificates would provide a method of financing other than through SAMA. The government could sell its pass-through certificates to the public in an amount equal to its deficit. This would be non-inflationary because the funds which the government would put into the economy would be matched by funds withdrawn via public purchase of certificates from the government. This procedure can be contrasted with the current situation, where any government budget deficit would be financed by a simple reduction in government deposits at SAMA—financed, in effect, by a money-creation process which would represent a net increase in public liquidity in the form of reserve money. Thus, the current procedure potentially could be far more inflationary than the pass-through proposal.

Summary and Conclusions

Saudi Arabia represents an interesting test case of the role of monetary factors in inflation. It would seem on the surface to be the least likely country to show any such influence, because (1) imports make up a very significant share of total goods and services available, and (2) government spending is the dominant source of changes in domestic aggregate demand.

The first proposition suggests that developments in the rest of the world, rather than domestic factors, largely determine the domestic inflation rate. The second proposition suggests that where domestic factors are involved, they should be due to fiscal rather than monetary policy.

This study has shown, nonetheless, that domestic monetary policy plays a significant role in determining the domestic inflation rate. The difference between the forces determining inflation in Saudi Arabia and in the world's major industrial countries is only one of degree and not of kind. For example, in the third section, we showed that identical equations can be used to explain the Saudi Arabia and U.S. inflation rates. These factors consist of (1) the expansion in the domestic money supply over the previous three-year period, and (2) the current rate of inflation in world prices, measured by export prices of the major industrial countries. The only difference between the Saudi and U.S. equations is the somewhat greater influence of world prices, and the somewhat lower influence of domestic monetary developments, upon the Saudi Arabian inflation rate. This, of course, is to be expected because Saudi Arabia is a much more open economy than the U.S. Nevertheless, Saudi Arabia can significantly influence its domestic inflation through control (if it chooses to exercise it) of its domestic money supply.

Three monetary aggregates represent potential candidates for targeting—M_0 (currency), M_1 (M_0 plus demand deposits) and M_2 (M_1 plus quasi-monetary deposits). Our results suggest that currency is the best of the three as a control vehicle. M_1 and M_2 growth are both strongly influenced by financial developments which are not *necessarily* associated with inflationary pressures. They may instead reflect the growth of financial intermediation and thus the financial deepening of the Saudi economy. The demand for currency, on the other hand, does not appear to be strongly associated with financial development, but rather is related to transactions needs, i.e., increases in aggregate demand.

To achieve stable domestic prices, policymakers should choose a target growth rate for currency which is roughly equal to the growth in the real demand for currency—that is, roughly equal to the growth in the nation's real income. Given her vast wealth of oil in the ground and foreign financial assets, Saudi Arabia's real-income growth is primarily a function of the "absorptive capacity" of the economy, which may be in the range of 20 to 30 percent per year. This would suggest that currency growth could be in the same range without adding significantly to inflation pressures.

As explained in the fourth section, the major factor influencing the growth of currency is government spending. Spending will lead directly to increased currency issue unless there is a leakage of spending, either abroad into foreign purchases or domestically into purchases of financial assets. The relation between government spending and currency is unique to Saudi Arabia, because government revenue derives from oil sales abroad rather than from domestic taxes. Government spending, when it leads to foreign purchases, is analogous to other countries' use of domestic tax receipts to finance their spending. But government spending, when not matched by foreign purchases, is analogous to other countries' use of the budget-deficit mechanism to finance their spending.

Saudi Arabia, like many other developing countries, can finance only a relatively small amount of its government "deficit" from domestic savings because of the rudimentary nature of its financial system. In these circumstances, the central bank must monetize most of the "deficit"—which in Saudi Arabia's case means all government spending that is not diverted into foreign purchases (including purchases by the private sector). This situation occurs even though the government budget is in surplus by standard accounting rules.

The process described above can be explained in terms of the SAMA balance sheet. Government spending will be reflected in a decline in government deposits at SAMA which if matched by an increase in foreign purchases will lead to an equal decline of SAMA foreign assets. This will neutralize the effect on the currency issue. If not matched by an increase in foreign purchases, the deposit decline will lead to a rise in SAMA's other liabilities, either in the form of currency or bank reserves. If matched by an increase in bank reserves, the deposit decline will reflect the financing of government spending by the *de facto* mobilizing of private domestic financial assets. (Bank reserves at SAMA would rise because of a rise in bank deposits from the public.) Finally, if not matched by a decline in foreign assets or increase in bank reserves, the government-deposit decline would necessarily lead to a rise in SAMA's currency issue.

Until now, SAMA has relied upon changes in reserve requirements as its major monetary tool. With this weapon, it influences the currency issue indirectly. For example, a rise in reserve requirements causes commercial banks to increase their demand for reserves, and thus sterilizes the effects of any increase in government spending; i.e., a reduction in government deposits is matched by an increase in bank deposits at SAMA, leaving currency unchanged. But the reserve-requirement tool, if carried too far, could weaken the banking system and prevent it from playing its necessarily important role in the process of economic development. Indeed, *defacto* reserve requirements are now between 40 and 50 percent, so that it would be unwise to use this tool any further to control the currence issue.

In this situation, we make three specific proposals designed to improve Saudi Arabia's program of currency control, and hence of inflation control.

1. Set a target growth of currency equal to the real growth rate of the economy.

2. Control government spending so that it conforms with the targets established for currency growth.

3. Encourage private purchases of foreign assets in amounts which are consistent with the economy's domestic financial needs, through the development of such techniques as pass-through certificates. (See section five.)

Reducing inflation is never an easy or costless task, in Saudi Arabia or any other country. However, the costs of inflation are very high. Policy makers at the highest level of government must determine for themselves whether the benefits of reduced inflation are worth the costs involved.

Notes

1. For example, if the price of oil were expected to appreciate by 5 percent per year, then a risk-free interest rate of 5 percent would just match the rest of return between oil in the ground and money in the bank. Changes in the inflation rate do not affect this calculation as long as the price of oil and the rate of interest are calculated in the same currency, such as the U.S. dollar.

2. Because oil revenues accrue only to the government, the only way to increase real income of the public is by increasing the prices of the things they sell, or by decreasing the prices of the things they buy. For the country as a whole, this requires a rise in the price of domestic (or non-traded) goods relative to the price of foreign (or traded) goods. There are only two ways this can happen: (1) exchange rate appreciation, which would transfer real purchasing power from the government to the public by reducing the domestic currency value of government oil revenue, and increasing the foreign purchasing power of privately held domestic currency; or (2) government spending with a fixed exchange rate, achieved either by (a) government transfer payments to individual Saudis with no increase in direct government purchases of goods and services, or (b) government spending via purchases of goods and services.

Both of these approaches would increase the nominal purchasing power of the private sector and, given an inelastic supply of domestic non-tradeables such as land, drive up its price. Because foreign (or tradeable) goods have an elastic supply, the price would not rise except as scarce domestic (i.e., Saudi Arabia) resources are added in the process of delivering imports to the public. Alternative 1 could be achieved without inflation.

Alternative 2 would lead to some domestic inflation. The actual approach followed in Saudi Arabia is closest to 2b with some elements of 2a. Alternative number 1 apparently has been rejected because, while it would have increased total real income, most of the benefit would have gone to those with the greatest wealth. This was considered undesirable, as it would not contribute to reducing the inequality of income distribution.

3. The assumption of a unitary transactions demand for money is not unreasonable on the basis of long-term U.S. data which underlie most of the work on this subject. Post-World War II data, especially data for the decade since the mid-1960's, suggest a less than unitary transactions demand for money. See David Legler's *"The Demand for Money"* for a further discussion of this issue. John Scadding has shown, however, that the Post-WWII result may be specious. The period is one of higher average inflation—and, therefore, higher interest rates which tend to reduce the transactions demand for money. However, Scadding shows when you account for the increased implicit interest paid on money balances, you get a transactions demand coefficient which is close to one, even with post-WWII data.

4. Two recent regulatory changes in the U.S. have substantially affected the demand for money: (1) the November, 1975, regulation which permitted corporations to hold savings deposits, and (2) the November, 1978, regulation which permitted individuals to make automatic transfers between their demand and savings deposits. Both actions reduced the real demand for demand deposits and, therefore, the demand for the M_1 measure of money.

5. These criteria are not mutually exclusive. Instability in the public's demand for money can reduce the central bank's ability to control the money supply, depending on the definition chosen. For example, if the demand for deposits unexpectedly increases relative to the demand for currency, the money multiplier between central-bank assets and the total money stock will change in an unanticipated way. This would impair the central bank's ability to control the money-supply measure which included deposits.

6. This measure of money could also reasonably be called M_3 because in the *International Financial Statistics* (IFS), the "other deposits" category or "quasi money" represents deposits of all financial institutions. However, non-bank financial institutions are relatively minor in scope in Saudi Arabia, or statistics are not available on their deposit balances. The latter includes such important financial institutions as money-changers, as well as banks located outside Saudi Arabia which accept deposits and make loans in riyals inside the country.

7. The legal system of Saudi Arabia is based on a strict interpretation of the Islamic Law, in which all interest payments are considered usury.

8. The legal prohibition of interest payments means that interest-rate data are not available. Real income data are available only on an annual basis from 1970 to 1976.

9. Banks have both responded to and helped develop this new financial wealth preference by opening new branches in many of the towns and villages where there were no financial institutions in the past. This has helped to break down the old suspicion of banks in the minds of many people, who find that deposits are more secure than domestic stores of gold and silver, and equally convenient when needed. There has, of course, been a substantial increase in the absolute quantity of traditional forms of real wealth, but because of the large increase in total wealth this is consistent with a more-than-proportionate increase in new financial forms of wealth. Judging by the stable ratio of currency to income, relatively little of this switch in asset holding is going into currency.

10. The discussion in this paragraph assumes that all of the increase in the observed reserve ratio is due to a change in the *de facto* reserve requirements. Alternatively, it could represent a change in desired excess reserves of the banking system. The available data do not allow us to discriminate between these alternative hypotheses, because required reserves vary with each bank's capital-deposit ratio. However, circumstantial evidence support the reserve requirement explanation. Typically, the demand for excess reserves increases in a period of increased risk and economic uncertainty. This was the U.S. experience during the Great Depression of the 1930s. But this hardly describes the economic experience of Saudi Arabia in the 1970's.

11. This relationship can be restated in the familiar Fisher equation of exchange:

$$MV = PT$$

Money (M) times velocity (V) equals the price level (P) times volume of transactions (T). Rearranging the terms and taking the rate of change would give the following transformed equation:

$$\dot{P} = \dot{M} + \dot{V} - \dot{T}$$

By assuming unit for T, the transactions demand, then V can be considered the financial demand for money. This is substantially the same equation as presented in the text.

12. Because of the unique characteristics of Saudi Arabian data, year-over-year changes rather than quarter-to-quarter rates of change are used in measuring all time series in this paper. Saudi Arabia follows the lunar calendar with 12 months, but its year is 11 days shorter than the Gregorian calendar year. There are procedures which allow for transformation of the Hijra-

year statistics into Gregorian-year statistics. However, seasonal variations in Saudi Arabia are largely related to religious observances—such as Ramadan, which occurs in the same month each year in the Hijra calendar, but which may shift from summer to winter when corrected to the Gregorian calendar. The standard seasonal adjustment programs have difficulty dealing with such "floating" seasonals. Also, seasonal dummies cannot be used in the non-seasonally adjusted data because seasonal changes move from year to year when translated into the Gregorian calendar. This violates the assumption that the coefficient values are constant over the sample period. The only effective seasonal-adjustment technique in this case is year-over-year changes. This procedure allows for the gradual movement of the (statistically significant) seasonal religious holidays, and does less violence to the assumption of stable coefficient values over the sample period. While year-over-year percent changes have problems of their own, they represent less severe constraints than quarter-by-quarter percent changes.

13. Between December 1970 and December 1973, the riyal appreciated by 5 percent, i.e., from 4.50 riyals per dollar to 4.28 riyals per dollar. From December 1973 to December 1977, the riyal appreciated an additional 3.2 percent to 4.148 riyals per dollar. These changes are small relative to the 100-percent increase in the dollar price of internationally-traded goods between 1970 and 1977.

14. Michael W. Keran, "Stabilization Policies in a World Context," Federal Reserve Bank of San Francisco, *Economic Review,* Fall 1976.

15. In this equation M_1 is the U.S. money supply (currency plus demand deposits). *DUM* is a dummy variable to account for the period of price controls from 1971.4 to 1972.4.

16. One of the authors has developed a detailed analysis for Saudi Arabia. See Ahmed Abdullah Al Malik, *The Money Supply Process in Saudi Arabia,* Chapters 5 and 6 (1970), University of Indiana.

17. The evidence behind this proposition is discussed below. Figure 12-6 shows the strong association between *RM* and currency, while figure 12-7 shows the link between *RM* and M_2. The major expectation is 1973, which is explained below.

18. The concept of reserve money has a long history in monetary analysis. Irving Fisher (1896) called it simply "money"; James Tobin (1960) called it the "demand debt of the government"; Milton Friedman and Anna Scwartz (1963) called it "high-powered money"; Karl Brunner and Allan Meltzer (1968) called it the "monetary base." The IMF uses the term "reserve money" in its monthly statistical publication from which the data in this article are drawn.

19. Michael W. Keran, "Towards an Explanation of Simultaneous Inflation—Recession," Federal Reserve Bank of San Francisco, *Economic Review,* Spring 1975.

20. The Ministry of Petroleum and the Ministry of Finance jointly prepare estimates of the government's annual revenue, on the basis of data they receive from oil companies and the government's policy regarding quantity of oil production. Since the budget is always balanced, then *anticipated* revenue must equal *anticipated* expenditure. However, actual expenditures may fall below expectations, because of procurement delays caused by such factors as manpower bottlenecks. The end result is a surplus in the budget, which is added to the General Reserve and thus leads to a rise in government deposits. In recent years, the gap between anticipated and actual expenditures has narrowed, but it is still positive.

21. In contrast to the first two leakages, this would have less than a one-to-one impact on reserve money; that is, R1,000,000 of government spending leading to an equal increase in deposit savings would increase bank reserves by only about R500,000, because the marginal reserve requirement is about 50 percent. The remainder would eventually go into currency holdings, as the bank receiving the deposits loaned them out.

22. On several occasions, SAMA has used another monetary tool—direct loans to commercial banks through transfer of government deposits. In 1961, SAMA transferred SR 25 million of government deposits from its Banking Deparment to the commercial banks, and in 1964, it reversed the process by withdrawing SR 26 million of government deposits from the commercial banks. See *The Money Supply Process in Saudi Arabia* (chapter 7) for further discussion of this monetary tool.

23. Reserve requirements were originally established in December 1957 at 15 percent of total deposits (demand plus time). The ratio was lowered to 10 percent in May 1962, but an additional liquidity ratio of 20 percent was then added, with the funds to be held in the form of vault cash, deposits with SAMA, or deposits with foreign banks. In November 1966, the reserve requirement on dime deposits was lowered to 5 percent. Finally, in June 1976, the statutory reserve requirement was raised to 15 percent on both time and demand deposits.

24. In private correspondence and discussion, Dr. Omar Chapra (Economic Advisor to SAMA) makes this point explicitly. "The crux of the money supply problem is not that SAMA is unable to influence the quantity and quality of bank credit, but that changes in such credit have constituted such a small proportion of total credit."

25. In one sense the change in reserve requirements is constantly working—there is a permanently lower level of money and thus prices. However, from the point of view of monetary control, each change in reserve requirements is a single influence on the rate of change of money and thus on the rate of inflation.

26. This would appear to be the reserve of the behavior of most other central banks, where currency is accommodated and bank reserves are con-

trolled. However, emphasis should be put on the word apparent. There is no technical reason why any central bank could not target and control currency growth. But it is generally not desirable to do so, because: (1) the public in most countries treat currency and various classes of bank deposits as highly substitutable in terms of usefulness in meeting transactions needs, and (2) the financial motive for holding deposits balances is a relatively stable and predictable function of income and interest rates.

On both counts, it makes more sense to control an M_1 or M_2 measure in countries which show these characteristics. In Saudi Arabia, however, neither of these conditions holds and, thus, it makes more sense to control currency.

27. The only difference between riyal- and foreign-currency denomination of contracts from a monetary point of view would be the different impact on commercial banks. The banks, acting as intermediaries between foreign contractors and SAMA, in the latter case would earn something on the spread between buying and selling rates for riyals. With riyal-denominated contracts, there would be an increase in reserve money equal to the earnings on these transactions. This would not occur if contracts were denominated in foreign currencies.

28. Some contracts are currently denominated in both foreign and domestic currencies. The government and the contractors denominate a certain percentage in local currency to cover the contractor's estimate of his local expenditure, and the rest is denominated in foreign currency.

29. An earlier version of this proposal was suggested by John Scadding, 1978 Visiting Scholar at the Federal Reserve Bank of San Francisco.

30. The foreign-exchange risk would be borne by SAMA, which would have both a foreign-asset and a local-currency liability. However, SAMA would experience no greater risk than it currently does in having its assets in foreign exchange and its liabilities (largely government deposits) in local currency.

Appendix 12A:
Alternative Measures
of Money and Inflation

The evidence presented in the second section suggested that currency was the best monetary aggregate for monetary control, because its demand was more stable than the other aggregates, M_1 and M_2. In the third section, we showed that the relationship between changes in currency and inflation was statistically significant. Below we present identical equations for M_1 and M_2.

M_1 and Inflation

$$(CPI) = -3.2 + \sum_{}^{4} 0.45 \, (Pw) + \sum_{}^{12} 0.52 \, (M_1)$$
$$(3.7) \qquad\qquad (6.7) \qquad\qquad\qquad (15.4)$$

$$R^2 = .93 \qquad DW = 1.63$$
$$SE = 3.27 \qquad DF = 35$$

M_2 and Inflation

$$(CPI) = -5.4 + \sum_{}^{4} 0.51 \, (Pw) + \sum_{}^{12} 0.57 \, (M_2)$$
$$(5.7) \qquad\qquad (7.8) \qquad\qquad\qquad (15.4)$$

$$R^2 = .93 \qquad DW = 1.63$$
$$SE = 3.25 \qquad DF = 35$$

In terms of overall statistical properties, the M_1 and M_2 equations are only slightly inferior to the currency equation. However, the key difference is in the value of the coefficient—.52 for M_1 and .57 for M_2, compared with the significantly higher .70 value for currency. The statistical reason for the difference is clear. M_1 and M_2 have grown more rapidly than currency, and thus the coefficient which describes how a 1-percent change in money affects inflation will be lower for M_1 and M_2 than for currency. The theoretical reason concerns the added financial demand for M_1 and M_2, which has been greater than the purely transactional demand for currency.

Thus the same increase in M_1 and M_2 would have a smaller impact on inflation.

If we were confident that the coefficient value would remain constant in the future, we could use M_1 or M_2 as a monetary target. However, such confidence is unwarranted because of the actual and potential variance in the financial demand for M_1 and M_2, as described in the second section. Added variance would increase the variance in the coefficient relating money to inflation—and thus would increase uncertainty regarding targeted money growth and hence inflation. Even the currency coefficient is biased downward, not because of financial demand but because of a substantial but unmeasurable rise in transactions demand since 1974. In the case of currency, we can assume on theoretical grounds that the appropriate coefficient value will be 1.0—which we cannot do in the case of M_1 and M_2. Consequently, currency is the best monetary indicator.

13 Saudi-U.S. Economic and Commercial Relations

Abdallah T. Dabbagh

My last three years have been spent in Washington and cities throughout this country trying, in some small way, to replace the *general image* of doing business in Saudi Arabia with the *simple fact* of doing business in Saudi Arabia. Thus this chapter will begin with the facts, first of the Saudi Arabian market, its recent past and its projected configuration, and then turn to the recent and projected performance of American business in this market.

There is little need to outline the many bonds between Saudi Arabia and the United States. Through the mass-media coverage of the Middle East, even the casual observer recognizes the depth of the connection between our two destinies.

The Saudi Market

The recent economic history of Saudi Arabia is indeed extraordinary. Only eight years ago our imports from the United States did not exceed 314 million dollars, and our exports were less than $200 million. Total Saudi imports in 1979 were estimated at $25 *billion*. They are currently increasing at a rate of 25 percent annually. United States exports to Saudi Arabia were estimated at about $5 billion in 1979 alone. Thus last year, the U.S. share of the Saudi Arabian market was approximately 20 percent.

In more graphic terms, Saudi Arabia is among America's *top ten* trading partners. Saudi Arabia is *sixth* among the top exporters to the United States. It is *ninth* among the top importers from the U.S., surpassed only by such countries as Canada, Britain, West Germany, and Japan; the value of Saudi Arabian imports from the United States exceeds those of Italy, U.S.S.R., and Brazil.

The recently announced third five-year development plan continues this extraordinary economic involvement. Total expenditures for the new development plan (1980–1985)—*excluding* military expenditures and military construction—are expected to exceed $285 billion. Like the qther two plans, this third five-year development plan has a character and a direction of its own. Whereas the Kingdom's second plan emphasized basic infrastructure—ports, airports, highways, and telecommunications—by allocating about 50 percent of total plan outlay, the third plan has scaled down investment in infrastructure to 35 percent.

On the other hand, more emphasis has been placed on the productive sector. The new plan has boosted total spending on industry, agriculture, and mining as a share of total plan spending from 25 to 37 percent.

Obviously, this shift in emphasis reflects the Kingdom's desire to diversify its economy by broadening its economic base, thereby reducing dependence on oil exports. Economic logic, as well as development policy, require that the Kingdom becomes the industrial processor of its raw material. The thrust of this industrialization is twofold: light industry will be established in cities and throughout the Kingdom, and capital-intensive heavy industries will be established in the two main industrial centers of Jubail (on the Arabian Gulf) and Yanbu (on the Red Sea). These and other towns will house up to seven petrochemical complexes (five of them with U.S. partners), an iron and steel complex, fertilizer, and other factories. Completion of a master gas system in 1983 will make Saudi Arabia the world's largest exporter of propane and butane and will eliminate most of the wasteful flaring of natural gas.

Other areas emphasized in the third plan are social services and education. The plan has earmarked more than $10 billion for the construction of hospitals and health services and about $20.4 billion for municipal development and services. In addition, the plan has allocated over $30 billion for education to continue construction, to expand existing universities, and to build more than 560 elementary and secondary schools. The number of enrolled students at all levels, male and female, is expected to increase by nearly 2 million.

In a recent International Monetary Fund (IMF) report on the world economy, the salutary impact of this massive program for the global community was a matter of some notice; it was pointed out that the Kingdom's high growth in imports of goods and services was such that Saudi Arabia alone in 1978 accounted for about one-half of the decline in combined current-accounts surplus of the entire bloc of oil-exporting countries.

The absorptive capacity of the Saudi economy, especially for high technology, is increasing. More than half of our imports from the United States now (in value) belong to the machinery and transport-equipment category. In 1972 the import of technology in the form of machinery and transport equipment was $194 million. In 1975 it was $928 million; for 1979 the figure was $2.8 billion. Again, although imports of consumer goods will not increase as dramatically, there will be significant opportunities in the fields of light industry and the creation of industrial estates (parks). The Kingdom is planning to spend close to $2.5 billion to increase agricultural production and about $1.5 billion to expand government-owned food-processing plants to achieve partial self-reliance in food production. When the programs for dealing with the continued massive migration of rural population into the urban areas are added to the list of projects, one can see no limit to the opportunities that such expansion will create for U.S. firms. But that is the bright side of the picture. How American business is taking advantage of these historic opportunities is another issue altogether.

Let us look at the current state of American participation in the Saudi Arabian market. Over the last five years the United States was able to supply about 22 percent of Saudi Arabia's import requirements for goods. Although the U.S. share in the Saudi import market fluctuated a little above or below this average, it did not show any significant growth. In fact, the U.S. share, which was 23 percent in 1975 and 22.6 percent in 1977, declined to 21 percent in 1978 and again to 20 percent in 1979. While the U.S. share of the Saudi market was constant or slightly declining, in the years from 1975-1979 (the span of the second five-year development plan), Saudi import activity was showing extremely high rates of growth. American exports were not matching other countries in their eagerness to capture a bigger share in the Saudi import market.

In the areas of services, design, construction, and maintenance, the showing of American companies looks rather bleak. The U.S. share in Saudi Arabia in this respect is declining. Recent data show that American companies obtained 9 percent of the value of construction contracts in 1975; in 1979 this figure is less than 3 percent. Of 163 contracts awarded, 20 have gone to American firms, 78 to European, and 55 to Asian. The American companies' share of contracts has dropped from 35 percent in 1977 to less than 5 percent in 1979.

One could go on and on citing studies showing this decline in U.S. participation in some of the fastest-growing sectors in the Saudi economy, but it may be better to look at two reasons for the decline: one is legislative and the other is what could be termed *attitude*.

Legislative Obstacles

First, there is the adverse impact of U.S. tax legislation, which adds to personnel costs for American companies working abroad. Despite the enactment of the Foreign Earned Income Act of 1978, Americans are still being taxed out of competition in overseas markets. This has prompted American companies in Saudi Arabia to reduce their American employees and substitute citizens of other countries for them. The percentage of American citizens employed by U.S. corporations in Saudi Arabia has declined from 65 percent in 1976 to 35 percent in 1979 and is expected to continue to drop in the future.

There is an even more important consequence to this substitution for American personnel by American companies in the Kingdom. Non-American engineers and technicians prefer equipment and specifications originating in their countries (Europe and Japan, for example), which represents a net loss in American exports to Saudi Arabia of goods and services in the long run. Thus, the United States is not only losing in the Saudi market through reduced employment abroad, it is also losing the potential for export of machinery, equipment, and other goods and services. According to the U.S. Bureau of Labor Statistics, each $1 billion of exported manufactured goods creates 30,000 jobs here in the United States. According to the American Businessmen Group of Riyadh, studies indicated that on the average, one American employee in Saudi Arabia generates thirteen additional jobs in the United States. Thus both balance of payments and domestic employment are affected.

The antiboycott laws continue to provide problems for American businesses. To be sure, the largest corporations with their battery of lawyers can get around the provisions enough to do business, but the small and intermediate companies are definitely being hampered. This hurtful effect will increase if only because of the particular demands for products from these small and intermediate companies built into the third five-year development plan. Many people think the antiboycott law provisions are behind us. It remains an impediment—there is no doubt about that.

A more positive direction, in the search for the causes of lost business in construction, does exist, and it needs serious attention. For example, a study by New York-based Engineering News Record attributes the drop in the American share of the Mideast construction market to twelfth place to different reasons. In addition to some restrictive federal regulations, the study points to a lessening of the U.S. hold on technological advantages of the trade. Contractors from Asia and Europe are reportedly offering stiff competition to American know-how even in highly sophisticated projects heretofore approachable only by a few U.S. firms. The business community is warned to be more responsible in updating technology as well as attitudes. A major weakness of U.S. firms is cited in the realm of attitudes.

Attitudinal Constraints

And here is a more delicate and sensitive area: the area of attitudes. It is time, I believe, to discuss these matters, sensitive or not. Aldous Huxley reportedly once said that the witchdoctor who manages to keep his job is the one who understands what a hoax it all is. Businesspeople may feel surrounded by witchdoctors: the consultants, the academicians, even those bureaucrats like myself. We "intermediaries" are supposed to have the magic to help create a healthy and profitable relationship between a businessman and a buyer. But the provision of "magic" is not enough—the "hoax" side of the export-import business needs to be undercut.

Let us look at some of these hoaxes and see whether or not understanding them makes a difference in attitude toward business in the Arab world. Most often they exist in contradictory but widely accepted statements as, for example, "Doing business in Saudi Arabia is just like doing business anywhere—the same principles apply in all business." "Saudi Arabians and their markets are so mysterious. The people, the laws, the prohibitions, and the customs are so difficult, it's nearly impossible to make a sale." "Those Arabs have so much money that just having the right connection is all that counts; price doesn't make so much difference with them." "Arabs, and Saudi Arabians in particular, are chronic nitpickers in price and bargaining, but, really, don't worry: they know they can't get American quality and expertise elsewhere, so they'll usually come around." This is the crux of it. Many Americans carry assumptions about Arabs and Saudi Arabians that not only block solid relations between the two countries but make it more difficult for American businessmen to compete. Even some businessmen who should know better are subscribing to these misconceptions.

Different business groups, lobbyists, and others have been trying to figure out the causes for this decline and loss of competitiveness in contracting business abroad, especially in the Middle East region. The focus has been on federal regulatory restrictions, tax policies, and different export controls, which have been cited as the major hindrance. There is a lot of truth to that, as the already-mentioned tax laws applying to Americans abroad and the antiboycott provisions. But there has been a tendency to lump *all* federal regulatory provisions together, undermining the legitimacy of the call for repealing the *truly* harmful restrictions. Nothing is more disturbing—in my view—than lobbying for the repeal of the 1977 Foreign Corrupt Practice Act (which is an antibribery measure) *along* with the call to repeal other restrictions such as tax laws or antiboycott provisions.

Last year, the chairman of the board of an important U.S. corporation, cited the Foreign Corrupt Practices Act as one of the disincentives to export along with other federal restrictions. (Incidentally, he cited also, as one of the disincentives, the imposition of U.S. environmental, health, and safety standards on exports to countries that do not share those standards.) More recently a request for repeal of the Corrupt Practices Act was made at a meeting of the International Engineering and Construction Council, the main lobbying group for American contractors at work overseas. If campaigning for bribery makes no sense to Americans, it makes no sense to Saudis either. And, certainly, the insinuation is most disturbing that what is being called "payment of commissions," in allusion to bribery, is an accepted norm in our region. Another example is the so-called Abscam event. Again we have another chance to undercut the commonly mistaken "hoax" that often hinders American businessmen. On the surface you may be sure that the selection by an agency of the U.S. government of an "Arab sheikh" with lots of money trying to buy American congressmen did not make Saudi Arabians think better of the United States. Beyond bad taste and insensitivity, however, this Abscam operation is important for what it tells us about the need for change in the American attitude toward Arabs in particular. When you think that congressmen allegedly believed this little scheme and allowed themselves to be taken in, that U.S. law-enforcement agencies were convinced enough such an assumption would be believed to spend thousands of taxpayers' dollars to make it happen—when you think about it, it is a pretty sad state of affairs. Think of what this Abscam implies: Arabs are easily tricked; Arabs have more money than they know what to do with; Arabs are willing to spend money to go around the law; Arabs normally do business through fixing officials with money under the table. Here again is the hoax: Saudi Arabia as a boom town of unwitting Arabs with gold in every pocket and no moral scruples.

It is my belief that Americans have always been concerned about the effect stereotypes have on relationships between people. The history of the United States in combatting these stereotypes, especially in recent years, is admirable indeed. In the case of the stereotyping of Arab peoples, there has been some improvement from the days when I attended college in the United States. Surely, with time, the Arab stereotype too will be erased and replaced with an image somewhat closer to the actual experience of Arab culture and life. But the period of history when there was plenty of time to allow more positive images to come about is definitely behind us. In the Arab world, we hear about Abscam as soon as anyone on Main Street, America. When such events go by without any real American protest, Arab people must just *assume* that Americans accept the negative stereotype.

Look at the situation that goes unprotested by Americans. Saudi Arabia has given American business and banking institutions the "edge" in the recycling of the revenues from our nonrenewable resource of oil. Saudi Arabia has been on the side of moderation in oil prices and has maintained production levels—to its own disadvantage—to meet Western nations' needs, especially in times of crisis. Yet the greater part of the mass media in the United States for many years has portrayed Arabs in the most negative stereotype possible. We have been given the role of the villain. We are the bad guys no matter what we do. If we invest in this country, we are trying to buy it. If we do not invest, we are not recycling our surplus dollars, and we are trying to sabotage the American economy. If we increase our oil production, we are greedy, trying to take advantage of the high oil prices. If we do not raise or keep output high, we are resorting to blackmail.

Unprotested media images and erroneous second-guessing have created an impenetrable fog between the positions and feelings of Saudi Arabians and the eyes and ears of the American people and their decision makers. The American businessman loses more of his competitive edge nearly every day. Each and every legal block to trading with the Arab world, each and every misinformed media event, each and every rumor that is taken for fact and left unprotested by those who know better thickens the fog of mis-understanding. These words may seem unpalatable; perhaps that very element is why they should be expressed.

The third five-year plan offers even more opportunities for American business. United States business is welcome, but the competition from other nations will not have a 911 tax law; they will not have an antiboycott law; and, finally, they will not have an Abscam.

14

Manpower in Saudi Arabia, 1980-1985

Clive Anglin Sinclair
and *J.S. Birks*

This chapter discusses the role of labor in Saudi Arabia's contemporary development, with special reference to the third five-year plan (1980-1985). It does so by first examining the structure and nature of various labor markets with respect to nationals and nonnationals. An assessment is then made of the labor requirement of the third plan and, in particular, of expatriate labor. This is done by studying the Kingdom's past economic performance, her presently planned expenditure, and likely revenue. From this exercise a number of significant features of Saudi Arabian development emerge. For example, it becomes clear that Saudi Arabia now has to trade off a level of oil production against a level of domestic expenditure and against a level of surplus petrodollars. It is her level of domestic expenditure that is of primary concern to us, and the conclusion reached in this chapter is that at presently envisaged levels of expenditure, additional migrant labor will be required in future years. This in turn has some significant and far-reaching implications for Saudi Arabian development in the longer run. We begin with an examination of the nature and structure of the labor market.

The Nature of the Labor Market

Saudi Arabia shares several labor-market characteristics with other capital-rich states in the Arab region. Her national work force (divided between nationals and nonnationals) is relatively small, the national participation rate is law as few women work in modern sector activities, and the majority of nationals are inadequately educated. The economy depends heavily on expatriate labor, both quantitatively and qualitatively. Nonnationals tend to dominate the construction and manufacturing sectors, whereas nationals work mainly in agriculture or in services, mostly government or quasi-

---

The views expressed in this paper are strictly those of the authors and do not necessarily represent the views of organizations with which the authors have been or are associated. *Editor's note:* Since this study was prepared (autumn 1980), some changes have occurred; nonetheless, although the results of their model may not have reflected these changes, the methodology remains valid.

government employment. In examining the relationship between economic growth and manpower in the Kingdom, this distinction is crucial. We therefore turn to the nature and growth of the two labor markets (national and nonnational) separately.

The national labor market is not divided between those living and working in rural areas—and so mostly working in traditional or informal activities—and those who have entered the modern sector of the economy, who are formally employed, and who tend to live in urban areas. This division of the national labor market can be illustrated by the following statistics. In 1963 some 475,000 economically active nationals were recorded as being "agricultural workers and bedouin," representing some 72 percent of the national work force. Eleven years later (1974), 52 percent of the national work force were recorded as working in "agriculture and fishing." During that time the sector changed relatively little.

Over that period urban labor markets sprang up that required labor of all levels and types prepared to accept poor working conditions. Many Saudi Arabians were neither qualified to participate in these labor markets because of their lack of modern sector experience, nor were they willing to endure long working hours. Neither were they able to pay the high rents necessary to secure housing in urban areas. Many elements deterred their leaving rural areas for the towns. At the same time access to housing grants, agricultural loans, and other cash benefits available as largesse in rural areas served as a very strong economic incentive to farmers to retain their rural life style. Paradoxically, the government's recent attempts to transform farming in Saudi Arabia (other than by instigating major large-scale projects) through the extension of loans and grants to small farmers with the object of aiding their mechanization and modernization have been instrumental in the preservation of a subsistence-based traditional rural sector. Loans and grants taken by farmers are not always used for investment purposes and are often spent on consumption. If invested, then the capital so provided remains underutilized, either because of poor management or for want of sufficient labor inputs. Thus grants and loans to farmers, directed toward investment in small-scale agriculture, are taken as income by the farmers. This income is not associated with intensive labor inputs and so is highly valued. Indeed, as income in cash, it alleviates in part the need to derive income from the farms themselves, which are allowed to stagnate or decline further. Thus funds directed toward modernization of small-scale farming arguably have the contrary impact to that which is intended: they serve to withdraw labor inputs from the land and to ensure that the population remains rurally oriented. In short, the agricultural sector is preserved in its relatively unproductive form.

In explaining the persistence of the rural traditional sector, it is appropriate to mention the premium that the rural Saudi Arabian population places on leisure. The disinclination to very formal or structured work, in particular, in manually strenuous jobs, is an important explanatory factor behind many Saudi Arabians' reluctance to enter a wide spectrum of employment in the modern sector. Life on the farms and in nomadic camps is not strenuous for the men, not subject to the rigorous disciplines associated with modern sector employment, and is not ordered by impersonal authorities that the tribesman has little reason or inclination to respect. There is thus a widespread disinclination among the rural population to be formally employed.[1]

Nationals who have entered the modern sector have tended to do so in selected occupations and sectors. The economic sectors that are popular with nationals are services, transport and communications, and trade and finance. Quite naturally the government administration attracts many nationals, as it does in virtually all capital-rich states. Trade and finance is also a natural activity, for many nationals are traders and merchants by family tradition. Looked at from the occupational perspective, the lack of qualifications or skills suitable for many modern sector jobs has meant that nationals are often employed in unskilled jobs such as driving or guarding. At the same time it should be noted that, in general, nationals occupy the key positions in government and industry. Industrial employment, however, with the exception of that within the oil industry, is not popular among nationals. Neither is the construction industry popular, and it is these two sectors, industry and construction, in which many migrants work. Table 14-1 details employment by economic sector and nationality in 1975.

Table 14-1
Employment, by Economic Sector and Nationality, 1975

	Total Employment	Nationals' Employment	Percent	Nonnationals' Employment	Percent
Agriculture and fishing	585,550	530,650	51.7	54,900	7.6
Mining and quarrying	27,000	15,400	1.5	11,600	1.6
Manufacturing	65,900	21,550	2.1	44,350	6.1
Utilities	20,350	7,200	0.7	13,150	1.8
Construction	239,300	35,900	3.5	203,400	28.1
Trade and finance	204,200	65,700	6.4	138,500	19.1
Transport and communications	103,800	72,900	7.1	30,900	4.3
Services	503,700	277,100	27.0	226,600	31.4
Total	1,749,800	1,026,400	100.0	723,400	100.0

Source: Based on: J.S. Birks and C.A. Sinclair, *Arab Manpower: The Crisis of Development* (New York, Saint Martin's Press, 1980), ch. 5.

The third five-year plan makes explicit government concern over the extent of "underutilized" manpower in the rural sector of the economy.[2] Much investment is directed toward infrastructural development in rural areas, the extension of schooling, the provision of low-cost housing, and the improvement of agriculture. All these are designed to facilitate a wider and deeper level of participation in the modern economy by the national population. There are signs that the government is enjoying success in this regard: the extension of education to rural areas alone will be of growing impact.

However, the plan incorporates one important contradiction. While greater emphasis is put on national participation, simultaneously industrial development is to proceed apace. National disinclination to participate at the present time in industrial ventures thus encourages and requires that migrants be employed. Some may argue that this is a temporary expedient necessary until attitudes and aspirations of nationals change. Nonetheless, there is another point of view that certain labor-market trends may be very difficult to reverse. For example, if in Saudi Arabia's industrial sites only nonnational labor is employed until, say, 1990, will it be possible to start employing nationals thereafter? It may be that a tradition will develop that only nonnationals work in certain jobs and sectors, which means that nationals will not accept employment in those occupations or sectors. This is a point to which we later return.

Turning to the nonnational labor force, the Kingdom has attracted migrants since oil revenues were first spent on domestic development in the 1950s. Initially, Yemen and Oman provided the bulk of migrants at the unskilled level while Levantine countries and Egypt provided more highly skilled manpower. The growth of nonnationals in the Kingdom largely parallels the growth of the modern sector and the growth of oil revenues.[3] Table 14–2 shows for various years (1962–1963, 1966–1967, 1975, and 1980) the growth of expatriate labor.

In 1975 migrants were working in all economic sectors, even in agriculture and fishing (table 14–1), but particularly in services, construction, and

Table 14–2
Employment of Migrants in Selected Years

Year	Migrant Employment
1962/63	60,000
1966/67	240,400
1975	723,400
1980	1,023,600

Source: Based on J.S. Birks and C.A. Sinclair, *Arab Manpower: The Crisis of Development* (New York: Saint Martin's Press, 1980), ch. 5.

trade and finance. Few occupations or economic sectors did not and do not rely on migrants to some extent, and, in some cases, heavily. Most migrants were Arabs, 69 percent coming from Yemen (Yemen Arab Republic or North Yemen), Jordan, Egypt, and Palestinians. Although only 5 percent came from Asia in 1975, their number and proportion has dramatically risen[4] (see table 14-3).

The growth of the Asian community and work force in Saudi Arabia, particularly those non-Muslims who are in many cases from Far Eastern countries, is symptomatic of many characteristics of the contemporary labor market. For example, it can change quickly, and responses come quickly to changed conditions. Second, the cheapness and efficiency of Asian labor in contrast to other labor has led to their widespread penetration of all sectors of the market. Official concern over the extent of Asians also shows how regularly "not everything that happens [in Saudi Arabia] is conceived by planners."[5] At present the government is moving energetically to monitory expatriates and, particularly in one important respect, residence and family reunion.[6] The implications for population growth among non-Saudi Arabians of family reunion are dramatic and appreciated by the

Table 14-3
Migrant Workers in 1975, by Nationality

Nationality	Number	Percent
Yemenis (North)	280,400	38.9
Jordanian (including Palestinians)	125,000	17.3
Egyptians	95,000	13.1
Yemenis (South)	55,000	7.6
Sudanese	35,000	4.8
Lebanese	20,000	2.8
Omanis	17,500	2.4
Syrians	15,000	2.1
Somalis	5,000	0.7
Iraqi	2,000	0.3
(Subtotal: Arabs)	(649,900)	(90.0)
Pakistanis	15,000	2.1
Indians	15,000	2.1
Other Asian	8,000	1.0
(Subtotal: Asian)	(38,000)	(5.2)
European and American	15,000	2.1
African and other	10,000	1.3
Iranians	10,000	1.3
Turks	500	0.1
Grand Total	723,400	100.0

Source: J.S. Birks and C.A. Sinclair, *International Migration and Development in the Arab Region* (Geneva: International Labor Organization 1980), Table 10, p. 134.

Ministry of the Interior. Some commentators think that government now has good control over migrant workers and their dependents. Others see the present successes of government as largely due to the slackness of labor demand. As soon as government spending in the third plan starts to bite, it may then be impossible to resist yet another wave of migrants into the Kingdom.

One of the most important aspects of the Saudi Arabian labor market today is the institutionalized nature of migrant labor and, increasingly, migrant families. It is the view of these authors that migrant labor is in Saudi Arabia, in some form or other, for an extended period if not permanently. This is important in two respects. One is that the growth of the immigrant work force will tend to slow the pace of entry of nationals into the modern sector; indeed, it may be that many segments of the national populace will be permanently excluded from certain areas of the modern sector. The second is that the more established the immigrant community becomes, the harder it will be for the Saudi Arabian authorities to impose strict immigration regulations on such questions as family reunion. While in a sense it may well be too early to predict the future of population development in Saudi Arabia, there are signs that both the previously mentioned points are likely, if not probable, developments.

Determinants of Future Employment Growth

The key factor in determining labor-force growth for 1980 to 1985 is the third development plan. The size and nature of the plan obviously is of major impact on the labor force and in particular on the nonnational component. Nationals' employment will increase more or less at rates set by population increases: the balance between national labor supply and global demand will be met by expatriates.

In broad outline, the plan has been announced. Total expenditure, including defense and aid, will total $363,000 million at constant (1980) prices. Total spending in the second plan was $133,000 million, again at constant (1980) prices. The emphasis in the third plan will be more on expanding production and relatively less on infrastructure. Human-resources development and rural areas emerge as two areas planners see as of major significance. Yet it is certain that industrialization will continue at Yanbo and Jubail, that the large petrochemical projects will proceed, and that several of the large projects such as King Khaled Military City, Riyadh University, and the Causeway will be affected. Most of these projects have their origins in the second plan, and although the third plan nominally has different objectives than the second plan, such changes will only become obvious toward 1985.

The plan has been announced in fairly bland terms, with comparatively little detail on some important aspects. One of these is manpower, on which only one detail was mentioned, namely, that in the third-plan period expatriate manpower growth will be limited to a rate of 1.2 percent per year as compared with the official estimate of the annual growth of expatriate manpower from 1975 to 1980 of 7 percent. To understand the implications of this constraint and to see the plan in the context of Saudi Arabian development, we here construct a model budget.

A Model Budget, 1980 to 1985

The task of constructing a model budget for Saudi Arabia is facilitated by knowledge of several key parameters. The price of oil in 1980 looks stable at about $31; Saudi Arabia's output has been running at 9.5 million barrels per day for some time (though present indications are that it will fall to 8.5 million barrels per day possibly early in 1981); total plan spending will be in the region of $363 billion.

Table 14-4 shows actual or provisional Saudi Arabian income and expenditure for 1978–1979 and 1979–1980 and an estimate of future income, expenditure, surpluses, and overseas holdings. Prices in 1978–1979, 1979–1980, and 1980–1981 are current; thereafter, they are constant in 1980–1981 terms.

The crucial element in our model is the projected growth of expenditure. This was estimated by converting expenditure in each year from 1975–1976 to 1979–1980 into constant prices so that real growth in expenditure could be analyzed. The trend of expenditure in that period was extrapolated forward for each year of the third plan, subject to the constraint that total spending could not exceed announced plan expenditures, that is, $363 billion. Our expenditure figures exceed this total by 8 percent, but because the fit obtained between 1975–1976 to 1979–1980 expenditure and 1980–1981 to 1981–1985 was good, we accepted this slight overrun. Figures for expenditure in 1978–1979, 1979–1980, and 1980–1981 are, as are all figures in those years, in current prices.

Important to this calculation, though less problematic to deal with, is oil output. For the purposes of table 14-4, this was assumed to be, from 1980–1981 to 1984–1985, 9.5 million barrels per day of which 9 million barrels per day is sold for a price of $31 per barrel. The effect of other levels of output or prices of oil can be easily demonstrated. (Interested readers requiring further information on the assumptions behind table 14-4 should consult the notes to that table).

Table 14-4
Budget in 1978/79 and 1979/80 and Estimated Budget, 1980/81–1984/85
(in Millions of Dollars)[a]

	1978/79[b]	1979/80[c]	1980/81[d]	1981/82	1982/83	1983/84	1984/85
Income							
Oil and related	33,483	61,070	105,115	105,115	105,115	105,115	105,115
Haj	5,029	7,000	1,000	1,000	1,000	1,000	1,000
Foreign investments			7,000	6,000	8,200	9,000	10,700
Total	38,512	68,070	113,115	112,115	114,315	115,115	116,815
Expenditure (including aid and defense)	42,724	57,270	62,000	70,000	79,000	87,000	96,000
Balance							
Surplus (+) or deficit (−)	− 4,212	+10,800	+ 51,115	+ 42,115	+ 35,315	+ 28,115	+ 20,815
Foreign Investments							
Total government holdings		$75,000	$ 85,000	$137,000	$179,000	$214,000	$242,000
Yield rate[e]		9.3%	7%	6%	5%	5%	5%
Yield		7,000	6,000	8,200	9,000	10,700	

Sources: Saudi Arabian Monetary Agency (SAMA), *Annual Report, 1979* (Riyadh: SAMA, 1980); *Middle East Economic Digest*, Special Report, July 1980, p. 88, May 23, 1980, pp. 3–4, and August 3, 1979, p. 7; other corroborative reports.

a Exchange rates used are; 1978/79, 1$U.S. = 3.45 Saudi riyal (SR); 1979/80, 1$U.S. = 3.37SR; 1980/81, 1$U.S. = 3.3SR. For the years 1978/79, 1979/80, and 1980/81, prices are current; for the years 1981/82–1984/85, prices are constant in terms of 1980/81.

b Data for 1978/79 from SAMA, *Annual Report, 1979.*

c Data for 1979/80 estimated as follows from *Middle East Economic Digest:* "Expenditure" and "Balance," May 23, 1980; "Income" estimated as the residual; in foreign-investments category, "Total Holdings," August 3, 1979, and "Yield," Special Report, July 1980.

d "Income/Oil and Related" estimated by assuming an annual production of 9.5 million barrels per day, less 0.5 million barrels per day which is consumed domestically and the remainder sold at $31 per barrel. In addition, revenue of $3.28 billion from natural-gas liquids (NGL) and refinery products assumed. It is assumed for 1981/82–1984/85 that if domestic consumption increases, output will expand and revenue will remain constant. Haj revenue of 1980/81 derived from various sources, including SAMA, *Annual Report, 1979.* "Yield" from foreign investments is the result of net additions to overseas holdings in the preceding year. Expenditure in 1980/81 and 1984/85 at a rate consistent with real annual growth, 1975/76–1979/80 and totaling $394 billion in constant 1980/81 prices, which is marginally higher (8 percent) than the official plan total in constant 1980/81 prices.

e For 1980/81–1984/85, "Yield Rate," is assumed to fall as Saudi Arabian holdings increase in size; it is assumed portfolio managers will spread risks more evenly. The yield rate is placed conservatively, but the overall budget is not sensitive to this rate compared with, say, the price of oil.

The Implications of the Model Budget

The first point to make about our constructed budget is that Saudi Arabia is clearly able to afford the financial costs of the third plan. Indeed, at a level of oil production of some 9.5 million barrels per day and at the anticipated expenditure, the Kingdom accumulates large surpluses. Figure 14-1 shows these surpluses graphically. In 1980–1981 they amount to $51 billion, and over the plan period are reduced to $21 billion. Recycling these will present the world's financial institutions with a considerable challenge. The second

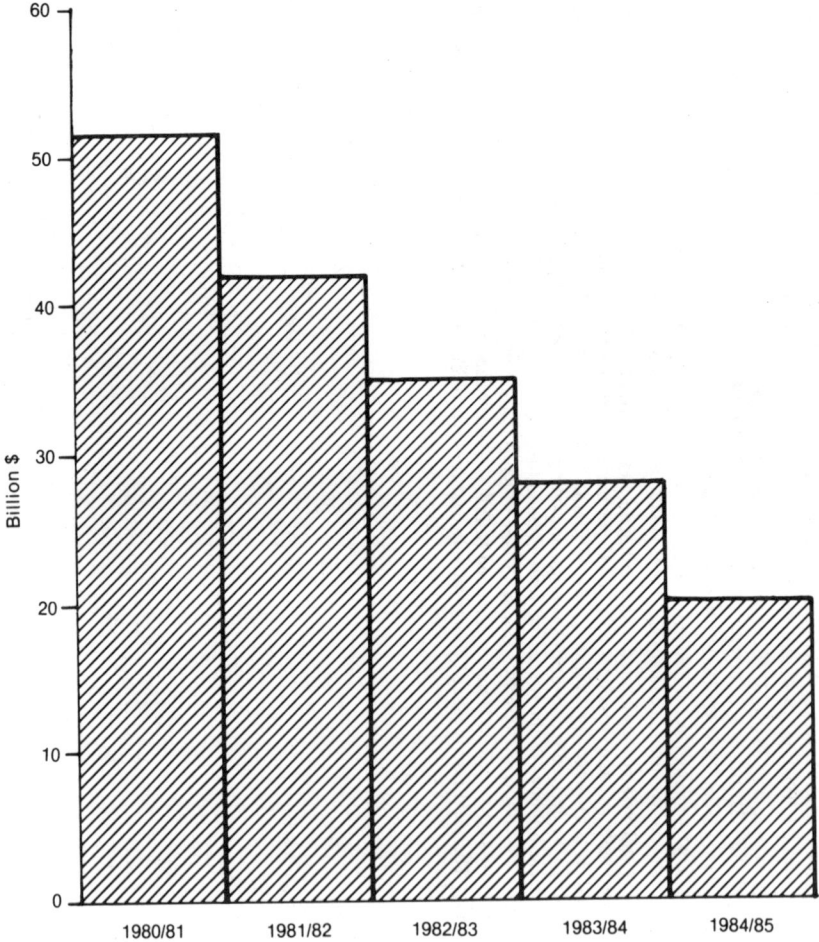

Figure 14-1. Financial Surpluses, 1980/81–1984/85 (in $ Billions of Dollars) with Oil Production at 9.5 Million *B/D* and Plan Expenditures as Stated

point is that with an oil price of about \$31 per barrel, Saudi Arabia need only produce about 5.5 million barrels per day in 1980–1981 to finance her envisaged development. Figure 14–2 shows exactly what level of oil exports would be essential in order to finance development after 1980–1981 (when it is assumed that oil exports are in fact 9 million barrels per day). In 1981–1982 Saudi Arabia's oil exports could fall as low as 5.5 million barrels per day, but thereafter they rise annually.

Third, Saudi Arabia's overseas holdings rise from an estimated \$85 billion in 1980–1981 to \$242 billion in 1984–1985 (constant 1980–1981 prices).

The Saudi Arabian government is in the interesting position of trading off three factors: oil production, development expenditure, and financial surpluses. A high level of oil production combined with conservative development expenditures produces large financial surpluses. Alternatively, a low rate of oil production (say, 5.5 million barrels per day) combined with presently envisaged development expenditures produces low financial surpluses. The triangular, interrelationship of these three phenomena and the broad implications that are associated with a change in any one make balancing them a difficult task. The level of development expenditure has a particular relevance for the present discussion since expatriate manpower and development expenditures are positively associated.

The impression is gained from Saudi Arabia's fiscal position that development as presently conceived is easily affordable, and the present plan is, if anything, a conservative picture of future development expenditure.

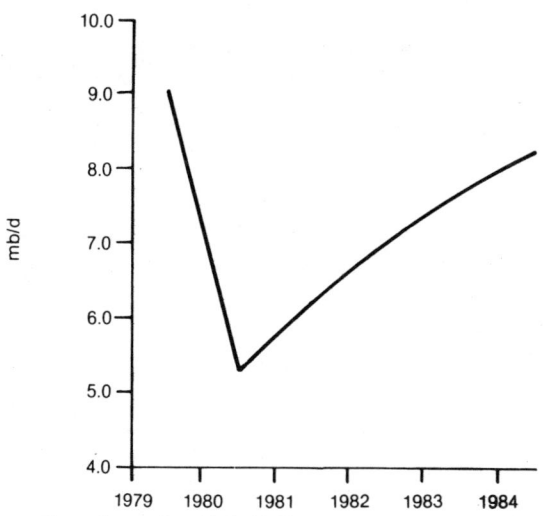

Note: Assumes nil surpluses after 1979–1980.

Figure 14–2. Minimum Level of Oil Exports Required to Finance Third Five-Year Plan, 1980/81–1984/85

However, to detail the manpower requirements of the plan, we require a great deal more information than we presently have. This might come from the plan itself or from a detailed statement of output growth by sector. We have neither of these, and we are therefore obliged to evaluate employment growth from 1975 to 1980 in the light of development expenditures and to make subjective judgments of likely future growth given what information we find in the plan.

Table 14-5 shows the growth of employment from 1975 to 1980 by economic sector. Some sectors grew more quickly than others, notably transport and communications (15 percent), construction (10 percent), and manufacturing (10 percent). By interpreting the stated objectives of the third plan and from a knowledge of the projects presently ongoing and from the trends of employment from 1975 to 1980, we have constructed patterns of growth, also shown on table 14-5. The construction sector is assumed not to expand in employment terms, although manufacturing employment grows more quickly; this reflects the objective of moving investment away from infrastructure and toward production. The agricultural sector, which was declining previously, begins to grow in employment terms as large sums are invested in rural infrastructure and in agriculture. Services, notably those of government, continue at a comparatively high rate of employment growth of 6 percent, reflecting the continuing growth of government administration, health and education provision, as well as defense and national security. The growth of utilities moderated slightly but is still quite high. Overall, employment grows at 4 percent per annum in the third five-year plan compared with 4.8 percent per annum in the second plan.

Essentially the growth of employment envisaged here is consistent with announced plan expenditures, erring possibly on the conservative side. The construction projects envisaged in the third plan may require an even larger work force than 385,000 persons; productivity on construction sites may be lower than we anticipate. The administration of this increasingly complex and diverse country may require yet more staff; the expansion of schools and hospitals may proceed still more quickly. However, as estimated here, total employment rises from 2.2 million in 1980 to 2.7 million in 1985, an increase of some 500,000 people.

Table 14-6 shows the growth of the national work force from 1.0 million in 1975 to 1.4 million in 1985, an annual rate of increase of some 3 percent. Deducing the expatriate element in the work force is not simply an arithmetical task, for reasons outlined earlier in this chapter. There are some spheres where nationals are unwilling to work, others where they are unqualified to work, and still others where only nationals are entitled to work. However, in a broadly based assessment such as this one, we make the assumption that we can deduce expatriate employment by subtracting

Table 14-5
Employment in 1975 and Estimated Employment Growth to 1980 and 1985

Economic Sector	All Employment in 1975	Annual Employment Growth Rate 1975–1980 (%)	All Employment in 1980	Estimated Annual Employment Growth in Third Plan, 1980–1985 (%)	All Employment in 1985
Agriculture and fishing	585,550	− 2	529,300	+ 2	584,380
Mining and quarrying	27,000	+ 5	34,460	+ 5	43,980
Manufacturing	65,900	+ 6	88,190	+ 11	148,600
Utilities	20,350	+ 10	32,770	+ 7	45,960
Construction	239,300	+ 10	385,390	0	385,390
Trade and finance	204,200	+ 5	260,620	+ 4	317,080
Transport and communications	103,800	+ 15	208,780	+ 5	266,460
Services	503,700	+ 6	674,060	+ 6	902,050
Total	1,749,800	+ 4.8	2,213,570	+ 4.0	2,693,900

Source: For 1975, based on J.S. Birks and C.A. Sinclair, *Arab Manpower* (New York: Saint Martin's Press, 1980), ch. 5, table 5.13, p. 108; for 1980 and 1985, authors's estimates.

Table 14-6
Employment, by Nationality in 1975, 1980, and 1985

	1975	1980	Annual Rate of Increase	1985	Annual Rate of Increase
All employment	1,749,800	2,213,570	4.8	2,693,900	4.0
Nationals' employment	1,026,400[a]	1,189,990	3.0	1,379,530	3.0
Expatriate employment	723,400	1,023,580	7.2	1,314,370	5.1

Sources: For 1975, national total based on J.S. Birks and C.A. Sinclair, *Arab Manpower* (New York: Saint Martin's Press, 1980), ch. 5; expatriate total based on: J.S. Birks and C.A. Sinclair, *International Migration and Development in the Arab Region* (Geneva: International Labor Organization, 1980), table 10, p. 134; 1980 and 1985 are authors' estimates.

[a]There is some uncertainty about this figure and the national population for 1975. It might be rather higher than the present figure suggests. However, adjusting the national work force would not affect the figure for the nonnational work force.

the supply of national labor from the total labor requirement. Thus, while expatriate labor increased from 1975 to 1980 at an annual rate of 7 percent and by some 300,000 people, it is projected here as rising annually at the reduced rate of 5 percent and by some 291,000 people.

An Expatriate Manpower Growth Constraint of 1 Percent Per Annum?

The view of these authors is that the stated third-plan expenditures are both well within the country's fiscal capacity and conservative in that the government is likely to be tempted to spend more rather than less. Projects may prove to be more costly, but also both internal and international pressures will be on Saudi Arabia to maintain high levels of development expenditures. Local merchants and the national populace benefit from government expenditure; the third plan aims to distribute wealth more evenly. Saudi Arabia is a major supplier of oil to OECD countries; a regular energy supply is essential for their economic growth. Within OPEC, Saudi Arabia extends her influence often by raising oil production. The demise of Iran as a major oil exporter and the disruption of Iraqi production following the war with Iran in 1980 will have a growing impact on the oil market. Iran and Iraq have been major oil producers. In 1978 their combined production was 8 million barrels per day, equivalent to Saudi Arabian output. After the Iran-Iraq conflict their combined production may fall to as low as 1 million barrels per day. The net effect of this will be to encourage Saudi Arabia to keep its oil exports above the 8.5 million-barrels-per-day level set as the optimum some years ago. The high price of oil will ensure enormous revenue and, even at presently envisaged levels of development expenditure, Saudi Arabia will accrue large surpluses. To diminish the task of recycling these surpluses, Saudi Arabia will be under pressure from the international community to maintain high levels of domestic expenditure.

The currently envisaged expatriate manpower requirement is some 291,000 persons, an annual increase of 5 percent. To reduce this to 1 percent implies one of two things: either a spectacular increase in productivity or a greatly reduced level of domestic expenditure. Constraining expatriate manpower growth to 1 percent per annum would be equivalent to severely restricting if not virtually halting development, a situation certainly not envisaged in the third plan.

Conclusion

We have examined manpower and manpower growth from two perspectives. In the first part of this chapter the structural and qualitative aspects of the Kingdom's labor market were delineated. The most important conclusions from that microeconomic analysis were that labor-market segmentation is growing. Nationals and migrants are tending to divide between two different labor markets and to work in different sectors of the economy. Second, it was found that quite pronounced differences exist within the labor market where nationals work between those whose existence is oriented to rural areas and those who have an urban life style. While the best efforts of government to modernize the rural economy and to utilize underemployed national labor may be having some success, on the other hand, the burgeoning ranks of migrant workers serve to exclude nationals from large areas of the modern economy.

Our second perspective was the likely scale of economic growth in the period 1980-1985 and the consequent demand for labor. Even when the fairly generous and possibly unrealistic assumption that labor is homogeneous is made, and when using fairly conservative growth assumptions, expatriate labor grows annually by some 5 percent and by about 219,000 people over the period 1980-1985.

The two main conclusions of this chapter are: if Saudi Arabia's development is to continue at anything like the pace envisaged in the third plan, additional migrant workers will be required in quite large numbers, and second, migrants are increasingly becoming institutionalized in Saudi Arabian economy and society in the sense that the economy cannot do without them and, since they will be around for some time to come, society must come to terms with their presence.

Notes

1. There is a sense in which the description of Saudi Arabia's rural economy as traditional is inaccurate. Some parts are unambiguously modern, in particular, the newly created irrigated farms. These though are small in terms of output and employment and often do not employ nationals. These modern capital-intensive enterprises we exclude from the description of the *traditional* economy. The inaccuracy in the term arises because quite frequently rural Saudi Arabians approach their traditional activities with modern technology. It is, for example, occasionally noted that "the bedouin have replaced the camel with the Mercedes truck." In part they have (and in the main they have not), but it is important to appreciate that modern technology has been employed only to preserve a traditional life style. A more extensive treatment of Saudi Arabia's rural sector is given in J.S. Birks and C.A. Sinclair, *The Kingdom of Saudi Arabia and the Libyan Arab Jamahiriya: The Key Countries of Employment,* World

Employment Programme Research (Geneva: International Labor Organization, 1979).

2. Summary details of the third five-year plan are given in *Middle East Economic Digest,* Special report, July 1980.

3. The growth of the modern sector of the economy and the contemporaneous growth of migrant labor is examined in more detail in J.S. Birks and C.A. Sinclair, "The Domestic Political Economy of Development in Saudi Arabia," a paper presented to the Symposium on State, Economy and Power in Saudi Arabia, Centre for Gulf Studies, Exeter, July 1980.

4. The entire question of contemporary labor migration in the Arab region is discussed in J.S. Birks and C.A. Sinclair, *International Migration and Development in the Arab Region* (Geneva: International Labor Organization, 1980).

5. *Middle East Economic Digest,* Special report, July 1980, p. 9.

6. This was reported in *Middle East Economic Digest,* September 5, 1980, p. 37.

15

The Third Development Plan of Saudi Arabia, 1400-1405 A.H./ 1980-1985 A.D.

Ragaei El Mallakh and
Dorothea H. El Mallakh

As the second five-year development plan drew to a close in 1980, the new third plan set development priorities for the next half-decade. The performance of the second plan could also be evaluated; overall, significant progress was achieved in meeting planned targets.

The gross domestic product (GDP) experienced an average annual growth rate of 8.04 percent, with the nonoil sector's average rate of growth at over 15 percent. During the 1975-1980 period, many of the major physical constraints to development—ports, roads, communications—although not eliminated have been diminished. Other constraints addressed by the second plan included an adequate labor supply and the absorptive capacity of the domestic economy. The former aspect received particular attention during the first two years of the second plan, resulting in an influx of labor from abroad and a sizable transfer of indigenous labor from agriculture to other sectors. The absorptive-capacity constraint, in fact, reflects some of the infrastructural limits already noted. By 1980 the Saudi economy's absorptive capacity had improved as seen in the consistently rising level of imports and in government actual expenditures, which surpassed allocated amounts by the close of the second-plan period.

During the 1970s as a whole, the real GDP of Saudi Arabia almost trebled with the per-capita GNP in 1979-1980 reaching Saudi riyals (SR) 44,500, or $13,400. The average annual growth rate of real GDP for the ten-year span of the first and second plans was some 13.2 percent. Noteworthy is the real nonoil GDP, which rose close to 350 percent—not insignificant considering the absorptive-capacity constraints.[1]

As the decade of the 1980s opened, a more favorable situation existed relative to the rate of price increase than that obtaining five years earlier. Inflationary pressure was building throughout the first-plan period (1970-1975), becoming severe in 1975 and during the first two years of the second plan. Government expenditure had risen steeply from SR 5 billion in 1969-1970 to SR 128.3 billion in 1976-1977—an annual rate of just under 60 percent. During the last three years of the second plan (that is, 1977/78-

177

1979/80), the government moved to reduce its spending growth rate down to 14 percent per annum. This tough-minded fiscal policy brought the GDP deflator and the cost-of-living index down from 61 percent and 35 percent in 1974–1975 to 7.2 percent and 1.8 percent, respectively, in 1978–1979, despite a rise of 10.5 percent in import prices.[2] Thus the third plan can begin with a better handle on inflation; imported inflation is expected to be the main source of inflation in the 1980–1985 span.

With inflation controlled, most of the Saudi population has been able to achieve a much higher standard of living at the beginning of the third plan than at the comparable period of the second plan. Average annual per-capita income from employment rose from about SR 4,800 in 1975 to approximately SR 8,200 (in constant 1979 prices). In addition, the government's social-welfare programs increased personal-income levels by an estimated 29 percent during the second plan.[3] Although distribution figures are not available, it can be asserted that the "average" Saudi was much better off in 1980 than in 1975—particularly with inflation dampened down.

With considerable developmental achievements under the second plan, nonetheless continued constraints to development have been recognized. In particular, the gap between demand and supply in manpower has been singled out as one of the issues basic to economic decisions in the coming five years. Simply, the number of new indigenous entrants into the Saudi labor force is inadequate to meet the burgeoning manpower requirements. As remarked earlier, during the second plan a trend developed in which labor drained from the agricultural sector to jobs in nonagricultural pursuits. This trend cannot be continued indefinitely without a significant negative impact on food production and demographic patterns. Nor is the manpower constraint merely one of numbers. During the second plan, the demand for labor (especially non-Saudi) was concentrated in such infrastructure as construction, transportation, and distribution, activities seen as "through-put" sectors that, although vital, contribute to the growth of the GDP in a supportive fashion. The employment of manpower in new and productive enterprises in agriculture and industry can be seen as a long-term objective in diversifying the Kingdom's economy away from the overwhelming predominance of the petroleum sector.

Plan Rationale and Objectives

The third plan departs from its predecessors in several areas. The ten years from 1970 to 1980 targeted high growth rates in all sectors; this carried with it a policy of allowing relatively free importation of foreign labor to satisfy demand. The next five years of the third plan should witness greater selectivity, opting for high growth in certain areas with proven potential. The thrust of this policy would be to contain the expansion of the imported labor force.[4] Departing from the second plan's emphasis on infrastructure development and thereby increasing the absorptive capacity of the economy, the new plan homes in on raising the efficient utilization of the labor force—domestic and foreign alike—in hydrocarbon (usually highly capital intensive) and other manufacturing industries, in the agricultural and in the mining sectors. Again the overall goal is to diversify the economic bases of the nation.

Briefly, three medium-range objectives have been identified and targeted: the structural change of the economy; the achievement of participation and social welfare in development; and greater economic and administrative efficiency.

Policies geared to achieving a structural change in the economy are linked to three areas of economic activity: oil and gas production, the expansion of productive sectors in agriculture, mining, and industry; and the continued development of infrastructure. Clearly, the oil and gas sector is preeminent; it is the primary foreign-exchange earner and thus underwrites the others financially. Decisions impacting on oil and gas development must of necessity impact on all the other sectors. The third plan's enunciated production policies vis-a-vis oil and gas is to lift these resources at a rate that seeks to conserve the reserves for the longest time frame while still managing to generate sufficient revenue to cover the financial requirements of the plan. Thus natural-gas production will continue to be developed (reducing the waste of this energy source, which in the past was flared at the wellhead). Crude-oil output will aim at optimizing the mix of heavy and light crudes as well as optimizing the life-spans of the various fields through careful attention to production levels.

The ongoing long-term goal of economic diversification requires development of the agricultural, industrial, and mining sectors. In the government view, the private sector can and should be instrumental in undertaking the expansion of these areas. Government support of the private sector is expected to take the form of the provision of information and research results, of a supportive financial framework and investment incentives, of the required infrastructure needs, and of the areas given priority for investment.[5]

Over time the structural change sought for the economy will be affected by infrastructure policies. The relative weight given infrastructure in the second plan has been reduced in the third plan in relation to the volume of investment directed toward other productive sectors. In the next five years, projects under way will be completed along with development of some seventy-three areas identified as requiring physical infrastructure to become growth centers for future productive economic activities. Municipalities and the industrial complexes of Jubail and Yanbu will continue to receive investment during the third plan.[6]

Human-resource development is the second goal enunciated in the third plan. This will entail the distribution of the benefits of the national wealth throughout the population but in a manner consistent with the Islamic tradition and the fabric of the social structure. Specifically targeted is to support the development of all regions by offering a full range of government services, thereby reducing any regional disparities in the quality of life available. This in turn should help to alleviate a portion of the rural to urban population drift, which usually marks the developing process of many nations. Also seen as human-resource objectives is the control of inflation and a reduction in subsidies without affecting the low-income groupings, coupled with services to assist in blunting the social dislocations that frequently accompany rapid economic growth.[7]

Planners have attempted to bring in a larger segment of the population in the third plan's implementation. A primary vehicle is through information services and education. Adult and vocational education are to receive direct governmental participation as well as community-development projects designed to encourage self-help principles, particularly in the rural areas. The manpower strategy outlined earlier calls for the number of foreign workers to be reduced; this will encourage a higher level of Saudi labor participation.[8]

As noted briefly, the negative aspects accompanying regional disparties in development have been addressed in the third plan.[9] Involved will be the institution of a system of national, regional, and district centers for the provision and coordination of services beyond the standard municipal services (electricity, schools, and so on). These new services will be of an administrative and support nature as, for example, agricultural extension activities. The regional-development policies seen as going hand in hand with other human-development programs aimed at stimulating citizen participation yet offering services that seek to cushion the problems of adjustment caused by rapid economic transformation.[10]

Excessive inflation has been acknowledged as an area requiring governmental attention in the third plan in order to avoid the stresses that can appear among the low-income groups. The struggle against rapidly rising prices in the second plan included the introduction of subsidies on various items as housing and essential foods. In the upcoming five years, these subsidies will be reviewed; the goal is to reduce or abolish them. This action will be possible if the government can restrain expenditures and thereby keep inflation within acceptable bounds—7 to 10 percent.[11]

Last, the social-development services in health, welfare, and culture in place at the end of the second-plan period will be expanded under the third plan, with preventive medicine, health education, and primary care being given more emphasis.[12]

The third medium-range objective calls for raising economic and administrative efficiency. Not surprisingly, the rapid pace of growth experienced by Saudi Arabia is straining its administrative apparatus. Four areas have been earmarked in the area of improved efficiency: administrative development, manpower development, preservation of national fixed capital, and fiscal management.

To improve efficiency through administrative development, a comprehensive study is under way, scheduled for completion in 1982. That study is expected to come up with fixed recommendations for where basic changes are needed in the administrative structure. There will be improvement in the collection of statistical data and more emphasis on training within the reorganization effort. During the third plan there will be restrictions on the recruitment of additional manpower; no additional government positions will be budgeted beyond those vacant at the beginning of the plan and those required for entirely new programs.[13] This decision will curtail government hiring except in those cases where an agency can verify that its existing level of vacant positions is low enough to merit an injection of additional manpower.

Improved efficiency in administration is seen as benefiting from the high priority accorded manpower development generally in the third plan. Upgrading skills of the indigenous labor force has the beneficial spinoff effects of increasing citizen participation and increasing stability. The element of stability is often related to the large numbers of foreign workers employed when segments of the Saudi population are underemployed.

Manpower development directly involves education, beginning with an adequate level of primary schools. The third plan envisages greater attention paid to making education beyond the intermediate level more responsive to national manpower needs. Students with more academic abilities will be directed toward university training while others will expand their capabilities in technical schools and specialized training institutes. It is hoped that the new educational policies and system will turn out sufficient numbers of skilled individuals to match the country's economic needs.[14] In this same line, government loans are available to the private sector for training programs for Saudis.

Governmental policy in the next five years will seek to upgrade administrative staff through training programs, to use incentives to stimulate workers to relocate geographically and sectorally into more productive activities, and to redeploy manpower with the introduction (where appropriate) of labor-saving technology.[15]

Turning to the issue of preservation of national fixed capital as a part of economic efficiency, the third plan views maintenance as a vital component in keeping the high investment in infrastructure in earlier plans viable. Maintenance has frequently been a bottleneck to efficiency on a number of levels in Saudi Arabia—a problem shared with other oil-exporting nations undergoing rapid growth. The plan has outlined standards for new projects with an eye to design and production technology that will minimize maintenance requirement as much as possible.[16]

Administrative efficiency also is sought in terms of fiscal management. To accomplish the plan's growth target but with consideration to the absorptive capacity of the economy and the rate of inflation, government spending will be closely monitored through the plan period. A system of a ceiling to allocations for expenditure by each government agency is being put in place; its object is to wield more control over expenditures in terms of the plan's priorities. A special review is scheduled in 1982 to reassess all planned programs and allocations for the remaining three years of the plan period.

Strategies and Patterns for Development

In the tradition of its immediate predecessor, the third plan is ambitious— $235 billion compared with the second plan's $149 billion (at current prices). The sum for the third plan includes a built-in 7-percent inflation allowance per annum; it does not include defense spending and foreign aid, which could hike the total to around $391 billion (compared, again, to the second plan's total of $210 billion). Table 15-1 visually shows the reordering of priorities for 1980-1985: infrastructure's share in spending will fall from 50 percent in the second plan to 35 percent; expenditure in productive activities as industry and mining will rise from 25 percent in the 1975-1980 plan period to 37 percent in the third plan.[17]

Planners see the 1980-1985 span as a time for consolidation, characterized by a more selective approach to the growth in GDP and a constraint in the form of manpower availability (table 15-2). The oil sector's growth is expected to be 1.34 percent annually, with most of that growth arising from refined products, including the output of the new gas-gathering project. Refined products play an increasingly significant role as industrialization has proceeded. For example, the value of refined products has had an estimated annual growth of 15 percent. Crude-oil production, however, which still makes up the lion's share of the petroleum sector's revenue-earning power, is determined by the government as part of a policy to conserve oil resources while generating adequate revenues to finance development. In 1979, the 9.5-million-barrels-per-day output earned some $79 billion; that level could go even higher, depending on international and domestic considerations.[18]

In the third plan, the projected annual growth rate has been set at 6.2 percent, down from the second plan's average rate of over 15 percent per annum.[19] This estimate was premised in part on the low rate of employment

Table 15–1
Government Expenditure on Development

| | Change in the Direction of Development Expenditure | | |
Function of Expenditure	Amount in SR Billion (Current Prices)	Second Plan[a] (Estimated %)	Third Plan (%)
Economic-resource development	261.8	25.1	37.3
Human-resource development	129.6	15.9	18.5
Social development	61.2	9.4	8.7
Physical infrastructure	249.1	49.6	35.5
Subtotal: development	701.7	100.0	100.0
Administration[b]	31.4	6.7	4.5
Emergency reserves, subsidies	49.6	15.9	7.1
Total civilian expenditure	782.7	122.6	111.6

Source: Kingdom of Saudi Arabia, *Third Development Plan, 1400–1405/1980–1985,* chapter 3, p. 88.
Note: The total excludes (a) transfer payments; (b) noncivilian sectors; and (c) foreign aid.
[a]Based on actual and estimated values converted into 1979/80 prices.
[b]Administration includes (a) ministries and agencies with primarily administrative functions and (b) judicial and religious agencies.

growth due to the third plan's conscious policy of constrained manpower supply and on the drying up of the indigenous labor outmigration from the agricultural sector to other activities. As with the second plan, the services sector is expected to out-perform the producing sector during the 1980–1985 period (tables 15–3 and 15–4). A major cause for this projection is that the producing sectors will be affected by decreases in construction activity. This is indicative of the process whereby the concentration in development shifts toward the creation of production capabilities (for example, manufacturing) and away from the construction of infrastructure.

The construction sector will exhibit a slight rise in activity during the first two years of the third plan as expenditure on already committed projects is fulfilled; thereafter, construction's share is expected to decline during the remaining three years (1983–1985). Not surprisingly, construction has been the leading sector in the nonoil economy, accounting on average for about 20 percent of nonoil GDP throughout the second plan.[20] Nonetheless, the extent to which government policy in the latter part of the third-plan period will effect the construction sector is uncertain; steady growth is still expected from the private and noncivilian sectors. Such private-con-

Table 15–2

The Growth of GDP in the Period 1966/67–1979/80

(Annual Compound Growth in Percent per Annum, in 1969/1970 Prices)

	1966/67–1969/70	First Plan 1969/70–1974/75	Second Plan[a] 1974/75–1979/80	Third Plan 1980/81–1984/85
1. *Producing Sectors*				
Agriculture	3.62	3.59	5.40	5.35
Other mining	5.56	21.07	17.14	9.78
Other manufacturing	11.76	11.39	15.37	18.83
Utilities	11.31	10.93	24.41	29.46
Construction	3.32	18.57	17.78	(2.48)
2. *Service Sectors*				
Trade	10.09	13.94	22.06	8.42
Transport	10.58	16.97	21.13	12.93
Finance	7.94	8.16	12.99	7.29
Other services	9.76	7.09	13.91	2.95
Government	4.39	7.75	5.96	7.16
3. *Nonoil Economy*	6.96	11.66	15.13	6.19
4. *Oil Sector*	10.34	14.80	4.78	1.34
5. *Total Economy*	8.75	13.41	8.04	3.28

Source: *Third Development Plan*, ch. 1, p. 19.

[a]Sectoral data for the first-plan period shown above include the old price system for 1974–1975; the second- and the third-plan figures, however, use the revised price system for each sector. Tables for the nonoil eocnomy, the oil sector and the total economy for the second and third plans are in 1979–1980 prices partly because the 1984–1985 composition of the oil sector's output has no equivalent in 1969–1970.

struction investment will not take up the slack left by the massive infrastructure spending by the government that marked the second plan in particular.

As emphasized throughout this study, the most sweeping changes in the third plan's priorities is the concentration on manpower and employment. With significant reductions to be effected in the foreign component of the labor force and with a slower average annual growth projected for the 1980–1985 span (1.16 percent as compared to 7.19 percent for the second plan), the government is committed to close monitoring of the economy's performance with reevaluation of policies when deemed necessary.[21] This is because the exact extent of constraint on the growth of the economy due to the manpower policy is not known.

Agriculture and construction will be the sectors losing the most workers (table 15–5). The other sectors, for the most part, will show a substantial decline in employment growth per annum because of the more selective

Table 15-3
Projections for Growth of the Nonoil Economy
(In Percent per Year)

Growth Rates	Producing Sectors		Service Sectors		Total Nonoil Economy	
	Second Plan	*Third Plan*	*Second Plan*	*Third Plan*	*Second Plan*	*Third Plan*
1. GDP	16.5	2.2	14.1	8.8	15.1	6.2
2. Employment	2.2	(1.5)[a]	12.5	3.1	7.2	1.2
3. Productivity, of which:	14.0	3.7	1.5	5.6	7.4	5.0
(1) Cost/price effects[b]	4.1	5.1	1.2	4.4	2.4	4.6
(2) Employment shift effects	9.6	(1.3)[a]	0.3	1.2	4.9	0.3

Source: *Third Development Plan*, ch. 3, p. 91.
[a]Annual rates of decline relative to 1979–1980.
[b]These figures represent lower unit costs and/or higher-value products.

Table 15-4

The Structural Composition of GDP in the Period 1966/67–1979/80

(In Percent of Nonoil GDP, Based on 1969/70 Prices)

	1966–1967	1969–1970	1974–1975a	1974–1975b	1979–1980	1984–1985
			(A)	(B)		
1. *Producing Sectors*						
Agriculture	13.9	12.6	8.7	9.1	5.8	5.1
Other mining	0.6	0.6	0.7	0.6	0.7	0.7
Other manufacturing	4.8	5.5	5.5	5.6	5.6	8.9
Utilities	3.1	3.5	3.4	2.5	3.8	8.9
Construction	13.3	12.0	16.2	19.1	21.3	12.6
Subtotal	35.7	34.2	34.5	36.9	37.2	36.2
2. *Services Sectors*						
Trade	11.8	12.9	14.3	14.9	19.9	19.9
Transport	14.5	15.9	20.1	10.0	12.8	15.8
Finance	12.1	12.4	10.6	16.8	15.3	14.5
Other services	2.8	3.1	2.5	2.5	2.3	1.8
Government	23.1	21.5	18.0	18.9	12.5	11.8
Subtotal	64.3	65.8	65.5	63.1	62.8	63.8
3. *Nonoil Economy*	100.0	100.0	100.0	100.0	100.0	100.0
4. *Oil Sector*	109.1	119.8	137.6	144.5	89.5	64.1

Source: *Third Development Plan*, ch. 1, p. 20.

[a]New data have been incorporated by CDS in the revised estimates for the years from 1974–1975 onward (except for agriculture). For this reason, figures from 1974–1975 onward are not strictly comparable with figures for earlier years. The column (A) shown above for 1974–1975 is based on the old system of prices; the second column (B) is based on the revised data.

[b]Ministry of Planning estimate.

Table 15-5

Changes in Civilian Employment in the Second- and Third-Plan Periods
(Comparison by Economic Activity)

Economic Activity	Employment Increase (Thousands)		Annual Growth Rate (%)	
	Second Plan	Third Plan	Second Plan	Third Plan
Producing Sectors				
Agriculture	(96.2)	(70.0)	(2.94)	(2.46)
Other mining	3.9	2.5	16.51	6.07
Other manufacturing	29.8	60.0	6.97	9.52
Utilities	15.4	15.5	14.37	8.33
Construction	157.8	(85.0)	13.89	(5.78)
Subtotal	110.7	(77.0)	2.20	(1.48)
Service Sectors				
Trade	157.0	29.0	15.12	1.80
Transport	100.1	60.0	13.39	5.05
Finance	21.7	10.0	21.58	5.18
Other services	252.3	23.0	15.96	0.94
Government[a]	74.3	100.0	5.41	5.57
Subtotal	605.4	222.0	12.46	3.06
Nonoil Economy Subtotal	716.1	145.0	7.21	1.16
Oil Sector	8.6	10.0	5.61	5.02
Total	724.7	155.0	7.19	1.22

Source: *Third Development Plan*, ch. 3, p. 101.

[a]Excludes noncivilian employment.

GDP growth estimates as well as from planned increases in productivity. The classification of "Other manufacturing" stands as an exception and serves to emphasize the third plan's concentration on the productive industries. Although government is estimated to increase slightly in its annual growth in employment, this is subject to the efficiency review due out in 1982.

The third plan's development strategy hangs to a large extent on an increase in productivity. Had not the second plan achieved a rise in productivity, the labor-force requirements would have been more than twice what they were. Similarly, the expected increase in productivity in the third plan would translate into 550,000 fewer workers needed—a figure of significance when compared to the 155,000 projected as required for the period. As the participation rate of the Saudis in the labor force has been declining slightly, the bulk of the workers who would be hired in the absence of increased productivity would be foreign. It should be noted that the decline in Saudi participation is a direct result of the expansion of educational and training programs.

Capital and skill-intensive improvements and developments within specific sectors will form the source for productivity growth. Despite a background of outmigration of labor, agriculture will contribute as a result of a projected modest growth to GDP. High-productivity projects, financed with the aid of the Saudi Industrial Development Fund, offer the basis on which manufacturing is to contribute. Energy, water, communications, transport, and storage are to contribute to an increase in productivity through capital-intensive activities.

The productivity growth of the third plan can be contrasted to that during the 1975–1980 period when gains were primarily a result of the movement of labor away from low-productivity agriculture toward high-productivity construction. The third plan notes some concern on whether the estimated productivity increase can be achieved; if it is not achieved, there could be considerable impacts on the manpower policy and the GDP growth projections.[22]

Another factor critical to the third plan's targets and the realization of such targets is the unknown elements in the role of inflation. High inflation, like that of the mid-1970s, could arise if inflation is not kept close to the 10-percent ceiling figure—a rate still deemed tolerable to the planners. Of course, the level of government expenditure is one potential source. However, the willingness of the government to impose fiscal brakes has been demonstrated earlier during the second plan. Should inflation get out of hand, expansionary pressures could set off heavy demand for skilled labor, demand beyond the economy's ability to meet. The "demand-pull" on wages that could result might generate a "cost-push" pressure that would only aggravate the inflationary spiral. Moreover, the private sector is capable of generating the same "demand-pull" condition since at present investment outlays represented less than half of gross profits, leaving sizable funds for potential use.[23] Yet another potential source of inflation emanates from the Kingdom's trading partners in Europe and North America that have been experiencing inflation rates above that in Saudi Arabia. All in all, inflation, controlled during the second plan, cannot be discounted as a disruptive influence of major proportions for the 1980–1985 period.

Turning to the foreign-trade sector, crude oil will continue to dominate exports. Refined products and gas should begin to enter international trade in larger quantities during the third plan. It has been estimated that the level of crude-oil exports per day (at May 1980 prices) needed to finance development expenditures during the third plan is just under 5.3 million barrels. This is significantly below the 9.5 million barrels per day output level of

1979. Nonetheless, the Saudi government's policy aimed at the support of global economic stability through adequate supplies of energy is likely to be maintained.[24]

Turing to imports of goods and services, there was a close one-to-one relationship with nonoil GDP during the second plan; this reflected the utilization of imported components in Saudi manufacturing industries. The high propensity to import is projected to continue in the third plan.

Prospects for Implementation

As noted earlier, the third plan is an ambitious blueprint. It is not that the projected growth rates are too high; realistically, the growth rates targeted are moderate and can be attained based on the second plan's experience. The third plan may confront obstacles to implementation arising from structural changes in the economy related to the manpower policy incorporated in the plan.

What then are the elements favoring realization of the third plan's goals? There will be adequate revenue to underwrite the development projects, despite some slackening in worldwide oil demand in the early 1980s. It has been pointed out already that, based on mid-1980 oil prices, Saudi Arabia could cut back oil production from its 1979 level of 9.5 million barrels per day to under 5.3 million barrels per day and still earn sufficient revenue to finance the third plan. Realistically, such a reduction is not likely to occur given the government's policy of seeking to maintain stability in the global oil market. It should be kept in mind that an 8.5-million-barrel-per-day level was pronounced several years ago as the optimum ceiling of oil production; the 9.5-million-barrel-per-day output was initiated to reduce supply shortfalls in 1979 and 1980 due to export cutbacks by Iraq and Iran at that time.

It is unlikely that inflation will be allowed to grow out of hand and threaten the third plan's viability. The government's ability to apply stringent fiscal measures has been proven in the 1975–1980 span.

Infrastructure development and its place in the absorptive capacity of the economy are unlikely to pose any major obstacle to achievement of the third plan's targets. The rise in absorptive capacity during the second plan not only saw actual expenditures matching appreciations, the initial appropriations were surpassed through supplementary allocations.[25] There is little reason to hold that, despite an increased level of spending planned, absorptive capacity will not be a major constraint in the 1980–1985 period.

Although physical infrastructure development will go on (as clear by the 35.5-percent share of total development funds allocated to this activity), progress during the 1970s was such that the third plan's allocations are below the 50 percent of total development funds earmarked for infrastructure in the second plan. Major programs are now geared toward support for industrialization (transport, communications) and toward distribution of the national wealth (municipal and rural-area development and housing).

With constraints, aside from possible manpower snags, manageable, there are two additional elements that bode well for successful implementation of the third plan. Since a 1976 Council of Minister's resolution, annual budgeting—the most effective means in controlling plan implementation—has been improved as part of the planning follow-up. The planning, budgeting, and follow-up departments in all ministries and governmental agencies have been integrated.

There is a second element in the third plan that is designed to increase its flexibility: at the end of the second year (1981–1982), the policies and programs will be reassessed for the remaining three years. The plan's strategy is not considered immutable; priorities and allocations can be changed. This type of planning approach (that is, toward so-called roll-over planning) is viewed an allowing an economy undergoing rapid economic growth to adjust to changing conditions.

In conclusion, the third-plan priority that will need the closest scrutiny during implementation will be in manpower—reducing the share of foreign workers in the labor force. The pressure on manpower may be significant since expenditures will continue to rise sharply (up more than 50 percent over the second plan) yet employment is to increase by an average annual rate of only 1.2 percent during 1980–1985: the gap is to be filled by increased productivity. Trimming the foreign work force in manual and semiskilled labor may be difficult, given the government commitment to upgrade Saudi labor through training and education. With an active, growing economy reflecting sizable demands for labor in the development process, enormous efforts might be needed to bring down the annual rate of growth in expatriate workers can be brought down from 7 percent to 1.2 percent as projected in the plan. Indeed, "Saudization" may well figure prominently in the next two to three development plans before indigenous manpower supply can meet the enormous demand generated by rapid economic growth.

Notes

1. Kingdom of Saudi Arabia, Saudi Arabian Monetary Agency (SAMA), *Annual Report, 1400 (1980)*, p. 1. (Hereafter cited as SAMA, *Annual Report, 1980.*)

2. Ibid., p. 11.

3. Kingdom of Saudi Arabia, Ministry of Planning, *Third Develop-*

ment Plan, 1400–1405/1980–1985, tables 2–7 and 2–8, ch. 2, pp. 37, 38. (Hereafter cited as the *Third Development Plan.*)

4. Ibid., ch. 1, section 1.4.2, p. 16.

5. Ibid., ch. 3, section 3.1.1.2–3.1.1.3, pp. 75–78.

6. Ibid., ch. 3, section 3.1.1.3, pp. 77–78.

7. Ibid., ch. 3, section 3.1.2, p. 79.

8. Ibid., ch. 3, section 3.1.2.1, pp. 78–80.

9. Ibid., ch. 3, section 3.7.1, pp. 107–110.

10. Ibid., ch. 3, section 3.1.2.3, pp. 80–81.

11. Ibid., ch. 3, section 3.1.2.4, p. 81.

12. Ibid., ch. 3, section 3.1.2.5, p. 81.

13. Ibid., ch. 3, section 3.1.3.1, pp. 82–83. The reorganization study is detailed in ch. 9 of the plan.

14. Ibid.; greater detail on education and training is available in ch. 5 of the plan dealing with human-resource development.

15. Ibid.

16. Ibid., ch. 3, section 3.1.1.1, pp. 84–85.

17. Ibid., ch. 3, section 3.2.2, p. 88.

18. *Middle East Economic Digest,* July 1980, p. 16.

19. *Third Development Plan,* ch. 3, section 3.2.3.2, p. 90.

20. Ibid., ch. 1, section 1.4.4.2, pp. 18–19.

21. Ibid., ch. 3, sections 3.4.1, pp. 97–99 and 3.4.2, pp. 99–102.

22. Ibid., ch. 3, section 3.4.3, pp. 102–104.

23. Ibid., ch. 3, section 3.5, pp. 104–106. A relatively extensive discussion of inflation-control measures are offered in ch. 9 of the *Third Development Plan.*

24. The import sector during the third plan is projected to have a 7-percent annual growth rate in relation to the 6.2 percent for nonoil GDP annual growth. The slightly higher figure for imports is a result of an expected rise in components that substitute for labor.

25. SAMA, *Annual Report, 1979,* pp. 11–12.

Index

About the Contributors

Ali D. Johany, faculty member and dean of the College of Industrial Management at the University of Petroleum and Minerals in Dhahran, received the Ph.D. in economics from the University of California, Santa Barbara. His nonacademic experience includes service with the then Central Planning Organization (now the Ministry of Planning). Dr. Johany prepares a weekly commentary on economics-related topics for the newspaper, *Al-Riyadh.* Among his publications is *The Myth of the OPEC Cartel: The Role of Saudi Arabia* (1980).

Farouk M. Akhdar, Secretary General of the Royal Commission for Jubail and Yanbu, received the Ph.D. in economics at the University of California, Riverside. He has taught at the University of Petroleum and Minerals in Dhahran and served as director of the Technical Department of the Ministry of Planning. His publications include a chapter in *Energy and Development,* edited by Ragaei El Mallakh and Carl McGuire (1974).

Fouad A. Al-Farsy, Deputy Minister for Industry, Ministry of Industry and Electricity, received the LL.B. degree from Beirut Arab University and the Ph.D. from Duke University. Dr. Al-Farsy's earlier positions include an assistant professorship in the Faculty of Commerce of the University of Riyadh and Assistant Deputy Minister of Information. Dr. Al-Farsy was an administrative assistant in the international conference on ''Islam in Global Perspective,'' convened at the Rockefeller Foundation's Bellagio Study and Conference Center, Lake Como, Italy. Among his earlier publications is *Saudi Arabia: A Case Study in Development* (1979).

Paul John Stevens received the Ph.D. from the University of London, School of Oriental and African Studies. Currently a lecturer in economics at the University of Surrey, England, the author also has taught at the American University in Beirut and the Polytechnic University of Central London. Among his publications is *Joint Ventures in Middle East Oil* (1976).

Saud Ounallah is manager of administration and finance, Petromin Participation and the Petromin representative for the Eastern Province. He graduated from Damascus University with a degree in business administration and received the master's degree in management. Mr. Ounallah was attached to the Arthur D. Little Institutes of Management and Petroleum Management in Cambridge, Massachusetts. Prior to pursuing graduate study, he was private secretary to the Minister Sheikh Ahmed Zaki Yamani at the Ministry of Petroleum and Mineral Resources.

Hugh George Hambleton, professor of economics, Department of Economics, Laval University, Quebec City, received the Ph.D. from the University of London. His earlier positions have included economic advisor to the government of Peru (1971); president of the Canadian Association for Latin American Studies; economic directorate, North Atlantic Treaty Organization (1956–1961); producer, Inter-Continental Films; Communications Division of the National Film Board of Canada. His publications include *The Petroleum Industry in Latin America* and *The Economic Decline of Spain in the Seventeenth Century.*

Talal K. Hafiz is executive vice-president of the Saudi Research and Marketing Company, Houston, Texas (head office in Jeddah), which publishes *Arab News, Saudi Report, Saudi Business,* and *Al-Asharq Al-Awsat.* A specialist in intercultural relations, Dr. Hafiz received the Ph.D. in communications from the University of Colorado (Boulder) and has been consultant to the Educational Mission of Saudi Arabia; 3&D/International of Houston; Skidmore, Owings & Merrill of Chicago; and the Washington Educational Research Associates.

Fahad Sultan Huraib received the B.S. in electrical engineering from the University of Petroleum and Minerals in Dhahran where he also worked as a graduate assistant. Mr. Huraib is currently a doctoral candidate at the University of California, Santa Barbara, and is also a project director of the joint Saudi-U.S. solar program, in charge of solar photovoltaic power and solar data-collection stations. A member of the staff of the Saudi Arabian National Center for Science and Technology in Riyadh, in 1980 he was seconded to the Solar Energy Research Institute (Golden, Colorado).

John Duke Anthony holds advanced degrees from the School of Foreign Service of Georgetown University and the School of Advanced International Studies of the Johns Hopkins University; he is associate professor of Middle East Studies at the latter institution. His experiences have included: director of cultural exchange projects in Iran and Egypt during the early 1960s; a Fulbright Scholar in the People's Democratic Republic of Yemen (1969–1970); coordinator of the Area Studies Training Program for American Personnel, U.S.-Saudi Arabian Joint Commission on Economic Cooperation; and Chairman of the Advanced Area Studies Program for the Arabian Peninsula Countries and Iran of the U.S. Department of State's Foreign Service Institute. Author of, or contributor to some two dozen works on the Middle East, his recent books include *The Middle East: Oil, Politics* *and Development; The Sultanate of Oman and the Emirates of Eastern Arabia;* and *Arab States of the Lower Gulf: People, Politics, Petroleum.* Forthcoming books are *Girding and Guarding the Gulf: Policy Challenges for the 1980s* and *Saudi Arabia's Influence in the Arab World.*

Abdulrahman H. Al-Said is manager of the Economic and Industrial Research Division of the University of Petroleum and Mineral's Research Institute as well as a professor at this institution. Dr. Al-Said has taught at both Kansas University and the University of Missouri; he received the Ph.D. from the latter institution. Dr. Al-Said is author of a forthcoming volume (in Arabic and English editions), *Saudi Arabia: The Transition from Tribal Society to Nation-State.*

Yusuf A. Nimatallah, executive director for Saudi Arabia, International Monetary Fund, Washington, D.C., received the B.A. from the American University in Beirut and the M.A. and Ph.D. degrees in economics from the University of Massachusetts. Among the author's prior positions are professor of monetary and international economics at the University of Riyadh; advisor to the Saudi Arabian Ministry of Finance and National Economy on finance, oil, and planning (1967–1973); advisor to His Majesty the Sultan of Oman on oil, finance, money, and banking (1967–1973); deputy chairman and president of the Central Bank of Oman (1973–1978); and deputy chairman of UBAF Arab-American Bank, New York.

Michael W. Keran is senior vice-president and director of research of the Federal Reserve Bank of San Francisco.

Ahmed Abdullah Al-Malik is director general of the Foreign Department, Saudi Arabian Monetary Agency (SAMA), Riyadh. Dr. Al-Malik received the B.A. in economics from the University of Riyadh and the M.A. and Ph.D. degrees from Indiana University. Prior to joining the staff of SAMA, Dr. Al-Malik was director general of the Defense Procurement Department in the Ministry of Defense.

Abdallah T. Dabbagh, commercial counselor and head of the Commercial Section at the Embassy of Saudi Arabia in Washington, D.C., received the B.A. from the University of Colorado (Boulder) and the master's degree in international public policy from the Johns Hopkins University School of Advanced International Studies. The author joined the Ministry of Commerce in 1967 as director of public relations and was later posted as director of international exhibits in the same ministry. He served as commercial attache, stationed in London, with responsibility for covering Western Europe from 1973 to 1976. During 1976–1977, Mr. Dabbagh left the ministry to become general manager of a manufacturing company in Riyadh, rejoining the Ministry of Commerce in 1977.

Clive Anglin Sinclair has been, since 1976, a research Fellow in economics of the Middle East, Department of Economics, University of Durham. Dr. Sinclair's other positions have included codirectorship of the International Migration Project (commissioned by the International Labor Office, Geneva) at the University of Durham; consultant to the Technical Assistance and Special Studies Division of the World Bank; manpower-assessment consultant for the International Labor Office to the government of the Yemen Arab Republic. Among his recent publications are *International Migration and Development in the Arab Region* (1980); *Arab Manpower: The Crisis of Development* (1980); and *Basic Data on Population, Economic Development and International Migration in the Arab Region* (1980).

About the Editors

Ragaei El Mallakh, director of the International Research Center for Energy and Economic Development (ICEED) and professor of economics at the University of Colorado, Boulder, is editor of the *Journal of Energy and Development.* He is the author of, or contributor to some sixteen books, and has written over eighty articles and reviews that have appeared in the *American Economic Review, Journal of Economic Literature, Kyklos, International Journal of Middle East Studies, Middle East Journal, Land Economics, The New York Times,* and the *Christian Science Monitor,* among others. Dr. El Mallakh has been consultant to, or a member of the World Bank; Federal Power Commission (Natural Gas Task Force); Joint Economic Committee of the U.S. Congress; and the U.S. National Committee on World Petroleum Congresses. He has received grants and fellowships from Harvard University, the Rockefeller and Ford Foundations, the Social Science Research Council, the National Science Foundation, and the Hoover Institution. Dr. El Mallakh also serves on the boards of editors of the *International Journal of Middle East Studies* and the *Middle East Journal.*

Dorothea H. El Mallakh, executive administrator of the ICEED and associate editor of the *Journal of Energy and Development,* received the Ph.D. from the University of Colorado. She has been awarded a Rotary International Fellowship, the University of Colorado Perrine Memorial Fellowship for graduate study, and three National Defense Rare Language Fellowships. Her publications include *The Slovak Autonomy Movement, 1935-1939* (1979) and contributions to, and editorship of *The Genius of Arab Civilization; Energy Options and Conservation;* and *New Policy Imperatives for Energy Producers.*